THE SOCIAL MEDIA PRESIDENT

THE SOCIAL MEDIA PRESIDENT

BARACK OBAMA AND THE POLITICS OF DIGITAL ENGAGEMENT

JAMES E. KATZ, MICHAEL BARRIS, AND ANSHUL JAIN

palgrave
macmillan

First published in 2013 by
PALGRAVE MACMILLAN®
in the United States—a division of St. Martin's Press LLC,
175 Fifth Avenue, New York, NY 10010.

Where this book is distributed in the UK, Europe and the rest of the world,
this is by Palgrave Macmillan, a division of Macmillan Publishers Limited,
registered in England, company number 785998, of Houndmills,
Basingstoke, Hampshire RG21 6XS.

Palgrave Macmillan is the global academic imprint of the above companies
and has companies and representatives throughout the world.

Palgrave® and Macmillan® are registered trademarks in the United States,
the United Kingdom, Europe and other countries.

ISBN: 978–1–137–38085–2 (hc)
ISBN: 978–1–137–38084–5 (pbk)

Library of Congress Cataloging-in-Publication Data is available from the
Library of Congress.

A catalogue record of the book is available from the British Library.

Design by Newgen Knowledge Works (P) Ltd., Chennai, India.

First edition: December 2013

10 9 8 7 6 5 4 3 2 1

CONTENTS

Part III   Perspectives and Outlook on the Social Media President

ACKNOWLEDGMENTS

AS WITH ANY SCHOLARLY PROJECT, AUTHORS INCUR A DEEP DEBT FROM MANY quarters. Here my coauthors and I have a chance to express appreciation to some of the many people who have shared generously of their time and insights. When I was at Rutgers University, the late Irving Louis Horowitz pressed me to initiate the project and Dean Jorge Schement gave encouragement once it was launched. Rutgers students Lora Appel and Daniel Halpern provided fascinating empirical backdrops to citizen participation in federal social media offerings that have done much to inform our thinking on the subject. Gratitude also goes to the Rutgers students who participated in my seminars on media and culture, especially Rhaman Johnson, Michelle Riley, and Marianne Stewart Titus. David G. Robinson and Ed Felten of the Princeton University Center for Information Technology and Policy provided a stimulating milieu in which to work. In 2012, I moved to Boston University where the intellectual leadership of Dean Tom Fiedler of the College of Communication has played an instrumental role in facilitating the book's completion. During the work's development, John T. Carey contributed thoughtful ideas about public involvement in policy via media as did Edward Tenner and Ron Rice concerning ideologies and historical antecedents. Beth Noveck generously shared her time and insights. Nancy Baym, James Shanahan, Kristóf Nyíri, András Benedek, Richard John, André Caron, Craig Calhoun, Michael Schudson, Barry Wellman, Fred Turner, Anne-Marie Slaughter, Eszter Hargittai, Joachim Höflich, Leopoldina Fortunati, Rich Ling, Jack Harris, Jeffrey Boase, Zeynep Tufekci, Aaron Shaw, Paul DiMaggio, Letizia Caronia, Paul Starr, Joe Turow, Scott Campbell, Andy Chadwick, David Greenberg, John Pavlik, Matt Weber, Jack Bratich, Dino Christenson, Douglas Kriner, Gianpietro Mazzoleni, Fausto Colombo, Peppino Ortoleva, and Aram Sinnreich offered valuable perspectives. Amanda McGarry and Allison Keir played vital roles at the infrastructural level, as did Allison DeAngelis. Joyce Walsh offered discerning advice concerning cover design. I benefited from the advice of editors Vicky Cullen, Scarlet Neath, and Brian O'Connor.

Manuel Castells was incisive and discerning in his advice at an early stage; Matt Hindman, Phil Howard, Dave Karpf, and Daniel Kreiss were extraordinarily helpful at the project's closing stages. The highly talented Liz Crocker, who joined my team in 2013, rendered invaluable assistance in conducting interviews, tracking down important leads, and at many junctures incisively contributed to the manuscript.

My coauthors and I are profoundly grateful to the many interviewees without whom this book would be much the poorer. They are quoted by name unless they requested anonymity, in which case they are simply referred to, in a general way, by their position.

Needless to say, all mistakes and all errors of interpretation and judgment rest with me alone.

James E. Katz
Kenmore Square
Boston, Massachusetts

PART I

FRAMING THE ISSUE

CHAPTER 1

INTRODUCTION AND OVERVIEW

"LET THEM DETERMINE ITS COURSE"

On July 8, 2013, President Barack Obama entered the White House State Dining Room to address a packed chamber of reporters and dignitaries and lay out his new management agenda. He spoke forcefully on behalf of his vision: harnessing communication technology, so effectively deployed in his campaign, for empowering citizen participation in government. His remarks compactly frame the theme of this book. He declaimed:

> Back in 2007, when I was first running for this office, I had the opportunity to visit Google headquarters in Mountain View, in Silicon Valley, to discuss ways we could use technology to allow more citizens to participate in their democracy, and bring a government built largely in the 20th century into the 21st century.
>
> After all, we had already set out to build a new type of campaign—one that used technology to bring people together, and then trusted them with that technology to organize on their own. And the idea was simple: instead of bringing more people to the campaign, we wanted to bring the campaign to more people, and let them determine its course and its nature. If you wanted to make phone calls or knock on doors, you didn't have to come into a field office first, you could just get the information you needed right on your phone and go out there and do it. If you wanted to get your friends involved, then we had the tools to help you connect.
>
> And I very much felt that some of the things that we were doing to help us get elected could also be used once we were elected.... Now, once we got to Washington, instead of an operation humming with the latest technology, I had to fight really hard just to keep my BlackBerry.[1]

THE PROMISE AND ITS APPEAL

President Obama's oft-repeated assertion is that he wants to draw on the power of digital engagement to tap into the wishes and talents of the American people. He believes that the remarkable results of the computer revolution include the possibility of public participation in national policy—that is, that widespread computer-mediated communication could give individual citizens a hand in affecting the destiny of their country. This idea has stirred not only the imagination of Barack Obama, but of some of the activists and thinkers across academia, industry, and advocacy groupings with whom he has interacted over the years.[2] The vision of direct public participation is embraced with particular warmth by those who long to use communication technology to effect dramatic social change.[3] Yet the idea also has tremendous resonance with many among the general public who would wish to have their views taken into account, and perhaps even gain widespread adoption. Surely this must be one of the more alluring prospects offered by the dramatic advances in social media technology. To the technology's most enthusiastic proponents, a new era of equity, democracy, personal empowerment, and interpersonal understanding is about to be realized.

In contrast to these enthusiastic visions, we offer not just a corrective that these dreams are a bit too sanguine, or that progress will be slow. Rather we go further to argue that, in fact, this social media-enabled future is exceedingly difficult to implement with foreseeable technology; its pursuit has real costs, and it may be counterproductive, even if it were to succeed.

Recent scholarship offers valuable insights along both theoretical and empirical axes that shed light on how social media impact the dynamics of elite cues, public opinion, and opinion transmission more generally. What is lacking, however, and what our study attempts, is to push toward a deeper understanding of how presidential social media engagement interacts with the public. We want to provide a sense of what drives policy formulation and implementation in the social media arena at the White House level. We want to survey the reactions and changes that have arisen from high-level social media engagements. Finally, we want to explore the implications for future governance in terms of high-level social media interactions.

MODELS OF AMERICAN GOVERNMENT

In this section, we sketch the evolution of social media and their role as seen by two competing visions of citizen engagement in government. We do this to provide a sense of the kind of citizen engagement endorsed by two Founders of the United States. Drawing on the contrasting models of US government favored, respectively, by Alexander Hamilton and Thomas Jefferson, and placing them in today's context, it can be said that the underlying tension in the debate over citizen participation in policy-making is between a desire for expertise, on the one hand, and democratic participation, on the other. Hamilton believed that a strong centralized government was needed for business and industry to grow, and for the rights of individuals and minorities to be protected. Jefferson, on the other hand, distrusted professional expertise: he wanted power dispersed among the people both on a philosophical level and as a way to prevent them from being exploited by elites. Hamilton wanted governmental officials to be insulated from the passions of the crowd; Jefferson wanted them exquisitely responsive to the will of the people.[4]

The US Constitution is designed to maintain a balance of power within the government, implicit in its establishment of checks and balances that induce cooperation and pressures across the three branches of government. The implication is that the Constitution not only favors deliberation but also promotes the blending of expertise with intermittent democratic participation. In fact, fear of "mobocracy" weighed heavily on many of the Founders of the United States. Hamilton in particular sought to have a Constitution capable of serving as a bulwark against the abuses of enraged crowds that he had witnessed at the outbreak of the American Revolution and intermittently in its aftermath.[5]

With the Constitution as a backdrop, and aware of the cross-pressures elaborated by Hamilton and Jefferson, we reason that relying on "the wisdom of the crowd" to set policy is a far less vital dimension of the political process than opposition and confrontation at the leadership level. Conflicts over broad national policy cannot, and should not, be avoided or short-circuited through reliance on ever-more-powerful social media tools. In the final analysis, social media-based town halls and aggregations of "likes" and tweets do not a representative democracy make.

On the other hand, engaged citizens do make a democracy. Drawing on the competing visions of Hamilton and Jefferson, we can conceptualize a continuum of citizen engagement. For illustrative purposes we can describe several points along the continuum. Starting at the lowest form of engagement, which we could say is close to nonengagement, the citizen takes no active part in governmental affairs but is merely law abiding. The citizen pays taxes and obeys laws but is otherwise inert in terms of governmental activity. The very-low engaged citizen does nothing to learn or express an opinion about politics or policy. A somewhat higher form of engagement is to vote but not learn about issues. The next highest form is to vote and learn about politics but give no meaningful expression to a viewpoint. Still higher engagement is to not only vote and learn about policy but also to take actions that reflect or propagate a viewpoint. This would include discussing politics with neighbors, contributing to a campaign, or taking other steps to make one's views known outside the voting booth (such as commenting or arguing on blogs or contacting elected officials concerning a policy). The highly engaged citizen is active in suggesting, evaluating, and formulating policy. The highest form of citizen engagement is to decide directly on issues.

The emergence of advanced communication technologies has both deepened and complicated the meaning of engagement. Philip N. Howard explains that "thin citizenship," where citizens impulsively respond to transient political urges without pondering deeper issues, is promoted by the growing aggregation of detailed personal profiles ready for manipulation. These "data shadows" and "silhouettes" command the sharp interest of political actors.[6] The implications of readily available silhouettes are profound. Elected officials, campaigns, or other political advocacy groups can use hypermedia technology to engage not only with individual citizens, but with their data "silhouettes" as well.[7] Along the spectrum from total disengagement to full engagement, social media platforms have engendered a number of additional possibilities—both with and without the full knowledge and consent of the individual citizen.

We might say that Jefferson favored the highest form, direct decision-making,[8] while Hamilton feared the excessive passions and poor judgments of people if brought together as crowds, and had little patience for ill-informed people participating in political free-for-alls.[9]

PLATO'S PUZZLE

Social media enthusiasts often embrace the notion that the wisdom of the people should dictate the actions of leaders. Generally, democracy is traced to ancient Athens, but that "cradle of democracy," of course, never allowed full participation of all its residents (i.e., only male adult citizens were allowed to participate); nor did those it empowered vote on all decisions. Rather, Athens practiced a republican form of government. Nonetheless, the idea of full participation by citizens was at least *considered* by ancient Greek political philosophers, though some such as Plato did not think it was a good idea. If we are to live together, the Greek philosophers asked, how are the rules for this shared existence to be determined? How are the goals of the society to be established? Who should have say over the direction?

Plato, for one, examined, and then rejected, the idea of society being steered by the will of the people. In an analogy from *The Republic*, Plato described how a ship's navigator must rely on his expert training and greater wisdom to guide the ship of state, rather than be guided by its brawling, ignorant crew. Moreover, Plato warned in his ship analogy that the crew (the mob) was not only incompetent to make proper judgments, but also would too easily be suborned by manipulators. Plato strongly rejected the idea that democracy should be used as the arbiter of governmental policy, and argued instead that sophisticated and wise experts should be relied upon. Although he never used the term "lobbyist" or "special interest," he certainly alluded to their ancient equivalents and warned of their corrosive influence. Plato's criticisms were based on his experience with early democracy as he witnessed it in Athens. Yet he was arguing not only against an early form of "wisdom of the crowds" but also against the philosophical tradition of shared power and responsibility. Like it or not, Plato was enough of a realist to recognize that democracy had taken deep root in Athens, and a degree of crowd wisdom was already being practiced. For the many philosophers and political leaders arrayed against him, an important question remained as to how the will of the people should be transformed into the actions of the leaders. Plato's objection to democracy notwithstanding, that question continues to bedevil all who want to see the noble impulse of democracy put into action. The problem is an enduring one, and the energy and excitement that go into addressing it not only continue unabated but have even intensified with the prospect of "crowdsourcing" the overthrow of old regimes, as witnessed by a series of ballyhooed social media revolutions arcing from Tunisia and Egypt to the Ukraine and Moldova, and whose reverberations trouble Iran and China.

LINES OF INQUIRY

DEMOCRACY THROUGH TECHNOLOGY

In essence, one goal of this book is to explore a well-intentioned program in pursuit of democratic ideals through technological dreams. To foreshadow our findings, despite initially vigorous pursuit of a program of participation via social media, and valuable steps toward transparency in some governmental operations, the possibility of democratic participation via social media remains hovering, mirage-like, on the horizon. While social media tools serve as useful devices for information dissemination and democratic *mobilization*, among large groups they are largely ineffective—if not undesirable—as tools of democratic *deliberation and decision-making* on major policy issues. (We make this judgment not on the basis of sentiment, since our own values lead us to favor democratic deliberation and decision-making, but rather on the hard realities of discursive practices, information processing, and human cognition.) Beyond the technical and bureaucratic reasons, we see that what is required are political leaders who struggle to persuade publics, no less than the opposition figures who challenge them. Leaders need these skills to fulfill their visions. Relying on technocrats armed with ever-better opinion aggregation tools, for example, would not lead to a system that would be "too big to fail" but rather to a system that is bound to fail.

DIGITAL MEDIA'S EVOLVING ROLE IN PRESIDENTIAL POLITICS

An important background topic of this book is the way digital media technologies have evolved over the past two decades to play a generally important role in presidential politics. We attend to this in terms of campaigns for the White House from 1992–2012, as well the ways the White House has historically used digital media to inform, guide, engage, and even propagandize the public in light of presidential-level objectives. We examine some attempts by the Clinton and Bush Administrations to use social media to reach out to the public and some of the benefits and achievements that have been forthcoming. In the process we also share some of the criticisms of them and identify some of the pitfalls that have been encountered. Though at times we are critical of such efforts, we also recognize that they are part of the nature of politics. In our evaluation, we highlight both what is new and what has remained constant in the use of social media to extend the unrelenting battle over controlling the vision and the fate of a nation.

SOCIAL MEDIA AS A PROMINENT FEATURE OF THE OBAMA WHITE HOUSE AND ADMINISTRATION

President Obama's election campaigns, transition teams, and executive offices have prominently featured the infrastructure of social media in public outreach strategies. We examine promises that he has made and the steps he has taken to fulfill those promises, focusing on the goals, operation, and impact of social media events from a political perspective. These social media initiatives have taken varied and fascinating forms, and we examine several in detail. These initiatives, though, have been structured largely in accordance with the Administration's preexisting policy and governance objectives. At the outset of the President's first term, the Administration used social media tools to broadcast government priorities and sought to engage citizens via channels of nonbinding input. Yet well into a second term, after a successful reelection, and despite some interesting technical innovations, the realization of mass citizen input through mediated channels of ever-advancing technology remains far off. Notwithstanding heavy use of social media for various collateral purposes, and despite programs that purport to offer public input via social media, the Obama Administration has primarily used social media as a way to put out its messages and viewpoints and mobilize the public in support of Administration objectives. Only secondarily have these platforms been used to garner public input (and even less frequently in a meaningful way). A typical illustration of this last point is a system that permits the public to ask short questions of the Administration, allowing officials to explain and propagate their policy perspectives. Yet social media have been used heavily in an attempt to mobilize the public to back Administration positions. These outreach efforts have advanced the Administration's objectives of getting its viewpoints across to the public and garnering support.

FRICTION BETWEEN AIMS AND ACCOMPLISHMENTS FOR SOCIAL MEDIA INPUTS TO ADMINISTRATION

The dissonance between campaign and Administrative overtures versus the realities of citizen engagement through social media channels has left some followers disappointed. Certainly the ambitions of those who advocated policy-determination systems via social media have not been realized, despite the fact that some believed Obama's election would create the opportunity to build such systems. The dissonance has also become a target of criticism from the press, particularly "technogeek" and activist commentators. Fairly or not, the public nature of social media overtures, extended on multiple occasions during Obama's 2008 campaign and subsequently, led many to interpret the Administration's activities as exemplifying specific pledges to enable public use of social media to participate in policy deliberations and influence the government's policies. The impetus for this optimistic logic derives from promises and desiderata uttered by candidates and, ultimately, President Obama. Similar promises and expressions were provided by his staff, and also appeared in Administration press releases, web postings, and public pronouncements. These words did not spring de novo from the head of Barack Obama, but drew from a broad ideological landscape associated with the utopian visions of advocates who believe in the deliberative, democratizing potential of advancing information and communication technology (ICT) tools.[10]

More importantly, the gap between inclusory rhetoric and exclusory procedures has led some enthusiasts to believe that all that is lacking for this input to materialize is either the right tools or the right leader. The impression is left that, if only the proper platform, procedure, algorithm, or post-partisan leader could be found, the dream of citizen steering of public policy would be realized. This optimistic impression, regardless of its validity, can be used for political advantage as well as political change; as such it is a critical thesis that we analyze in this book.[11]

Finally, given its self-generated emphasis on accountability and public responsiveness, it is only fitting to hold the Administration accountable for its performance predicated on the goals it has set for itself. While these goals are ambitious, and progress toward them may be impeded by unforeseen constraints and undesirable circumstances, the metrics of performance must remain intact.

SOCIAL MEDIA FOR POLICY CODETERMINATION AND CITIZEN ENGAGEMENT

Given President Obama's advocacy of citizen engagement, we wanted to explore the viability of using social media tools for mass exercises in direct, participatory democracy with binding outcomes. We also want to consider less stringent, and less binding, ways for social media to be deployed in terms of citizen engagement: for gathering information about the status and wishes of the population, providing information to the public, and using social media to persuade the public.

Our argument builds outward from modeling considerations, spanning both in-depth case studies and more compact examples of social media policy in the White House. Chapter 2 provides key definitions and operational frameworks. Proceeding from these definitions and frameworks, we identify three critical modalities of social media communication: gathering input from the public, pushing information to the public, and codetermining policy with the public.

Chapter 3 presents a compendiary historical perspective on social media in presidential politics. We track the rise of digital platforms from the first White House website to the advanced incorporation of social media into campaign machinery for fundraising, outreach, and mobilization. We also provide numerous examples that illustrate the persistence of the three communication modalities.

Chapter 4 examines the creation of the Transition Team's Citizen's Briefing Book (CBB). Through reviews of documents, public statements, and interviews with expert personnel inside and outside the Administration, we uncover the major challenges of the CBB project, explaining that in the wake of highly ambitious rhetoric and expectations, meaningful engagement proved difficult.

Chapter 5 analyzes the dynamics of the White House's Online Town Hall. The Online Town Hall, like the CBB, illustrates the Administration's ability to use the social media interactivity of an ostensibly open forum to nevertheless gather information and promote already established policy positions.

Chapter 6 details the vision and experiences of the White House's Expert Labs, the Administration's most ambitious crowdsourcing engagement project to date. In addition to examining how the Grand Challenges program activated the three social media communication modalities, we explore the relevant bureaucratic, political, and logistical roadblocks that impeded the progress of this ambitious body of initiatives, extending the trends of curtailed collaborative engagement.

Chapter 7 considers the counterfactual examples of Supreme Court vacancies and the complex maneuvering in pursuit of the Patient Protection and Affordable Care Act. We show that where the White House chose to deploy social media, they did so with considerable caution, maintaining maximal control of messaging and limiting public participation to safely contained forums.

Chapter 8 considers an array of contests, awards, question forums, and event overtures including the "We the People" petition portal, Google+ Hangouts, White House "office hours," Reddit's "Ask Me Anything" forum, the Presidential Citizen's Medal, and the opportunity to text the President concerning student debt issues. The dynamic of using these tools to propagandize is framed in the context of free moral labor, the ensuing recruitment of the public to broadcast executive priorities. The examples in this chapter also demonstrate the Obama Administration's sophisticated micro-targeting of its messaging apparatus and illustrate the circumscribed limits of citizen engagement, which we figuratively dub the Glass Suggestion Box.

Chapter 9 considers the broader integration of social media platforms across the federal bureaucracy. Here, the macro-level impact of the Obama Administration's orders and memoranda on transparency, federal agencies' attempts to interpret and implement these directives, and Congress' role in curtailing various initiatives are all considered. The metaphor of the Glass Suggestion Box is revisited with a wider scope that also considers international examples of social media engagement initiatives.

Chapter 10 provides an analytic foray into the reasons underlying the successes and failures of these initiatives. From one perspective, we assume earnest intentions on the part of the President and the White House, explaining outcomes as the result of various legal, bureaucratic, logistical, and political hurdles. However, we also consider the possibility that limits to social media engagement with the citizenry stem from the deliberate, strategic restriction of these platforms in order to maintain control of critical message flow.

Chapter 11 concludes, assessing these undertakings in terms of the general implications for using social media in governmental policy-making. We weigh the merits of more direct engagement with an eye to rational interest versus technocratic models, also considering the collateral phenomena of civic empowerment and fragmentary data presence. After offering predictions for social media engagement trends in the coming years, we revisit our overall outlook: even with ambitious efforts that deploy the most sophisticated social media technology, there are political and practical limits to direct citizen involvement in the implementation of substantive matters of policy.

A brief word about this book's audience: our writing is directed to sophisticated generalist readers, advanced undergraduate and graduate students, policy enthusiasts, and scholars. We believe that a social science-theoretic perspective on the social media president, which we present in the Appendix, helps frame the book. As such, interested readers are invited to visit this section.

As we wrap up our introduction, let it be clear that our narrative is driven by no political party commitment or partisan cause. Rather, our pursuit is a critical intellectual inquiry into an increasingly important topic.

CHAPTER 2

SITUATING SOCIAL MEDIA AND CITIZEN PARTICIPATION IN THE OBAMA ERA

ALEXANDER HAMILTON, THE FIRST US SECRETARY OF THE TREASURY, DID NOT mince his words when he bluntly assessed the much-debated notion of using the wisdom of the crowd to inform governmental policy decisions. The masses, Hamilton complained, "are turbulent and changing. They seldom judge or determine right."[1] Hamilton believed that experts knew best how to govern the populace; he wanted the processes of government regulated centrally. At the other end of the dispute stood Thomas Jefferson, Hamilton's fellow Founder (and, ultimately, nemesis). Jefferson, the principal author of the Declaration of Independence, contended that it was every citizen's duty to engage in shaping fundamental policy decisions, because codetermination of government policy, when all was said and done, was not only a natural right but necessary for democracy to function effectively. For Jefferson, "It is an axiom in my mind that our liberty can never be safe but in the hands of the people themselves."[2]

Over two hundred years later, this debate still lives with us, amplified by the popularity and power of social media. The marriage of cellular communication to the Internet spawned electronic media expressly suited to social interaction. The new technology, embodied in social networking sites such as Facebook, microblogs such as Twitter, and other methods of exchanging digital messages, had the potential to transform communication among far-flung parties into interactive dialogue. The implications for political communication were immense.

DEFINITIONS: DIGITAL ENGAGEMENT, SOCIAL MEDIA, AND THE SOCIAL MEDIA PRESIDENT

In the prior chapter, we defined the active citizen and citizen engagement. Here we expand our terminology by contextualizing our use of the term *digital engagement*.

By this term, we mean people using integrated circuit (computer chip) based-devices to send, receive, or interact with data concerning societal or governmental matters. Such devices include desktop and mobile computers, tablets, cell phones, and gaming consoles. By data, we include all forms of information (such as text, photos, videos, as well as web interfaces) and by implication its cognitive and emotive effects on users. Engagement includes one-way, bilateral, and multilateral interactions and responses. It refers as well to the co-creation of new insights, information, attitudes, organizations, and relationships that stem from the use of digital resources.

Social media can be defined as digital multiway channels of communication among people and between people and information resources and which are personalized, scalable, rapid, and convenient. They are characterized by user-generated content and interaction among users. The term social media also has a connotation of drawing its power from an ideology emphasizing freedom of expression, individual empowerment, and collective action.[3]

Above, we considered what is traditionally meant by an engaged citizen. Here, we want to characterize what we consider to be "meaningful engagement of the public" as it applies to White House policy and social media—namely, the question of what is the appropriate role of social media technology in actual governance. A helpful definition in this context is operational: what decision by the President or White House was modified because of ideas tendered or deliberated by the public? That is, what was done differently than the White House originally intended because of some idea, statement, or piece of information drawn from the public via social media platforms? This is, of course, not the same thing as altering policy direction because of lobbying, public outrage, or personal influence—all of which are common events that have led this and prior White Houses to choose to act differently. The promise of social media was that they would allow the former, giving the public input or even discovering previously unappreciated ideas, with the concomitant consequence of reducing the role of entrenched power and political influence, particularly on the part of privileged special interest factions with longstanding levels of access. The outcome of this change would supposedly lead to better policy.

As reflected in this book's title, we aver that Barack Obama is the *social media president*. On what basis can we make such a claim? We do so not only on the strength of his own statements about his ambitions when he was running for president, but even more on what he has said and done since then. We also do so on the basis of how attentive publics interpret and respond to his declarations and actions.

Barack Obama is not the first "digital" or electronic president; his White House predecessors broke new terrain in that regard (as discussed in chapter 3). But even from the early days of his campaign at both the ideological and tactical levels, Obama sought to achieve the status of the social media president.

In terms of how this came about, the social media dimension was important in framing his 2008 campaign when candidate Obama's rhetoric struck a chord with millions. Three themes came into view through his campaign speeches: populism, active citizenship in government, and digital communication technology as a mechanism to convey the will of people to a responsive government. He used the informality of social media to present himself as a candidate of the people. For instance, on April 1, 2008, during a town hall-style meeting in Wilkes-Barre, PA, a coal mining town hurt by the plummeting economy, Obama, then seeking the Democratic nomination, invoked a populist theme when he said: "The American Dream is slipping away." Obama said, "They call it an ownership society but basically the idea is that you're on your own. Well, that's not what America is about."[4] In other, similar speeches, Obama declared he wanted a government that would not just provide for people, but for people to feel they had a stake in the government.

Another recurring theme in his campaign speeches was that he was in tune with the spirit of the people, hearing their voices, and acting on their behalf to defend them. In fact, "hearing the voice" of the people became an important subtheme of the Obama campaign and subsequently his Administration. And social media would be the way in which this voice could be heard and even influence policy. In his campaign speeches (and in speeches after his election) he repeatedly called for "active citizenship." On December 5, 2007, early in the election cycle, he made his call to service in a speech at Mount Vernon, IA: "I won't just ask for your vote as a candidate; I will ask for your service and your active citizenship when I am President of the United States. This will not be a call issued in one speech or program; this will be a cause of my presidency."[5]

In an April 30, 2008 campaign stop in Indianapolis, IN, he spoke of how he wanted to use a revamped White House website to have citizens become involved in major issues:

One of the things I'm really proud of about this campaign is I think we've built a structure that can sustain itself after the campaign...So now we've got a database with a couple million people on there who are activated and inspired. And they know each other and they are communicating with each other through the Internet...And what I want to do is continue that after the election. Number one, we're going to keep on having town hall meetings. I want to keep on having conversations like this where I'm listening to voters. I want to really open up transparency in our government so that you guys know on a day-to-day basis what's happening. And I want to revamp our White House website. I know it's nice to take a virtual tour of the china room and all that stuff. But I want people to be able to say today this issue is going on...Just creating the kind of situation where if they want to get involved they have the information to do it and it's even easy...The more we can enlist the American people to pay attention and be involved, that's how we're going to move an agenda forward.[6]

Barack Obama was swept to power on a platform of hope and change that included using social media to effectuate that change. Many pundits underscored the Internet's role in bringing him to power. For instance, Al Gore, the former US Vice President, Nobel laureate, and 2000 Democratic Party presidential standard bearer, declaimed that Obama's election win "could not have happened without the Internet." He described the Internet as an "electrifying redemption of America's revolutionary declaration that all human beings are created equal."[7] Or, as another commentator declared, Obama was "the president that the Internet elected."[8]

Ample facts and statistics certainly supported that claim. Obama not only had enormous support from the Internet's ordinary citizens, or "netizens," but also from its leaders. Among his high-tech backers and advisors (as mentioned in chapter 1) were Google's chief executive, Eric Schmidt, and Facebook cofounder, Chris Hughes.

For the dimension of active citizenship, Hughes captured the essence of the Obama campaign—and later, of the Administration—that real democracy could be achieved through digital communication: "There's huge potential for people that haven't been involved in politics to discover that, yes, this is something that impacts me. The fundamental premise was to help put the political process into people's own hands."[9] That sentiment was echoed by an important figure in the 2008 Obama campaign, Kate Albright-Hanna, who served as its Director of Video for New Media. She told us that while she was disappointed by later developments, when she worked for the Obama campaign she believed in that hope. "The promise," she said, "which was spelled out pretty clearly in some of the emails, was that if you donate to this campaign that means that Barack Obama is going to have to listen to you when he becomes president. And you're buying in."[10]

Now it might be argued that what Senator Obama said on the campaign trail concerning citizen engagement and social media were rhetorical flourishes calculated to help him get elected, and, that like so many promises, no one took them seriously. However, some of his supporters obviously did take him seriously and expected him to act on his promise, as noted immediately above. And the argument that there were no meaningful promises actually made by candidate Obama is also gainsaid by the transparency declaration he issued on his first day in office, January 21, 2009. On the occasion of welcoming his senior staff and cabinet secretaries he underscored for them the importance of an open government. He asserted:

> commitment to openness means more than simply informing the American people
> about how decisions are made. It means recognizing that government does not have
> all the answers, and that public officials need to draw on what citizens know. And
> that's why, as of today, I'm directing members of my Administration to find new ways
> of tapping the knowledge and experience of ordinary Americans—scientists and civic
> leaders, educators and entrepreneurs—because the way to solve the problems of our
> time, as one nation, is by involving the American people in shaping the policies that
> affect their lives.[11]

FROM ONE-WAY TO MULTI-WAY COMMUNICATION: A GATEWAY TO BECOMING A SOCIAL MEDIA PRESIDENT

In terms of elections, digital technologies were initially seen as a way to win political campaigns by mobilizing supporters, soliciting funds, and gaining positive attention. This understanding meant that the campaigners' jobs in this field were primarily to use the technology to push information to voters or offer information to voters who came to them via these channels. Only as an afterthought was attention, faint though it was, given to using the electorate as a source of policy guidance or ideas that might usefully inform the campaign.[12] But once the idea of "crowdsourcing" via the Internet leaped from a means for getting advice on fixing computers, finding recipes, and subverting governments to a possible means of making national policy, the potential for drawing on public opinion as a source of ideas and legitimacy for policies became an idée fixe for a new generation of technology-loving activists. They felt that, at long last, tools were available to effect great society-wide change.[13] This belief grew despite the fact that earlier technologies, such as the telephone, radio, fax, and television each also seemed to offer effective multidirectional communication in democratic systems, but they were successful only to a limited degree in terms of citizen influence on national policy.[14] Amid this much-changed communication landscape, the lingering question of whether the untapped wisdom of the public should be harnessed in governmental decisions suddenly commanded a fresh look, as social media increased the capability of governments worldwide to more fully involve ordinary citizens in policy-making. Although in the next chapter we address the rise of digital technology in the White House for citizen engagement, we will next situate Barack Obama in regard to his stature as the social media president.

On the strength of the 2008 presidential contest in which social media played a fundamental role, President Obama can legitimately be called the "social media president."[15] The campaign team of the US Senator from Illinois deftly used technology to shatter fundraising records, organize supporters locally, repel attacks, and get out the vote en route to a strong victory over Obama's Republican rival, Sen. John McCain, whose campaign, by comparison, seemed woefully slow, underfunded, and lacking in imagination.[16]

Throughout the race, there was an ideological component to Obama's candidacy that was inherently about more than just winning an election, ending the war in Iraq, and repairing the crumbling economy. It was even about more than electing the first politician of African-American heritage to the most powerful office in the land. It was also about a hope for major change, centered on the rhetoric of empowering citizens to regain control of the machinery of government and to provide direct and meaningful democratic involvement in federal policy-making and governance, including the generation of new policy initiatives.

And the idea of empowerment via digital means, it was promised, was no mere sloganeering. As to Chris Hughes' earlier commitment, that the campaign's "fundamental premise was to help put the political process into people's own hands," he assured Obama supporters that this principle "was the value from the start of the campaign, that was the value at the end of the campaign, and it's not going away."[17]

STRUCTURES OF USAGE OF THE PUBLIC'S VOICE IN WHITE HOUSE SOCIAL MEDIA EXERCISES

Our fascination with the question of how democracy can and should work has guided our selection of the illustrations and mini case studies that we used to examine the social media activities of President Obama and his Administration. The major activities we cite seek to exemplify the nature and types of the Administration's efforts. Some of these seem to be designed to uncover great ideas, reveal unappreciated truths, encourage people to work together to solve problems, or pinpoint unarticulated and latent desires of the American people. Others seem designed to let people know about government programs and initiatives from which they might benefit. Yet other examples seem to have different aims, such as attempting to persuade the public about the wisdom of an Administration initiative, or getting a White House policy adopted.

In terms of the last set of examples, two approaches are often taken. In the first, a political leader will ask for the public's concerns in a specific area in order to galvanize the public to take action or to demonstrate the leader's responsiveness to those concerns. This can be shorthanded by the popular term, "having a conversation" (although this can also be a temporizing strategy). The second is communing with the spirit of the people, or more simply, "listening." This type of gamesmanship could be considered, at best, manipulative, primitive "crowdsourcing." This example shows how those who control the agenda can easily manipulate what can be described as the seeming "will of the people," even without fancy technology. But we show later that social media and related communication technology can be even more easily controlled. Amid all the overemphasis on social media and how they can alter who wins an election, it is often believed that the technologies can also change how policy directions are set. While it is easy to misconstrue the power and possibilities of technology, the fact is that the skills, objectives, and processes involved in actual leadership are not the same as those brought to the idealized view of social media-generated leadership; in fact these skills, goals, and processes are quite different.

This disparity, then, makes our examination of the Obama White House's use of social media more meaningful: not only do we use it to demonstrate the hopes and dreams of people who worked for Obama's 2008 election campaign and Administration in terms of the political direction they wanted, but we also point to why the government's social media initiatives, in terms of directing federal policy, were rendered ineffective despite a resounding electoral victory. And in a reinforcing line of argument, the 2012 election demonstrated anew the power of social media in elections, despite their nugatory ability to set national policy.

On the one hand, social media can be extremely useful in identifying procedural flaws, incompetence, corruption, or other forms of waste and abuse. They can also identify process improvements that help the government operate more efficiently or address overlooked issues. On the other hand, the technologies' use is wanting (at least as practiced thus far in the White House) as a source of policy preferences and for decision-making.

THREE MODALITIES OF SOCIAL MEDIA INTERACTION BETWEEN GOVERNMENT AND CITIZENS

There are many ways to address our guiding questions about the patterns and impact of social media communications. A particularly useful approach is to analyze the multidirectional flow of information between government and the citizenry.[18] An important view of this process was shared with us by Macon Phillips, the White House Director of New Media. From his perspective, the job has three parts: publicizing the President's message, increasing the visibility of White House activities for the public, and creating opportunities for citizen input in government. In his words:

> We all come to work thinking about three things, which is one, how we can amplify the President's message as technology changes how and where people get information...The second is opening up the work in the White House both in terms of being transparent

and sort of good government and open government priorities but also just fundamentally making our work accessible to regular people. And understanding that in 2013 when people have a question about Barack Obama and education or Barack Obama and immigration, they're going to type those words into Google... And the third is, how do we give people a meaningful opportunity to participate in their government? And this has sort of taken a number of tracks and continues to be the biggest challenge for us.[19]

His assessment generally concurs with our vision of this process, though he, of course, is discussing his work at the White House specifically, while we want to look at the problem somewhat more generally, though still at the apex of government. We distinguish among three different modalities in which the public's use of social media interfaces with the government. Although we treat these three as separate categories, there is overlap among them, and each is partly defined by the intention of the government as much as by the intention of the citizen-social media user. These are:

GATHERING INPUT FROM THE PUBLIC

The first modality is as a *source of information for the government*. This includes surveying, systematically or otherwise, public opinion. It also includes scanning for problem identification or solutions from the field, much like an old-fashioned suggestion box, but in virtual form. It also includes passive data collection and surveillance of electronic traffic and content. Here, it is again worth noting Philip N. Howard's conceptualization of thin citizenship and data shadows. The thin citizen's silhouette offers an array of dispersed opportunities for actors and agents, both public and private, to gather fragmentary information that can inform political strategies.[20]

PUSHING INFORMATION TO THE PUBLIC

The second use of social media is as a channel through which the government can *inform and propagandize* the public. In terms of directional flow, the first form—problem identification—represents a "pull" of information into the center. The second form—propaganda and information—represents a "push" of information from the center. Sometimes the motive for this push is simply to help citizens via education, to enhance their understanding, or help them be more effective in reaching their personal or community goals. And certainly getting information out to citizens is an important aspect of this use. Presumably citizens will appreciate such efforts, responding with sentiments that the government, and particularly its leadership, is concerned about their well-being. Still, such efforts may also be guided by what is on the presidential agenda. Hence, some of these "push" forms of information dissemination are undergirded with, or even prompted by, a call for action on behalf of agenda items. At the very least, they aim to reduce resistance to the presidential agenda. Though the word "propaganda" has pejorative connotations, such as being intentionally misleading, we use it here to embody its less negative denotation of dissemination of information as a political strategy, often to promote a political cause.

The question-and-answer format is an interesting combination of forms 1 and 2. The question reveals much about the asker, and perhaps the audience, and thus pulls information from the question answerer (form 1). But the answer not only conveys information but also allows an answer that can move the dialogue in a certain direction and can motivate the auditors to take action (form 2).

CODETERMINING POLICY WITH THE PUBLIC

The third modality is the gathering of citizen viewpoints and opinions as a *form of power-sharing*. Here, the public would be directly involved in setting policy for the government. Such gathering may be citizen-initiated or invited by the government, and is distinguished by the fact that the input will *affect governmental policy*. This is different from the first form, gathering information, since it means that the public's voice must be heeded, rather than mined as an additional source of data that a policy-maker may wish to consider.

For us, it is this third style—power-sharing—that is of central interest. While the push and pull modalities are important and certainly alter the terrain of political life, they are in many ways the same in terms of the people's relationship to those invested with decision-making authority; in neither case is the latter constrained by communications of the former. Social media remain an entirely discretionary source of power for those in authority. Power-sharing via social media, on the other hand, represents a potential transformation in citizen empowerment, democratization of governmental processes, and the fundamental legitimacy of those in power. Therefore, in our book we highlight this topic, though attending to the other two as well.

TOPICAL FOCUS AND CASE STUDY SELECTION

Concerning our scope, case selection, and interview methodology, we focus our examination on aspects of social media engagement primarily *by or with the president* and only secondarily with the *executive branch* when they appear connected to presidential leadership. Even within that subset, given the gamut of social media activities emanating from the White House and used within the executive branch, we had to be selective, seeking illustrative cases rather than an exhaustive enumeration. We therefore bypassed important areas, such as electronic rule-making (e-rule making) for instance, since they would have taken us too far afield. Nor do we devote ourselves to systematically investigating the reception of President Obama's social media initiatives in the blogosphere or through crosscutting public opinion perspectives, which, while meriting book-length treatments of their own, fall outside our scope. We also do not explore models of e-government that focus on service delivery and provide information because these vast topics, while vital, do not speak directly to the critical questions of citizen engagement and presidential-level policy formulation.[21] By concentrating more on the President himself, we can deepen our analysis and participate better in the lively discussions of the community of presidential scholars, the broader public and the media, all of whom are intrigued by activities at the apex of political power.

Regarding the cases we have selected, we were guided not by an attempt to achieve statistically representative or randomly sampled examples. Rather, we sought instances of social media use that had one or more of the following characteristics: (a) they involved Obama himself, or were (b) drawn from White House operations, (c) of high salience against the background of presidential political discourse, (d) exemplary, in that they demonstrated a pattern or feature, or (e) exemplary of the negative or nonuse of social media, that is, illustrated opportunities foregone. Thus we have chosen both cases of action and inaction for their relevance to our analysis.

In terms of whom we sought out for interviews, we cast wide our net of solicitations. In addition to calling directly upon recognized experts in the field, we also pursued a "snowball sampling" strategy to identify interviewees. As well, we contacted media relations and digital engagement units at the White House and leading federal agencies, asking to speak with a specialist or expert. Though by no means were all such interview requests granted, we did make substantial exertions to locate interviewees who could offer exemplary views and insights, based on firsthand experience, or who could speak from different institutional perspectives. Interviews were conducted by telephone unless otherwise noted. We made repeated requests for an interview with staff of the White House Office of Public Engagement (OPE) and the Executive of the President's Office of Management and Budget. Staff members whom we contacted informed us that they would be willing to be interviewed but would need permission from their superiors. Accordingly, we requested permission from their superiors repeatedly over several months but our requests for permission went unanswered.

Before delving into details of these social media exercises, an historical-evolutionary perspective is useful in providing a background for the power, and especially the limits, of technology for citizen engagement. Hence in the next chapter, we trace the growth of digital communication technology for citizen engagement.

CHAPTER 3

DIGITAL MEDIA AND ELECTORAL POLITICS: AN ABBREVIATED HISTORY

THIS CHAPTER BRIEFLY SKETCHES THE RISE OF DIGITAL MEDIA IN RECENT AMERICAN presidential elections and offers snapshots of the victors' digital engagement approaches. Our retrospective analysis of presidential elections from 1992 through 2012 reveals emergent patterns concerning social media's role in presidential politics. The period shows dramatic growth in the size, scope, speed, and diversity of online media connections between campaigns and the public. These connections are ultimately relevant because every winning campaign must transition from this mesh of interactivity to the more multispectral demands of governance and the complicated balance of collecting, disseminating, and collaboratively using information. Social media can be thought of as tools for citizen engagement, but both social media and citizen engagement can be thought of as a corollary of the unceasing electoral practices that precede and succeed a campaign. These practices have been captured in the concept of the "permanent campaign."[1] This concept is instructive, both for examining the difficulties of translating campaign strategies into practices of governance as well as for comparing the actual use (and limits) of digital media technologies outside of campaign cycles.

It is useful when considering campaigns, to bear in mind that while attention naturally focuses on the victorious campaigns and their innovations, it is also the case that many losing campaigns, including primary campaigns, have been extraordinarily innovative. Daniel Kreiss incisively reminds us of this when analyzing the trailblazing but ultimately unsuccessful presidential bid of Howard Dean.[2] The fact that a campaign might not have been victorious does not diminish the importance and effects of the breakthroughs it achieved. Moreover, one must consider that even a losing campaign may have been far more competitive than without its pioneering social media effort; this was certainly the case with Howard Dean and his campaign's social media advances. Many social media innovations have been picked up

22 THE SOCIAL MEDIA PRESIDENT

and used in subsequent campaigns, by competitors no less than successors. Hence we direct our attention in the recapitulation that follows to breakthroughs on both sides of the electoral ledger.

ELECTIONS AND GOVERNANCE AS DIGITAL MEDIA EMERGES

THE EARLY DAYS

While the rise of digital media is a major development in the history of political communication, it would be a mistake to overlook longstanding efforts aimed at direct communication between the president and the public; these have marked the American political landscape for much of its history at both the level of the campaign and of governance. Andrew Jackson, who had imbued his 1828 campaign with strategic rhetoric of the "common man," attempted to invite the public into the White House—literally—following his inauguration, for an "open house." As the White House was ransacked during several hours of revelry, the exercise became an infamous disaster. Less raucous overtures to engage the public include Franklin Roosevelt's use of radio for his Fireside Chats, the first real-time communication with a mass audience. Further expanding a sense of communication between the president and the people has been the growth of presidential television appearances, institutionalized press conferences, and widespread opinion polling. Hence the Obama Administration's public outreach through the latest media platforms inherits a legacy of more than a century's worth of innovations, shifts, successes, and failures.[3]

1992: CHANGE AND THE INFORMATION SUPERHIGHWAY

We will pick up the analytical thread with the 1992 Presidential Election, which coincided with dramatic advances in networked computational technology—phrases such as "information superhighway" depicted the concept of a connected public exchanging information and ideas. The existing platforms (e.g., AOL, CompuServe, Prodigy, and TelNet) served as rudimentary conduits for email, bulletin boards, and chat forums. The Clinton Administration launched the WhiteHouse.gov domain in 1994 and began featuring email as a way to communicate with the White House. This feature, however, was largely a novelty, as emails were collected, printed, and replied to via White House form letters. The technology would not be used for any internal, interbranch, or external communication for several more years.[4]

The highly charged and power-shifting midterm election of 1994 swept Republicans into control of both Houses of Congress for the first time since 1954; it also coincided with the development of browser applications such as Netscape Navigator. Computer-based communication became conceptualized as a web—an apt metaphor for the world of increasingly networked computers. New levels were achieved in terms of graphic presentation and easy-to-use interfaces. Crucial to this process was the adoption of the practice of website construction by commercial enterprises, from major newspapers and magazines to tour operators and florists. Businesses' embrace of the World Wide Web not only provided a way for consumers to become educated about its usefulness but also to become fluent in the argot of cyberspace. It also allowed new, independent, and often irreverent or idiosyncratic online voices to come to the fore, thus readily introducing oppositional voices to the debate.[5]

Richard Lytel, who edited the White House's original website, organized it by "the three ways the White House wants to present itself to the world: the home of the president, the seat of government, and a living museum of American history."[6] The Clinton Administration embraced an expansive vision of information efficiency as a centerpiece of its executive operation; it thereby created an expectation that new levels of access and information would be offered to citizens. In fact, the first White House web portal described itself as an "Interactive Citizens' Handbook." Nevertheless, the Clinton Administration phased out the term, and mainly featured greetings from the President and Vice President, biographical information, and miscellaneous facts about White House tours and its building and grounds. Significantly for our recapitulation of the evolution of social media and the White House, the site did urge interactivity in the form of sending President Clinton an email. In the course of Clinton's presidency, hundreds of thousands of emails were sent to the White House. But overwhelmed, the staff could only respond via "snail mail" form sending letters acknowledging the email's receipt.

After the 1994 midterm election, Congress followed the White House's lead, and began adopting widespread use of email and websites. Not only were members of Congress given access on an individual office-level, but on party and institutional levels as well. The new Republican House majority adopted the technology—but again, less as a functional tool for legislative operation or civic engagement than as a symbolic tool for competitive posturing vis-à-vis the White House. Major policies of the Contract with America were publicly available on numerous House office and Committee websites, for instance, and the new House Speaker, Newt Gingrich, showed a greater level of individual attention to the adoption and integration of emerging communication technologies across the information messaging activities of the House.[7]

1996: SYMBOLIC ENGAGEMENT AND THE BRIDGE TO TOMORROW

1996 marked the first instance in which campaign websites were prominently featured by the Republican and Democratic nominees; both parties sought to engage large swaths of the electorate.[8] While frequently promoted, the Clinton-Gore and Dole-Kemp websites were ultimately limited in their impact due in part to wide gaps among user capabilities. Additionally, both had fundamentally narrow visions of the link between the technology and appropriately tailored content. For instance, both campaigns posted audio and video files of convention speeches and rally appearances, offered opportunities for interested citizens to receive campaign email updates, and posted press releases and event schedules. For most users, however, accessible information repeated campaign information already transmitted via television, direct mail, telephone, fax, and other traditional outreach activities. Websites were ultimately reduced to functioning as extended pamphlets, simply projecting existing information into an online realm. Further, in 1996, most Internet users were connecting through basic dial-up modems, and the websites were not optimized for the most common connection speeds, so the impact of any audio-visual content or interactive features was severely curtailed.

Rita Whillock argues that the two campaigns pursued different approaches to using their websites to advance their goals, holding that while the Dole-Kemp campaign actually offered a higher degree of interactivity, the Clinton-Gore operation more effectively utilized the technology for image projection and agenda-setting.[9] Bill Clinton and Al Gore continually referenced their website at rallies and during press interviews, and even though their website contained little new information, the effect was the "training" of the media to turn to their website for press briefings, event schedules, and policy points.

While the 1994 midterm electoral victory of the Republicans constrained Bill Clinton in his first term, the scandal resulting from the President's affair with White House intern Monica Lewinsky and ensuing impeachment proceedings constituted the major crisis of his second term. The scandal, initially arising as a tangential offshoot of the Whitewater investigations (which officially began in 1994, but whose roots reach back to the 1970s), dominated news coverage and public attention throughout most of 1998. In addition to showcasing the rising awareness, reach, and impact of Internet-based media, the progress of scandal-related exposés through Internet-based communication yielded surprises of their own in terms of insights about how these new media forms were affecting the relationship between the White House and the public. Bruce Williams and Michael Delli Carpini posit that digital media played a pivotal role in the breakdown of traditional journalistic gatekeeping processes—independent Internet-based investigators and reporters (Matt Drudge, in particular) were able to circumvent the mainstream press in their investigative processes, and would ultimately compel the mainstream press to accept and circulate the information they had uncovered.[10] The dynamics behind the eruption of the Monica Lewinsky scandal represent an important turning point in the White House's abilities to manage the press, and in its informational relationship with the American public: the Internet could no longer be ignored as part of the communication pathways that link the public with the White House. An equally important caveat to the lessons of the prominence of digital information flow—one that is highly relevant to the status of the White House's ability to broadcast its own perspectives to the public—is that Bill Clinton survived impeachment proceedings and emerged from the scandal with his public opinion standing largely unscathed. Indeed, it was Republican margins in Congress that suffered during the 1998 midterm elections. While the Lewinsky scandal illustrated that the White House could not ignore the growing content and uses of digital media, it likewise showed that the damaging information flows created by an existential scandal could, in fact, be effectively managed.

In 1999, with about a year left in his second term, Bill Clinton signed the "White House Memorandum on Electronic Government." Among other items, it directed heads of all agencies to "permit greater access to its officials by creating a public electronic mail address through which citizens can contact the agency with questions, comments, or concerns."[11] After years of urging by denizens of the Internet, this memorandum represents the tangible institutionalization of email communication across federal agencies. But significantly for our overarching thesis, and even more so for millions of email-using citizens, the memorandum outlined no provision for any kind of response requirements.

2000: HANDICAPPED ENGAGEMENT IN A CHANGED MEDIASCAPE

The growth of digital media presence in presidential campaigns closely mirrors the growth of the relevant technologies in other industries. Between 1996 and 2000, email and web presence transformed from common, but not necessarily critical, tools to essential internal and external communication platforms. Across the spheres of education, commerce, industry, and advocacy, the norm had shifted to a general default organizational minimum: to be credible they had to have email access and web presence.

For the campaigns of both presidential candidates George W. Bush and Al Gore, email was a regular internal and external communication tool. Their campaign websites purveyed extensive information. Positions, schedules, links to endorsements, links to relevant news stories, full drafts of policy documents, events videos, campaign advertisements, and contacts for volunteering and donating were all hosted on both the Bush-Cheney and Gore-Lieberman domains. As in the 1996 cycle, both candidates routinely pointed the press, their supporters, and the electorate at large to their websites for additional detailed information and general reference.

One important innovation of the Bush-Cheney campaign was the localization of its web presence. The campaign website was customized to deliver specific content based on user location. As Dave Almacy, former White House Internet and E-Communications Director and an important figure in the 2000 and 2004 Bush campaigns, told us:

> [I]t wasn't just GeorgeWBush.com and you went there and there was one message for all. What they literally did is they built about 50 websites and a few more if you include all the territories...So it meant you could go to GeorgeWBush.com/ Maryland and within Maryland there would be specific contact information about your state and each individual city where there was a George W. Bush campaign that was being developed. So you could find out who the precinct chairmen were. If you lived in a certain zip code we could put you in touch with the local volunteers so that you could do either phone banks, or lit drops, or attend town hall meetings...There were always ways to get more people involved.[12]

Almacy also noted that the role of Internet personnel in national campaigns had crossed key thresholds in accordance with the continually rising prominence of Internet-based outreach to the electorate. He explains, "We've gone from the Internet director approach, from 'this is the guy who slaps content up after the fact,' to now the Internet plays a role in everything that a campaign and an organization is doing, and they have a seat at the table when they didn't before."[13]

Despite expansive growth in the depth and range of content, however, issues of user-provider gaps persisted. Many home users lacked the necessary connection bandwidths to access content. Most Internet users were using higher-speed modems than in 1996, but newly complex levels of data packaging had surpassed recent progress in users' connection speeds. The two campaigns were not effectively able to convert the large footprints of their websites into offline mobilization—the wealth of additional information still paralleled existing channels of communication, and neither campaign's web strategy was able to solicit significant levels of additional volunteering, registration, event attendance, message spin, or fundraising. Lastly, there was little coordination with supportive advocacy groups outside of the campaigns proper.

George W. Bush's Administration held similarly elevated goals revolving around a different, more accessible and transparent White House. A Bush spokesperson said the site would be revamped to "reflect Bush's serious self-effacing approach to serving the highest office in the land" and that the website would "be friendlier to look at and interact with and easier to search. It'll be deeper in content, and there will be a new organization of the site with a more creative approach."[14] Despite suggesting an enhanced, more efficient use of the Internet, the G. W. Bush Administration, like Clinton's before him, ultimately chose to dispense with the pretense of using email to easily communicate with the public. Emailing the White House became a more elaborate—and less anonymous—process. Users were required to provide their name, address, and organizational affiliation, as well as indicate whether their email concerned their support for, or opposition to, a specific Administration policy. While the Bush Administration launched "Ask the White House," and did hold discussion forums that addressed questions from users, the platform included filtering that limited interaction and allowed the White House to choose which questions to engage.

JIMMY ORR, WHITE HOUSE INTERNET DIRECTOR, ON EARLY DIGITAL ENGAGEMENT

"April 2003 I pitched something called Ask the White House and what that was, was a live chat. The purpose of that live chat was to allow the American people to communicate with the White House. The way I pitched it— communication staff around any president is going to be very protective. And they have to be…And since the Internet was fairly new I could launch a lot of things. Ask the White House I had to go through more formal channels to get the ok. I remember pitching it to Dan Bartlett and saying, 'Listen man, this is the safest medium in the world and the reason for that is we ask for questions from the public and then we take the questions we want to answer and we publish just those. People don't see all the questions coming in. We just answer the questions we want to answer.' Which is in communications that's what they tell you anyway…If someone asks you something, answer the question you want to. On Ask the White House we'd have a 30 minute chat with whoever, we'd pick the question, and the official would write up the answer, and that would all be live. I thought it was a good way to communicate with the public and it was another way to drive people to the website. It can't be press releases. That doesn't work. It can't be speeches. That doesn't work. It has to be unique content. Content that we create. So Ask the White House would do a couple things. One, it would allow the people to interact with the White House. Two, it would give reporters—reporters would actually write on it. They would see this chat and see that news was being made. So it was another way to get our message out. So the way I pitched it to Dan, as I said, was, 'We pick the questions so we're totally in control of it Dan. We're totally in control of it.' Ok. So after he green lights it Andy Card [the White House Chief of Staff] was the first person on. The very first. And this was in April 2003... He was so likeable—he was a natural politician and I use that in a flattering way. He is wonderful and he doesn't flinch. So the question comes in, 'Where do you think Saddam Hussein is?' And Andy Card types out before we can say anything, 'I think he's dead.' The next day newspapers across the America and networks and everything, 'White House Chief of Staff: Saddam Hussein is Dead!' He was still out there. Dan Bartlett calls me to his office the next morning, 'You told me this was the safest medium there was!' And I just said, 'Well Andy said it!' 'Well you're in there to protect that from happening!'"[15]

Indicative of the ultimate reality of engagement is the experiences concerning the content of the White House website over time. While initially approached as a valuable gateway to meaningful information-seeking and political conversation, the website of the Clinton years morphed largely into a combination of campaign pamphlets and tourism brochures. The Bush Administration's most important online engagement adventure may have been Barney Cam. Following the attacks of 9/11, the White House was closed to visitors. As a way to offer the public glimpses into the White House, originally during the 2002 holiday season, a web camera was attached to the President's pet dog, Barney, and viewers could observe the White House Holiday Party from his perspective as he ambled about the mansion. Garnering 6 million views in one month, it became an Internet (and network news) sensation and a spectacular success. This new window offers several insights:

(1) In one realm, the popularity of Barney Cam illustrated the surprising strength of more passive forms of engagement. Jimmy Orr, who from 2001 to 2004 was the White House Internet Director, said, "Traffic to the website then just exploded. It went through the roof. All these people who came to the White House website (YouTube wasn't there yet) who wanted to see this simple video of the president's dog running through the White House. It was unreal."[16] This experience spotlights the attraction of passive versus active information access, and substance vis-a-vis entertainment as engagement pathways. These concepts also interplay with the public mood, sentimentality, and relationship to national institutions.

(2) In another intriguing outgrowth, the Barney Cam was noticed and linked to many numerous outside news organizations, who then linked to various policy documents, speeches, press releases, and other relevant items. This chain of events illustrated the powerful ability of digital media—even when not immediately substantive in the traditional sense—to be reabsorbed into traditional information platforms and spark wider discussion of administrative policies.

(3) In a third mode of interaction, the public interest in White House entertainment signified a transition toward elements of embrace of the First Family akin to the British public's interest in the Royal Family. Events, regardless of their relevance (or lack thereof), nevertheless inspired a degree of committed focus from durable audience segments. Bush and his advisors may have recognized this early on. For the second Barney Cam, Orr was reluctant to request that President Bush participate only to receive a call at 7 AM on a Saturday that the President wanted the film crew to come in for Barney Cam because it had snowed the night before.

(4) The Barney Cam's format and content allowed for large-scale apolitical outreach to the public that could then be translated into political outreach to a larger audience than would have otherwise been receptive to Bush Administration messages. David Almacy, who was deeply involved in the project, explained its resonance:

> What was interesting about this video is that it had a much broader appeal as opposed to your day-to-day messaging... Because regardless of your personal faith or political beliefs, there were certain things about this video because it featured the President's pet and it featured beautiful decorations. It featured the White House, which is an institution that I think is so immediately recognizable by many people, not just in the United States but around the world... It was a fun thing that had broader appeal.[17]

(5) Barney Cam had a spontaneous and unscripted aspect that connected in an important way. It was authentic in some surprising ways, and authenticity (or at least seeming authenticity), as will also be seen later, is an important dimension for presidents to successfully resonate with audience segments. When it came to spontaneity, it would be hard to surpass having a dog wandering around the White House. Orr reinforced this point, telling us,

> When the over-communicating communications people—when you start putting in people who are too "public relations specialists" and they think that everything has to be staged and everything has to be perfect. That everything has got to be exact that's when you don't connect anymore. There has to be looseness, levity, and behind the scenes stuff that most of the time people don't see. It is so important that they see it. It really is. When we overdo it and we think something has to be too perfect and too staged that's when you no longer connect.[18]

Through the linking processes described above, White House perspectives and priorities could seamlessly be accessed through an extremely wide array of portals, simply because of the proliferation of Barney Cam. Almacy described the mechanics of this linkage through nascent platforms defined by social sharing elements that were critical precursors to the integrated social media platforms that would soon arise:

> [W]e really had to [ask ourselves] was it more important to track how many video watches were coming directly from [our] website, or was it more important to leverage all the other websites that are out there that are housing our content and potentially reaching individual audiences that we could not reach on a daily basis on WhiteHouse.gov?

But now we're reaching a wider audience via these blogs, mainstream media, and other sorts of websites that were posting their versions of it.[19]

Almacy explained that despite the soft nature of the initial content draw, the proliferation and pursuit of Barney Cam story placement was a critical element in a broader strategy of engaging the public through the emerging media milieu of that time:

> It really went to the core of how it changed our strategy, which was if we treat every piece of content this way on WhiteHouse.gov, can we in fact expand the reach of our content on a daily basis, and not just around holiday time? And so then you add the advent of social media and this concept of engagement and the Web 2.0 approach. And now all of a sudden it is a conversation about policy issues, and immigration, and social security, and national security, and all of these things that were not occurring on WhiteHouse.gov specifically.[20]

2004: DIVERGENT ENGAGEMENT

Access to and capabilities of Internet technology grew for both citizens and politicians between 2000 and 2004. Not only had email become a standard internal and external communication tool for all realistic political campaigns, it had now grown to engage substantial numbers of campaign email subscribers, offering the Bush and Kerry campaigns the opportunity to create their own receptive audience spheres. More importantly, the two campaigns' websites not only conveyed information—they also served as organizational resources. In addition to keeping up with press releases, speeches, event schedules, policies, advertisements, media appearances, endorsements, and media spin, the two campaigns effectively used their online presence for organization and mobilization, but with significantly different emphases. The Bush-Cheney operation coordinated digital media primarily for physical organization. In addition to providing event information, the Bush-Cheney website allowed registered users to download lists of registered Republicans in their voting precinct. It also offered strategies for physical outreach and provided a suggested narrative for door-to-door meetings. While the Bush campaign used its web presence to decentralize outreach efforts, effectively empowering their supporters to seize the initiative and locate and reach out to like-minded neighbors, most of Bush's fundraising occurred via traditional formats of face-to-face greetings, dinners, and prominent bundlers collecting written checks. In contrast, the Kerry campaign, faced initially with a yawning fundraising gap, devoted much of its online efforts to closing that gap—to great effect. The Kerry-Edwards operation came quite close to finishing the general election sprint with parity in fundraising.

Though owing to radically different causes, George W. Bush, like Bill Clinton, faced a major crisis of leadership during his second term when, in the wake of Hurricane Katrina, the fundamental operational integrity of the Bush Administration came under severe public scrutiny. Whereas Clinton's standing came into question because of issues of ethics and character, Bush's eroded because of basic questions of competence. Just as Internet-based media had filled a niche of investigation and

dissemination overlooked by the mainstream press during the critical early phases of
the Lewinsky scandal, blogs, citizen journalists, and digital news outlets broadcast
stories, images, and perspectives directly to the public, and also fulfilled a number
of other functional roles as the Bush government's crisis of competence began to
grow.[21] Bush's Administration, like Clinton's in 1998, was caught off guard, and
was initially unable to wield managerial controls to implement the traditional gatekeeping functions of the mainstream press. Two additional parallels are important
to note. First, just as with the Lewinsky scandal, the mainstream press eventually integrated the content and practices of the alternative digital community and,
second, the White House eventually regained control of the narrative and of the
broader information flow and engagement with the public, even if it was achieved
through "stagecraft over substance."[22] While the damage had been done (and the
Bush Administration and the Republican Party would accordingly suffer in the
2006 midterm elections), it is again important to reflect on the ability of the White
House, even under severe strain, to nevertheless use its influence to regain control of
the dynamics of public engagement (with news information, at the least).

2008: IMBALANCED ENGAGEMENT

From the start of Barack Obama's bid for the White House, his campaign broke
new ground in its embrace of Internet technology. Speaking as someone who was
close to Obama on the campaign trails, Teddy Goff, Director of New Media for
Obama's 2008 campaign (who later became Director of Digital Media for his 2012
campaign), saw firsthand Obama's commitment to using Internet technologies to
mobilize campaign workers. The commitment was professional, but also reflected
personal dedication on Obama's part. Goff said, "First of all the candidate himself,
Senator Obama, was a person who cared about the Internet. Cared about technology. And it was important to him that he be a savvy operator." Goff continued,
describing the impact of this mindset on the campaign, adding, "I think the Internet
is sort of animated by a lot of the values that caused him to become a community
organizer when he was young. I mean, he famously moved to Chicago with his goals
of forging connections between people and empowering people and all that. And
that is sort of what the Internet does."[23]

At the level of technological advances between 2004 and 2008, the full-blown
arrival of social media platforms had a dramatic effect, particularly on the Obama
campaign. More than anything else, these platforms are most notable for putting
personal interactivity at the forefront of the interface. Yet, also quite important is
the integrated incorporation into one platform of email, chat, bulletin board, and
news media access. This blended approach to online interaction allows for a more
seamless transition across spheres of activity that had previously required (minimal)
navigation across compartmentalized nodes. 2008 marked an interesting transition
in the race between politics and industry: although the commercial world had not
yet embraced it as a necessity, the Obama campaign fully immersed itself in the
world of social media engagement. An even more significant transition in the 2008
campaign was the relegation of the two campaigns' official websites to their broader
engagement of social media.

Whereas the two campaigns of 2004 tacked in different directions for their online engagement, both Barack Obama and John McCain adopted social media engagement for all forms of information dissemination, physical organization, mobilization, and fundraising. Where the two campaigns differed, however, was simply in their respective levels of digital media engagement. The McCain-Palin campaign continually, and unsuccessfully, struggled to keep pace with the Obama-Biden media relations, ground coverage, and fundraising machines. Republican operatives appear to have fully grasped the relevance of social media platforms to their multifaceted outreach, fundraising, and organizational tools (such as shareable talking points, strike lists, and event schedules)—but they possessed neither the financial nor the manpower resources to adequately convert engagement into action with any competitive parity.

Chris Hughes, co-founder of Facebook, then 24 years old, brought with him a belief forged from Facebook's founding principles, namely, that supporters would foster more meaningful connections by attending neighborhood meetings and calling on people who were part of their daily lives. This view matched Obama's line of thinking. "One of my fundamental beliefs from my days as a community organizer is that real change comes from the bottom up," the *New York Times* quoted Obama as saying. "And there's no more powerful tool for grassroots organizing than the Internet."[24]

Hughes' key tool, My.BarackObama.com, helped the Obama campaign to reach beyond its base of young, Internet-savvy supporters. As Ellen McGirt reported in a March 2009 profile of Hughes for *Fast Company*, "He helped develop the most robust set of web-based social-networking tools ever used in a political campaign, enabling energized citizens to turn themselves into activists, long before a single human field staffer arrived to show them how."[25]

Indeed, My.BarackObama.com was "a surprisingly intuitive and fun-to-use networking website that allowed Obama supporters to create groups, plan events, raise funds, download tools, and connect with one another—not unlike a more focused, activist Facebook."[26] MyBO, the short name for the website, also let the campaign reach its most passionate supporters "cheaply and effectively." The website also contained a page, FightTheSmears.com, to deflect potentially damaging online rumors, including that Obama was not born in the United States.

MyBO also allowed the campaign to mount a response immediately after the *New York Times* published an op-ed piece by William Kristol claiming that Obama was in the pews on the day the candidate's spiritual adviser, Rev. Jeremiah Wright, delivered a controversial sermon. Sharp-eyed Obama supporters posted Obama's schedule in Florida to the listserv, drawing it to the attention of the *Times* and requiring the Gray Lady to issue a correction.

Hughes said: "People have always communicated, organized around campaigns. We just made it easier." Indeed, by the time of the November election, My.BarackObama.com had more than 161,000 active users. Obama volunteers had created more than 2 million profiles on the site, formed 35,000 groups, and posted 400,000 blogs. They also raised $30 million on 70,000 personal fundraising pages, and planned 200,000 offline events.[27]

By any estimation, the Senator from Illinois had become an Internet superstar. The candidate's Facebook page had 3 million followers, his MySpace page 845,000 friends, and his Twitter account 123,000 followers. Trendrr.com reported that Obama's name was mentioned in more than 500 million blog posts, his YouTube videos received 14.5 million hours of playing time, and he had his own "virtual campaign" in the cyber world, on Second Life[28] (a virtual world in which "residents" can create an identity in the form of an avatar who meets people, buys land, and generally lives a "second life").

In terms of the Internet, Barack Obama had achieved breathtaking results. His email list contained 13 million addresses; his campaign sent more than 7,000 different messages, many targeted to specific donation levels. In total, more than 1 billion emails were generated by his campaign. By comparison, just four years earlier, another Democratic presidential hopeful, Sen. John Kerry of Massachusetts, had 3 million addresses on his list, while his rival in the Democratic primaries, Howard Dean, had 600,000.[29]

Mobile phones were also ringing for Obama. A million people signed up for the candidate's text-messaging program. *The Washington Post*'s Jose Antonio Vargas underscored how important mobile phones had become to the Obama campaign by reporting that: "On the night Obama accepted the Democratic nomination at Invesco Field in Denver, more than 30,000 phones among the crowd of 75,000 were used to text in to join the program."

"On Election Day," Vargas wrote, "every voter who'd signed up for alerts in battleground states got at least three text messages. Supporters on average received five to 20 text messages per month, depending on where they lived."[30] In an act that symbolized Obama's heavy reliance on texting, his campaign text-messaged the announcement of Joe Biden, then a US Senator from Delaware, as Obama's pick for a vice-presidential running mate.

Obama was the candidate with his own iPhone app. The application's features reinforced supporters' commitment to their candidate. One feature, dubbed Call Friends, was advertised as "a great volunteering tool" that allowed users to "make a difference" by prioritizing their contacts by key battleground states, allowing them to "make calls and organize results all in one place." Another distinctive function of the app was "Call Stats," which allowed users to "see nationwide Obama '08 Call Friends totals" and find out how their own call totals compared to "leading callers." The app also provided "the latest news and announcements via text messages or email," and it let users browse media coverage of national and local campaign news.[31]

It is important to note that efforts such as the iPhone app were effective in pulling people along on Obama's march toward the White House. Yet, by the act of signing up as Obama supporters, individuals were taking much more positive steps than simply agreeing to passively await instructions. The declaration of support fed strength of support, a result predicted by cognitive dissonance theory, which suggests that people will change their attitudes, beliefs, and actions in order to reduce the uncomfortable feeling, or dissonance, caused by holding conflicting ideas simultaneously.[32]

Ultimately, Obama raised a record $745 million in his presidential campaign—including an unprecedented half a billion dollars online.[33] Needless to say, this allowed him to outspend the overmatched McCain by a huge margin. According to a 2008 University of Wisconsin study, Obama spent $21.5 million to McCain's

$7.5 million, from October 21 to 28. Even before the final advertising blitz, Obama had spent $190.2 million on media, compared with $76.7 million by McCain. Through October 15, Obama also spent $46 million on staff salaries, more than double McCain's $20.1 million, helping to open field offices and build a get-out-the-vote operation.[34]

Thus, money and messaging were of critical importance in propelling Obama into the White House on November 4, 2008. But they were only part of the picture: image also was important. In particular, media photographs and video showing Obama as a frequent user of mobile email using a BlackBerry smartphone complemented an image of the president-elect as a hip member of the "digirati," or the elite of the computer industry and online communities.

As the era of the Obama Administration got underway, a blog post on the website Easy and Elegant Life, devoted to "the search for everyday elegance and a study of the art of living well," reflected the love affair with Obama's chic connected image: "I understand that the Secret Service may not allow President Obama to continue to wear his beloved BlackBerry on his belt, citing it as a security risk," went the January 19, 2009, blog, by the "Elegantologist." "Personally, I think that they are simply forcing him to live up to his own elegance."[35] (There was a minor controversy after the election when President Obama wanted to keep his omnipresent BlackBerry mobile device, despite sharp argument from his national security team about the risks that its use posed. Extensive steps were taken so that he could keep his BlackBerry, a point he alluded to in his 2013 statement about social media engagement that begins this book.)

Throughout his first term, the image of Obama as a mobile and connected president lingered. Aside from media photographs showing the Chief Executive of the United States talking on a cell phone (for instance, arriving on Marine One in Baltimore, on January 29, 2010, which resulted in widespread republication), this portrayal was largely due to the fact that Obama was, on his own, a social media story: through social media the President could commune with the people, and every voice could be heard (if not necessarily heeded). Thus, social media represented an opportunity to achieve a fully democratic society.

Yet, the story was still more complex. President Obama's image no doubt benefited from other factors, including the perception of both social media and candidate Obama as exciting new forces on the communication landscape, the culmination of years of frustration with the outgoing Administration, and the economy's nosedive: all these events set the stage for the emergence of a fresh leader who could lead the country out of its deep malaise.

Social media were a critical element in the success of Barack Obama's pursuit of the presidency. From Facebook to YouTube, and cell phone apps to online campaigns, these Internet-based applications were a way for him to marshal his support and gain campaign contributions. Social media also became part of the narrative of the campaign, and a hallmark of Obama's style. In essence, they became a fundamental part of his brand. Branding is a powerful motivator for human purchasing behavior—for presidents no less than for beer, cell phones, or blue jeans. Yet, they were only part of the story of Obama's victory. Despite the highly significant role social media played, it was against the backdrop of a crumbling economy, an uninspiring opponent, the opportunity to repudiate grotesque chapters of racism in America's history, and a generally favorable press.

Additionally, the expectations were high in many quarters that social media would be used to help guide Administration policy. That expectation was not born out of thin air. Hughes wrote on My.BarackObama.com, shortly after the 2008 electoral victory:

> My.BarackObama has always been focused on using online tools to make real-world connections between people who are hungry to change our politics in this country. And the site isn't going anywhere. The online tools in My.BarackObama will live on. Barack Obama supporters will continue to use the tools to collaborate and interact. Our victory on Tuesday night has opened the door to change, but it's up to all of us to seize this opportunity to bring it about.[36]

Yet in terms of social media as a form of citizen empowerment, there is another element to Obama's campaign—a story that bears mentioning. It seems that the call for citizen engagement was taken quite seriously by some Obama volunteers who wanted him to come out in opposition to the Foreign Intelligence Surveillance Act of 1978 (FISA), which they saw as intrusive on their civil liberties. Daniel Kreiss relates that when his supporters did not get him to change his position, they "took to the blog to demand a strategic voice in the campaign given its perceived failures, but such a voice would have conflicted with staffers' tight control over communications and decision-making."[37] As a result, their rebellion was snuffed out. This incident remains the most significant attempt by social media-driven volunteers to redirect their candidate's position. That this was a failure despite the rhetorical stance of openness to precisely such guidance suggests that the ends of practical politics—winning—takes precedence over the means, in this case lofty rhetorical commitments to policy as a participatory process.

2012: BALANCED INTENSITY

The period from 2008 to 2012 saw few major qualitative advances in social media platform technologies. This was true despite the fact that technologies have grown faster, more efficient, and more seamlessly integrated, and that general suites of software are broader. Yet many incremental changes have affected the landscape as well. The three most significant advances from 2008 to 2012 are:

(1) Existing social media platforms have expanded across numerous interface technologies—digital media portals are now widely, and often fully, accessible on desktop, laptop, and mobile devices;

(2) Social media engagement is viewed as an essential component of running any commercial or political operation that depends on interaction with the public at large; and

(3) The tempo of engagement has increased—social media coverage of news and events involves markedly more rapid cycles of observation, dissemination, interpretation, reuptake, and amplification by both journalists and audiences alike.

The 2012 Presidential Election season witnessed financially matched operations engaged in a full-press duel via digital media technologies. It is possible that given greater financial resources, the McCain campaign would have done the same in 2008. However, given their monetary constraints, McCain's team opted to fuel more traditional ground operations. The Romney campaign, from the start, featured a less ground-intensive operation than the Obama campaign, and never sought to match the Obama campaign's engagement via digital media platforms.

In the week leading up to the 2012 vote, the Romney campaign announced the deployment of ORCA, a secretly-developed, highly sophisticated turnout tracking tool that would enable unprecedented Election Day mobilization. ORCA was designed as a smartphone application, distributed to approximately 34,000 volunteers who would have immediate access to shared strike lists (a.k.a. "walk lists") that would inform everyone connected whether individual targeted voters—down to the precinct level—had voted yet. The dispatched campaign volunteers would conduct their own informal exit polling by contacting the targeted person, and then update the strike list. Those who had not yet voted could then be contacted by other volunteers and encouraged to do so.[38]

ORCA offered three innovations: it was exclusively tied to a smartphone application, it was completely centralized, and it was designed to operate in real time. The application interface was designed to be user-friendly to the volunteers and to avoid the possibility of incorrect targeting or redundancy in last-minute voter outreach. Centralization was intended to allow the campaign headquarters to have ultimate discretion over how, and where, to target last-minute efforts. The real-time element of ORCA had the purpose of maximizing the utility of action and resources against a ticking clock. Despite the expert technical design and financial resources that went into designing ORCA, the endeavor ultimately failed: as data from field volunteers rushed in, the application system crashed. This left the thousands of field volunteers without access to the precinct strike lists, and the campaign with no accurate way to estimate where, and to what extent, targeted outreach had succeeded or fell short. It is worth noting that in 2008, the Obama campaign's voter tracking system, Gordon, crashed on Election Day. Nevertheless, a backup plan was in place in the form of traditional methods: frequent and frantic phone calls, and the manual updating of printed lists.[39]

The collapse of a much-touted, secrecy-shrouded initiative made for a compelling storyline, but its ultimate effect on the outcome of the Election was minimal. Eric Fehrnstrom, communications director of the Romney campaign, told us, "The meltdown of ORCA was overblown... The fact that it was not working on Election Day did not have any significant impact. I am reminded of the fact that the Obama campaign had something similar to ORCA in 2008...and it crashed on Election Day. And I don't think it affected the outcome in 2008 either."[40]

That said, ORCA was another example of social media being used from a central command post to give overall supervision to engaged campaigners carrying out the details of tactical activities with a limited degree of autonomy. As is the case with most other campaign technologies that use social media, it had minimal channel signaling capability, which limited volunteer ability to communicate with the central command post.

The outcome of the election is attributed to social media more than it ought to be—the negative characterization of Mitt Romney that the Obama camp so early and effectively orchestrated during the campaign, did far more to create an electoral edge than differences in social media strategies. The Obama campaign's own tracking system, Narwhal, was similarly centralized. Analytics teams would examine and sort vast amounts of incoming data, and volunteers would eventually receive targeted outreach messages from the campaign through a variety of interfaces. Like ORCA, Narwhal was constructed along upwardly aggregating pathways rather than along horizontally connected peer networks. The difference between the Obama and Romney campaigns' tracking and turnout systems was not due to substantive differences in public engagement—it was due to differences in the quality of physical design logic. Beyond the specific lessons concerning scalability and centralization, the ORCA experience revisits broader questions raised earlier about the ability to convert information and feedback into active participation, and the ability to use digital media interactivity for active, rather than passive, engagement.

In terms of tempo, Eric Fehrnstrom related to us the example of Democratic strategist Hilary Rosen who appeared on national television to say that Romney's wife, Ann, though she had raised five sons, "had never worked a day in her life." Fehrnstrom recounted, "It happened late in the evening. We first learned about it via Twitter, and at that point, Ann had not inaugurated her Twitter account, so we used that occasion to set up her account and then deliver her first tweet, which was "I chose to stay home and raise five boys, believe me, it was hard work."[41]

Would the outcome have been different had social media not been available? (Though there are obviously limits to such thought experiments, the counter-factual exercise can be illuminating.) Before social media existed, campaigns always used the "best available" technological tools (as they did in 2008): telephone banks, handbills, targeted mailings, and in-person canvassing. Nonetheless, the belief remains strong that social media not only could win campaigns but also could be used as a tool of citizen empowerment and mobilization to direct governmental policy.

In terms of the Obama campaign's use of social media, Alan Rosenblatt, former Associate Director for Online Advocacy at the liberal Center for American Progress, commented that, compared to 2008, "they definitely improved. As the campaign went on, they became more interactive, they became more social in the process. The President started to share a little more personal stuff—a picture of him celebrating with Michelle became the most tweeted picture ever."[42]

But still more important were his unofficial surrogates and self-directed supporters. These were individuals who self-activated and reached out to their own social networks. Rosenblatt said,

uncounted and unmeasured in this process is the whole network of surrogates and supporters and volunteers who are using their own accounts by the millions, probably, to influence other people not through Obama's Twitter account, not through OFA [Organizing for America]...but through their own personal pages. People were picking up stuff that they were getting via Twitter and just repurposing it...I think in the long run, the whole idea of a social media campaign, in order to make it effective, you have to get your audience to own your issues, own your success and use themselves as sort of strategic partners who share a stake in the outcome. That way, they are self-motivated to really champion the candidate in ways that the candidate couldn't ask them to do.[43]

This point is important in that loose confederacies of like-minded transient collaborators who use social media were influential in 2012 and should be even more so in 2016. This style of organization has already been prominent in coalition formation in online groups, and will increasingly spill over into the world of campaigns.

DIGITAL MEDIA AND THE PRESIDENCY: THE CHALLENGE OF GOVERNANCE

Campaigns set high bars for expectations of interactivity and responsiveness—in many instances campaigns can credit critical successes to such interactivity and responsiveness. However, the transition from the campaign battleground to the White House introduces every administration to a dynamic field of complex navigational hurdles. Regardless of any administration's stated intentions, which always sound laudable, they will inevitably arrive at the point where pursuits of transparency, engagement, and responsiveness are subordinated to the realities of institutional, legal, administrative, strategic, and logistical challenges. Moreover, based on the logic of having run successful, path-breaking campaigns that established new operational norms, every administration is likely to find itself in the position of having to roll back from prior proclamations of more meaningful engagement and transparency.

One of the take-aways from this chapter's overview is that social media are of increasing value in campaigns because of the feeling on the part of volunteers of intimacy with the candidate, ownership of campaign process and content, and a sense of autonomy in carrying out tactical activities in a larger electoral strategy. But another take-away that has implications for the unfolding of citizen engagement under the Obama Administration has been largely overlooked: namely, the myth of an election in the hands of the candidate's supporters. During 2008 and 2012, social media were used from a central authority to direct volunteers, and the opportunities for volunteers to influence the campaign were virtually nil. They did have an opportunity to act innovatively and autonomously, but only within narrowly constrained dimensions. While individual citizen efforts were important to the success of the Obama campaigns, and there was great enthusiasm for his candidacy among many demographic categories and ideological groupings, he depended heavily on bundlers and large contributors for his campaign to get off the ground and go on to set new fundraising records. These facts are overlooked in what has become the myth of the freeform citizen-empowered campaign.

Jeff Howe, a *Wired* magazine writer credited with coining the term "crowdsourcing," told us, "You had a campaign that was kind of being touted as the first crowd driven campaign, and you can make the case that Obama was really good at crowd funding…But when you really started to dig into the details it just really kind of wasn't true." He explained that misunderstandings about crowdsourcing obscured popular understanding of the underlying facts. He added, "From everything I heard talking to [media strategy and technology firm] Blue State Digital and the guys who were central to the campaign, there was not a lot of autonomy at the precinct level. There were marching orders, they came down, and they were followed very well." Howe's overall assessment contradicts the popular conception that many retroactives apply to the Obama campaign, noting, "I didn't get the impression that you had decision making from the grassroots up, which would be much more of a crowdsourcing model."[44]

Because of the myth, it is easy for both the President and his army of volunteers to want to invoke for governmental processes, the same (improperly understood) mobilizing tactics that led to his electoral victories. That is to say, the myth is attractive to all parties, and they all tend to believe it. Therefore they invoke the myth (which they believe is true) to mobilize people in the way they (thought they) did for the election to improve governmental processes. The echoes of the myth reverberate through many of the citizen engagement initiatives that followed, both during his transition, and throughout his first and second term in office.

PART II

THE OBAMA PRESIDENCY

FRAMING THE "PEOPLE'S WHITE HOUSE": CROWDSOURCING AND THE CITIZEN'S BRIEFING BOOK

THE NEXT SEVERAL CHAPTERS DELVE MORE DEEPLY INTO THE OBAMA ADMINISTRATION'S practices for digital engagement, considering in finer detail how these practices use social media to gather, broadcast, and collaboratively engage political information. We cover several mini-case studies, "counterfactual" examples of social media input, and a sampling of White House and Obama Administration social media initiatives. This chapter looks at a Transition Team social media engagement experiment, while later chapters examine the Obama Administration once it came to power.

EXPECTATIONS OF CHANGING THE WAY WASHINGTON WORKS

In the weeks after the 2008 election, the notion that America might be on the threshold of a new era of citizen participation in governmental decision-making excited technology enthusiasts. That view was due partly to the Obama team's highly effective use of social networking sites to gain power, as well as to the huge following of Internet-savvy supporters who helped put the first African-American US president in office.

David Carr, the *New York Times* media columnist, wrote that the incoming president would have "not just a political base, but a database, millions of names of supporters who can be engaged almost instantly." And, Carr continued, "There's every reason to believe that he will use the network not just to campaign, but to govern. His e-mail message to supporters on Tuesday night [election night] included the line, 'We have a lot of work to do to get our country back on track, and I'll be in touch soon about what comes next.'"[1] Such words lifted the hopes of those who yearned for change in the way the nation's capital did business; and indeed, President Obama would soon be "back in touch" with the American people to address that issue.

THE WHITE HOUSE WEBSITE SETS THE TONE

In the beginning, the most visible symbol of change in Washington, aside from Obama himself, was the website of the White House, www.WhiteHouse.gov. Redesigned just prior to Obama's inauguration, the site tried to humanize the image of the President's residence while reinvesting it with elegance. WhiteHouse.gov reflected the tone that Obama himself had set during the campaign: its language was upbeat, but not excessively hyperbolic; its format was eye-catching, but not overly pretentious. Most significantly, the site's home page included links to such social media tools as Facebook, Twitter, Flickr, MySpace, and YouTube, implying a desire to connect with the public. There also was a feature called the White House blog, ostensibly a symbol of the new openness and transparency in the chief executive's office.

One interesting feature was the splash (startup) screen that welcomed first-time visitors to the White House webpage and asked them to leave their email addresses so they could receive updates and further information. Though optional, visitors had to either accept or decline the invitation before they were allowed to proceed to the webpage. This arrangement further reinforced the impression that the Obama Administration was interested in using "push" social media to get its message out to the public. The fact that one was asked to sign up ("opt-in") to receive electronic communications from the White House could easily be construed as subtle pressure to agree to be contacted in the future. Though sophisticated people may well have recognized that choosing to withhold one's personal information from the White House may not have influenced the availability of information being sought, or some future treatment by the government, there was no way to ensure that this would not be the case for less sophisticated visitors.[2]

Thus, the nature of the splash page was one-way communication: you could get a message *from* the Administration, but there was no easy way to get a message *to* the Administration. While this in itself was not surprising, since all large organizations look for ways to lower the resource demands required to serve unique customer needs, it did highlight the yawning gap between the aspirations of easy access and the realities of fending off distractions while pursuing political objectives. Finally, in the early days of the Obama Administration, a form was available on the website that allowed people to ask questions, but this disappeared quickly, as even automatic sorting systems were overwhelmed by the volume of requests.

CROWDSOURCING'S EMERGENCE: DREAMS OF SOLUTIONS TO GOVERNMENTAL PROBLEMS

As the Obama era began, or was about to begin, attempts were made to engage citizens in the presidency through projects that, in one form or another, exemplified "crowdsourcing." The term, coined by journalist Jeff Howe in the June 2006 issue of *Wired* magazine, described a web-based business model that "harnesses the creative solutions of a distributed network of individuals through what amounts to an open call for proposals."[3] Daren Brabham has extolled crowdsourcing as a problem-solving tool that can "harness the collective intelligence of the crowd" to benefit government projects.[4]

In classic crowdsourcing, an open call for solutions to a problem goes out to a large mass of potential solvers. The solvers form an online community, and the sourcing organization and the crowd both submit and filter solutions, searching for the superior ones. On the one hand, it is argued, crowdsourcing permits the rapid, and relatively inexpensive, exploration of problems by a wide, external talent pool, allowing solvers to build a kinship with the crowdsourcing organization. On the other hand, it can produce results of inconsistent quality, and has raised some concern among trade unions, given its sourcing of cheap—or even free—labor.[5]

Another concern about crowdsourcing is its scalability. Large corporations use it to solve problems drawing on employees from their global workforces. But could it work on a national scale for a contentious issue, such as decision-making on the healthcare initiative under the Obama Administration? Howe told us that he did not think so, but thought someone might be able to convince him that it would. Yet he did admit that it could work on a state-wide level, explaining, "It is at that local level I think that it can be really effective. I think even the state level starts pushing it."[6]

One pre-Obama application of federal-government crowdsourcing, or more accurately, peer production via collaborative democracy, was the Peer-to-Patent Community Patent Review project for the US Patent and Trademark Office (mentioned briefly in the Appendix). Peer-to-Patent was announced in 2006, during the Bush Administration's second term, and developed by Beth Noveck, who would eventually become Obama's Deputy Chief Technology Officer for Open Government. Peer-to-Patent engaged "citizen experts" to supply the patent and trademark office with information relevant to assessing the claims of pending patent applications.[7] Noveck's idea caught the attention of Obama's campaign staff and "in his campaign's technology platform, President Barack Obama called for incorporating Peer-to-Patent into the US PTO's regular procedure."[8] (The Patent Office had a seven-figure backlog of patents at that time, and serious questions were raised about the adequacy of examiners' expertise in light of a wide range of topics.[9]) Noveck's aspiration was to use digital tools to create what she describes as collaborative democracy, explaining, "Unlike crowdsourcing, which aggregates the responses or preferences of individuals throughout a network, collaborative democracy emphasizes shared work by a government institution and a network of participants."[10] Her model, however, depends on expertise and detailed involvement of trained and committed individuals, although she also asserts information might come from nontraditional sources, such as a "person [who] may be an expert on wetlands because she lives near one."[11] Her approach influenced the Expert Labs/ Grand Challenges scientific outreach, an example of crowdsourcing combined with participatory democracy that will be discussed later.

CROWDSOURCING IN THE OBAMA ADMINISTRATION AGENDA:
THE CITIZEN'S BRIEFING BOOK

In late 2008, after Obama won the election and was preparing to take power, the Transition Team was busy not only laying plans for the new Administration, but taking steps to articulate the vision of hope, change, and citizen engagement that had been part of the campaign. The Transition Team dubbed its website "Change. gov" with the subtitle "The Office of the President-Elect" (and quickly dropping a much-mocked special "president-elect" emblem to accompany it). One of the team's early steps was to declare that the people would have both the opportunity and capacity to participate to some degree in setting policy priorities and have ready access to the same information that was received by the Transition Team members.

TRANSPARENCY AND A SEAT AT THE TABLE

On December 5, 2008, John D. Podesta, the Obama-Biden Transition Project co-chair, set the bar high in terms of citizen access and involvement. He announced that all policy documents from official meetings with outside organizations would be publicly available for review and discussion on Change.gov. He thus kicked off an initiative that was called, "Your seat at the table." The website declared "we're inviting the American public to take a seat at the table and engage in a dialogue about these important issues and ideas—at the same time members of our team review these documents themselves."[12]

Michael Strautmanis, the Administration's Director of Public Liaison and Inter-governmental Affairs, commented on the Transition Team's website,

> Our role really is to open doors of the transition and give people the opportunity to come in and talk to us. We're doing things differently. We're posting all the materials that come into us on change.gov. You have an opportunity to respond to the things that other people are saying, to the things that other people are presenting. Transparency is the process that leads to real change. And transparency is the process by which people have confidence that things are really going to be different, that they will have that seat at the table.[13]

Julius Genachowski, co-chair of the Transition Team's working group on Technology, Information and Government Reform, explained that one of the group's goals was to develop a platform that "catalyzes active citizenship and partnerships in shared governance with civil society institutions."[14]

Though the words were lofty, it was unclear just how open the process was and to what extent official meetings allowed for public input. But again, the stated objectives for procedures set a standard by which the Obama Administration, once it took power, could be judged in terms of transparency (and not just transparency's existence as a bureaucratic policy but also, as outlined by Michael Strautmanis, its significance for citizen engagement and governance) once it took office. However, one mechanism that was put into place to gather citizen views, and to give voice to proceedings, if not necessarily a "seat at the table," is discussed next, namely the Citizen's Briefing Book.

CITIZEN'S BRIEFING BOOK: AN OPPORTUNITY FOR CITIZEN ENGAGEMENT

The Transition Team's Citizen's Briefing Book (CBB) was a broad-based attempt at crowdsourcing. Visitors to the Transition Team's site were invited to post recommendations for changes they wanted to see made in the governing of the United States, and they were also able to vote on other users' recommendations, as well as participate in a comment process. The collected ideas were to be presented to President Obama in book form after his inauguration.

Reside, a Minneapolis-based company, helped develop the software for the CBB, using technology from partner Salesforce.com, a maker of software that helps manage customer information about sales, marketing, and customer support.[15] Valerie Jarrett, the Transition Team's co-chair, informed viewers in a YouTube video that the CBB was a way for the transition process to remain "open and transparent."

Jarrett said, "Hundreds of thousands of you have sent in suggestions, ideas, and you've shared your personal stories. And we've thought of a way of bringing personal stories and suggestions directly to the President, and it's going to be called the Citizen's Briefing Book."[16]

The CBB would be a way to communicate "ideas and suggestions" from citizens "directly to him (Obama)," the transition co-chair said. She added that "your participation is key to our success."

Jarrett asked viewers to log on to Change.gov and "give us your ideas." The topics could be "energy, health care, reduction of our dependence on foreign oil, you decide whatever is important to you." She added, "Others will then be able to read your ideas and make comments and suggestions. You may even hear from the Transition Team." She explained further, "After we've compiled them all, the most highly rated suggestions will rise to the top and we'll include them in a Briefing Book for the President. The Citizen's Briefing Book will come directly from the American people."

Jarrett closed by summing up the planned exercise as "yet another way we will ensure that this transition is the most open and transparent one yet. You have participated in truly inspiring numbers," she said. "We hope that will be the case for the Obama-Biden Administration too. We need your help. We want to hear from you. Thank you."

Jarrett's message was in line with the idea of putting government in the people's hands, particularly when she added, "You have participated in truly inspiring numbers. We hope that will be the case for the Obama-Biden Administration, too." Noteworthy about these remarks was their personal tone, and her emphasis on "you," the viewer/contributor. There also was an attempt to empower the viewer, through her words, "you decide whatever is important to you." The simplicity of the language was also notable, suggesting an attempt to reach out to a wide cross-section of people, including those who might be only minimally familiar with or who might not know how to use mediated communication. In short, this introduction promised great leaps in American government, with social media bringing the wisdom of the crowd to decision makers.

RESULTS OF THE EXERCISE

On Friday, January 16, 2009, three days before Obama's inauguration, a blog post-ing on Change.gov by Dan McSwain, an Obama Transition Team staffer, called the CBB a "tremendous success."[17] The blog said the CBB "enabled everyday Americans to share their expertise and insight with President Obama." In a video posted on YouTube, Strautmanis said more than 70,000 people participated in the CBB, cast-ing half a million votes, and offering "tens of thousands of wonderful ideas."[18] Yet, though initial attitudes were positive, the Transition Team later began to feel dis-couraged. In our interview with him, McSwain said, "At the time I was personally frustrated with the Citizen's Briefing Book because I thought it could have played a bigger role or it could have been distilled in a more powerful way. Or something like that."[19] He also noted that this process was much more difficult than it may have seemed from the outside, explaining, "there was no way for the executive office to take public comments like this. And because of things like the Paperwork Reduction Act, setting up a platform to accept comments that then become some kind of gov-ernmental record is really difficult."[20]

The completed CBB, however, was not released until nearly four months later. It was finally unveiled on May 11, 2009, coinciding with the announced renam-ing of the Bush Administration's Office of Public Liaison as the Office of Public Engagement (OPE). The renaming sought to reflect the Obama Administration's hope that the office would be the point of contact for citizens as they interacted with the executive branch.

As a press release said, the OPE would "help build relationships with Americans by increasing their meaningful engagement with the federal government." Serving as "the front door to the White House," OPE, the release said, "will allow ordinary Americans to offer their stories and ideas regarding issues that concern them and share their views on important topics such as health care, energy and education." In addition to its traditional White House operations, OPE would now also focus on "getting information from the American people outside the Washington beltway through special public events as well as activities on the website." The office, it said, "will have a strong on-line presence, including blog postings from OPE staff and other interactive elements."

The OPE's first official act was to release the finished CBB.[21] The introduction to the 32-page booklet echoed Jarrett's sentiments of months earlier, as well as those of the OPE name-change press release, pointing out that the idea of the CBB was to create a "grassroots version of the research binders that presidents receive every day." Instead of advice from top government officials, the CBB was presenting "ideas sub-mitted by ordinary people and reflecting the enthusiastic engagement from the pub-lic we saw throughout the course of Change.gov." The introduction said "125,000 users submitted over 44,000 ideas and cast over 1.4 million votes, with the most popular ideas accumulating tens of thousands of votes each."

The completed CBB contained "some of the top ideas, broken into groups by issue area." Each idea's popularity was indicated by a number that appeared next to it, representing how many people voted for the idea, with ten points awarded for each positive vote. In addition, a "word cloud" for each category of ideas represented the "frequency with which various words and concepts appeared through the entire process." The introduction concluded by saying, "out of the tens of thousands of submissions, these ideas found the most support; here they are, unvarnished and unedited." Some top CBB ideas, by category, are shown in table 4.1.

What was apparent in the CBB was that, though it brimmed with proposals and votes, it lacked novel thinking and the potential to set a new direction for the Administration. There were no thrilling breakthrough ideas among the top vote getters. Instead, they were well-trod issues of candidate Obama's core supporters, and for the most part themes previously endorsed by him. The ideas topping the

Table 4.1   Top-rated Citizen's Briefing Book ideas (January 2009)

Economy
- Revoke the George W. Bush tax cuts for the top 1%. (57,080 points)
- Let's make reduced-scale farming profitable! Less dependence on imported foods! (42,070 points)
- More stimulus focus on green jobs. (30,470 points)

Education
- An end to government-sponsored abstinence education to be replaced by an introduction of age-appropriate sex education. (65,350 points)
- Focus on the arts and creativity. (12,970 points)
- Libraries of all types need our support. (10,810 points)

Energy & Environment
- Commit to becoming the "greenest" country in the world. (70,470 points)
- Bullet trains and light rail. (65,100 points)

Foreign Policy
- Permanent closure of all torture facilities (such as Guantanamo and Abu Ghraib). (61,250 points)
- Reevaluate aid to Israel. (37,240 points)

Health Care
- Stop using federal resources to undermine states' medicinal marijuana laws. (66,170 points)
- Get the insurance companies out of health care. (55,080 points)

Homeland Security
- No more wars on abstract concepts. (38,250 points)
- Eliminate "Don't Ask, Don't Tell": so we don't lose any more soldiers. (35,840 points)

Technology
- Boost America's economy with legal online poker. (46,890 points)
- Restore net neutrality protections to the Internet. (46,220 points)
- Vote and debate all bills online and show what industries contribute the most to each representative's campaign. (40,080 points)
- Each of the 50 state governors should create a version of this site to gather ideas from their constituents. (25,730 points)
- National Wi-Fi. (23,540 points)

Additional Issues
- End marijuana prohibition. (92,970 points)
- Revoke the tax exempt status of the Church of Scientology. (52,470 points)
- People talking to government. (41,740 points)
- Marriage equality. (26,400 points)
- Bush Administration investigation. (23,820 points)[22]

list included more spending for light rail, solar power, a green environment, and education. They also included items seeking to repudiate Bush Administration policies. These issues were at the core of candidate Obama's Democratic base support. Special and single-cause interests were also well represented: libraries, small farms, anti-Scientology, pro-Internet poker, pro-gay, and pro-marijuana. Among the top-ranked items was a clear urge to use technology for access to levers of governmental powers. Examples included "people talking to government," national Wi-Fi, having governors offer citizen-input opportunities similar to the CBB, and voting and debating "all bills online." Opinions in favor of legalizing marijuana showed up in different places and, as a foreshadowing, would continue to do so.

Once the exercise was completed, the project managers were confronted with what to do with all the information. They wanted to make it public, of course, but how should the information be used to affect Obama Administration policy? One challenge they had was taking all of this information and making it meaningful and useful for the Administration. Dan McSwain said, "There is lots of feedback coming in from the citizens. How do we distill that feedback and pass it on to decision makers and administrators in a meaningful way? And at the same time show the public that their considerations, concerns, and questions are being seen? I think this is probably still one of the most challenging questions."

Word clouds were used, McSwain said, because it was important to get "everyone involved in the transition to understand what was going on with the top-line thirty-thousand foot view so we could see what was a hot topic for people. But I think that parsing all of that information was really challenging. Word clouds were an ineffective way of doing that. It leaves a lot to be desired."[23] The President, speaking of the CBB in a YouTube video, was ambiguous in his presentation of the results of this exercise. He noted that "many of the ideas [the public] offered, from improving light rail transit, to modernizing our energy grid, to a new national service corps," had "been embraced by my Administration."[24] On the one hand, this comment could have been taken to mean that the public's feedback helped to set a new direction for the government; on the other hand, it could have meant that the public's input helped to reaffirm an existing position. Evidence for the latter is the fact that all of these initiatives had been endorsed well before the CBB exercise. This suggests that the response was a post hoc justification for actions already intended.

If Obama's aim was to avoid appearing too committed to one position or the other, ambiguity was a good strategy. To the extent that any items appearing in the CBB were previously favored by candidate Obama, it was easy to point to the book as a rationale for pursuing them. In the event that President Obama wished to defer acting on any such items, it was equally easy to ignore them. But beyond their being easily manipulated, it was noteworthy that none of the items in the CBB prompted a novel policy direction.

In fact, as we noted, and which will become a recurring theme, the government's follow-up moves suggested an effort to justify stances already taken, or to remain vague when it suited politicians' or staff members' purposes. For example, shortly after the CBB's release, video replies to some of the more popular suggestions were made by White House officials and posted on YouTube. In a nearly four-minute clip, Nancy Sutley, Obama's then chair-designee for the White House Council on Environmental Quality, addressed the topics of mass transit, energy efficiency, and green jobs, but disclosed few legislative details, aside from mentioning that the forthcoming economic stimulus plan would respond to these concerns.[25]

Although the CBB gave the impression of expanding the public's access to a presidential administration, Sam Stein, a columnist for the liberal-leaning *Huffington Post* website, noted "the engagement" went only so far. "There remains," Stein wrote, "a crucial limitation on follow-up interactions, whether it be about policy pitches or question, unless another user picks up the baton."[26] For instance, Stein noted that *ABC* television journalist George Stephanopoulos, taking his cue from the CBB, asked Obama whether the incoming president would consider prosecuting members of the Bush Administration for breaches of the Constitution in connection with the use of torture to interrogate military prisoners tied to the September 11, 2001, terrorist attacks on New York and Washington. Stein noted that "Obama fielded the question—his website, citing a policy of not commenting on national security matters during the transition, had offered a previous response from [Vice President] Joe Biden—but then was pressed twice more to explain his answer." These observations illustrated how the ideas of citizen participation and transparency inherent in the Obama campaign may not have fit well with post-campaign reality.

The credibility of the CBB itself was questionable in light of the arbitrary ten-point system used to evaluate its biggest issues and the ease with which interest groups could attempt to stuff the virtual "ballot boxes." Nancy Scola, a blogger for *techPresident*, noted that a weakness of the CBB was that it allowed "for linking to individual ideas, making it easier for activists to rally support for their contributions."[27]

IMPACT OF REPORT

So the question remained: What was the purpose of the CBB? The Obama team invested significant effort in making ordinary people feel as if their views had been registered, but, of course, the participants could not be considered representative of anyone but themselves. Nor was there any commitment to act on any of the proposals. So, it may have been that the site designers thought that the mere sense of "being heard" was sufficient to meet, or at least a first step toward meeting, the goal of citizen involvement via social media. (And in this they are probably not mistaken, at least in terms of the majority of users.) As will be noted later, many citizens who engage in social media for setting policy directions understand they will not necessarily have an impact; but just having an opportunity to register their views can be satisfying. We have heard this not only from users in interviews, but also from insiders, including Macon Phillips, the White House Director of New Media.[28] David Almacy, the White House Internet and E-Communications Director under President George W. Bush, also perceived this to be the case. He told us that people get psychological pleasure "when you do these online poll kind of things or when you give people the perception that when they email in they are reaching the highest echelons of politics and impacting policy." However, rather than changing anything, "you get credit for just having those channels open."[29]

Dan McSwain also felt that this exercise allowed them to change the internal infrastructure dramatically so that future interactions could occur:

> I think looking back, the real accomplishment was actually the infrastructural part. Getting in a platform that could take all of these questions that we could assemble some of the data and then keep these records as the executive agency in a government tech regulatory environment that really didn't know how to handle stuff like this. That was a huge accomplishment. And I think we were all kind of amped up on just having won that—we were not really appreciating these challenges for what they were. But now a few years on and having gone through a lot of battles during my time at the FCC and watching my friends continue to do it I realized that was a very significant win even if it didn't feel like it at the time. So I'm happy for that aspect of it.

McSwain said the exercise also broke down some barriers in attitudes within the White House:

> The infrastructure changes were very significant but they also led to a change in understanding for the Administration about what these tools could really do...I think that myself included and some of our colleagues were very impatient with that at the beginning because to us it just seems like the logical next step. And we couldn't really understand why some of the more risk adverse parts of the Administration felt the way that they seemed to feel about these things. But I think that they've come around in a really positive way.

The former Obama campaign strategist does think that some issues still remain. "And now that a lot of the tech barriers have either been lifted or demolished I think there are still some cultural barriers inside the White House about how these tools can be leveraged," he said.

"Did the Citizen's Briefing Book directly impact policy?" McSwain asked. "I have no way of knowing that. But did it achieve the goal of showing people both inside the Administration and citizens that technology was going to enable a two-way flow of information to the executive branch in a way that had never happened before? Yeah, I think the Citizen's Briefing Book was part of that overall effort that enabled that."[30]

CONCLUSION

The CBB was launched amid promises of expanded opportunities for public input in policy discussion. In one sense, the experience of the CBB illustrates that the potential exists to create, manage, and maintain some of the critical infrastructure for collaborative engagement. More importantly, the exercise also demonstrated a pattern of implementation that more convincingly incorporated the modalities of information gathering and agenda broadcasting by the White House.

In the next chapter, we will turn to another White House crowdsourcing experiment: the Online Town Hall. This exercise had the potential to provide a meaningful two-way communication forum and to be valuable in spurring direct citizen involvement in setting policy. The analysis will suggest that, once again, this was an opportunity that did not end up realizing its full potential.

CHAPTER 5

WHITE HOUSE ONLINE TOWN HALL

BILLED AS "THE FIRST OF ITS KIND" ONLINE, THE WHITE HOUSE ONLINE TOWN HALL, held March 26, 2009, allowed questions submitted by ordinary Americans via the web to be paired with those from a live White House audience. President Obama would answer each question in detail over the course of the 75-minute event.

SEEKING TO ENGAGE THE AMERICAN PUBLIC VIA SOCIAL MEDIA

"President Obama is trying to talk directly to the American people, these days," reported the *New York Times*, "making the case for his ambitious agenda in forums as varied as Jay Leno's late-night television show and a news conference on Tuesday. Now Mr. Obama will have a chance at even more direct engagement," the *Times* continued, "in what the White House is billing as the first Internet video news conference by an American president."[1]

Truth be told, Obama was not the first president to engage in online chats with ordinary Americans: former presidents Bill Clinton and George W. Bush had both answered questions over the Internet. Clinton likened the virtual town hall meeting at which he presided in November 1999 to Franklin D. Roosevelt's Fireside Chats and John F. Kennedy's live-TV news conferences. He praised the use of "the most modern technology for...old-fashioned communication between the American people and their president."[2]

Obama, however, was the first to communicate in a live video format, streamed directly from the White House website. The event's importance was further elevated because, following the success of his 2008 election campaign, the President's use of social media was news in and of itself.

The virtual town hall came just three months after the President, in his first executive act, issued a "Memorandum on Transparency and Open Government" that stated: "We will work together to ensure the public trust and establish a system of transparency, public participation, and collaboration." Openness, the short note added, "will strengthen our democracy and promote efficiency and effectiveness in government."[3]

To kick off the initiative, the White House website posted a short video introduction by President Obama that invited public participation. Obama described the initiative this way:

> One of my priorities as President is opening up the White House to the American people so that folks can understand what we're up to and have a chance to participate themselves....We're going to try something a little bit different....We are going to take advantage of the Internet to bring all of you to the White House to talk about the economy....Anyone can submit a question about the economy or vote on other questions.[4]

The Online Town Hall was promoted on WhiteHouse.gov under a banner reading "The White House is Open for Questions." All told, by the time the exercise was completed, 92,937 people submitted 103,978 questions and cast 1,782,650 votes (votes were allowed for more than one item), according to the White House website.[5] "Taking a page, perhaps, from reality television shows like American Idol," which invited viewers to vote for their favorite contestant in a singing competition, the *Times* reported, "the White House has asked Americans to vote on their favorite questions."

The President opened the online town meeting by declaring, "When I was running for president, I promised to open the White House for the American people. This is an important step toward achieving that goal." Obama then launched into a long prefatory statement on his programs and their progress.[6] This was followed by a series of screened questions that covered the well-trod ground of education, housing, and the economy. Jared Bernstein, Chief Economist and Economic Policy Adviser to Vice President Biden, acted as the "facilitator" for the meeting, selecting and reading out the questions, which were shown on huge video screens in corners of the East Room. Two video-recorded questions also were selected and played for Obama. As the President answered each question, he directed his remarks mainly to the live audience in the room.

The President answered six questions submitted online, including the two sent in by video, and another six from some of the 100 handpicked guests identified by the White House as "teachers, nurses, small business owners and community leaders." Obama also decided to answer a seventh online question—about whether marijuana should be legalized—that was not chosen by Bernstein.

Among the variety of questions, the one concerning the legalization of marijuana was visibly the most popular, voted upon by visitors across the many categories of topics, including green jobs and financial stability. A typical question was: "Mr. Obama, thank you for allowing us to ask our questions to you, unfiltered. What is your stance on legalizing marijuana federally, taxing it and regulating [it] much like alcohol and tobacco? I believe that the Drug War has failed, and needs overhaul."

According to *Los Angeles Times* blogger David Sarno, "some of us expected Obama to sidestep the politically sensitive topic." President Obama, Sarno observed, instead slipped his response in between questions from Bernstein. Although Bernstein and Obama had originally agreed to answer the most popular question, Sarno nonetheless gave the President extra credit for going "out of his way" to take the question "head on"[7], as shown in the White House transcript:

> *The President*: Can I just interrupt, Jared, before you ask the next question, just to say that we—we took votes about which questions were going to be asked and I think 3 million people voted or—
>
> *Dr. Bernstein*: Three point five million.
>
> *The President*: Three point five million people voted. I have to say that there was one question that was voted on that ranked fairly high and that was whether legalizing marijuana would improve the economy—(laughter)—and job creation. And I don't know what this says about the online audience—(laughter)—but I just want—I don't want people to think that—this was a fairly popular question; we want to make sure that it was answered. The answer is, no, I don't think that is a good strategy—(laughter)—to grow our economy. (Applause.)[8]

CRITICS EVALUATE THE ONLINE TOWN HALL

In the end, no tough or probing questions were posed (which is a clear advantage of calling upon "ordinary citizens" to pose questions to a president). Mitch Wagner, a blogger for *Information Week*, observed that even though the White House selected questions by asking citizens to vote on them in advance using a crowdsourcing tool based on Google Moderator, "the questions (Obama) answered were pretty much the same ones you'd expect to see in any forum, Web 2.0 or otherwise."[9] Jose Antonio Vargas, who blogs about the presidency for the *Washington Post*, compared the virtual town hall to "a press conference streamed via the web" with the "same stock of generalized, predictable questions answered by the same stock of generalized, tried-and-tested policy responses."[10]

Like the Citizen's Briefing Book (CBB), the Online Town Hall appeared to portray the Administration as sharing power with citizens, but it also showed the President using his social media platform to build support for established positions. The tone for this exercise was set when, before taking questions, President Obama spoke about his economic recovery plan. The cadence, syntax, and language of his speech made it sound as if it belonged in an election campaign:

> "We, as a nation, have already begun the critical work that will lead to our economic recovery," Obama said. "It's a recovery that will be measured by whether jobs are being created and families have more money to pay their bills at the end of each month. That's why we're preventing teachers and police officers from being laid off, and putting Americans to work rebuilding our crumbling roads and bridges and dams, creating or saving 3.5 million jobs in the coming years. And that's why we're putting a tax cut into the pockets of 95 percent of working families who will see that tax cut in their paycheck by April 1st."[11]

In light of the Online Town Hall's billing as a vehicle for conversation between the President and the public, critics looked askance at what to them seemed like Obama's rhetoric-laced attempt to whip up enthusiasm for his plan to revitalize the economy, which was inappropriate, not to mention anathematic to two-way communication. Actions like these prompted one detractor to say Obama's use of social media "looks like one of those corporate all-hands planning meetings where the employees are told that everyone will be listened to and all ideas are on the table—and the decision at the end is pretty much exactly the same as what the bosses figured out before the meeting started."[12]

The Online Town Hall's design as a television event raised further questions about its credibility as a vehicle for dialogue between the President and the citizenry. Throughout the proceedings, video screens showed the name of the crowdsourcing tool, "Open for Questions," like a brand. However, it was difficult to understand how a meaningful dialogue could take place if multiple questions could be posed without an opportunity for substantive discussion or interaction due to the tight time limits.

QUESTIONS OF CONTROL AND PREDICTABILITY IN OPEN FORUMS

For politicians, open forums provide an opportunity to demonstrate their popular touch, command of the facts, and ability to connect with audiences. It also allows them to get a sense of what at least some of the people are thinking. Plus they are generally easy to control since the audience is usually not able to do much in the way of follow-up or in-depth probing. They are risky, too, since odd questions can arise or groups can organize themselves to protest or wall-in a politician. That is why even most "open forums" are choreographed and controlled by staff in ways that are not always obvious to participants. The positives and negatives of open forums are magnified when using social media.

Wired magazine's Jeff Howe noted that the CBB and the virtual town hall under-scored the government's failure to recognize that participation "goes both ways." The experiments, the journalist said, demonstrated the Administration's use of crowdsourcing as a "listening device."[13] Kim Patrick Kobza, the Chief Executive of Neighborhood America, which develops social software for business and govern-ment, has said that "the whole point of [such crowdsourcing exercises] is not to find the question that the whole group wants to ask and that is predictable, but to enable cognitive outliers to ask the unpredictable question, to promote ways of thinking about problems (and solutions) that are uncommon."[14]

But the Obama Administration showed little interest in hearing from the fringe members of its audience. For example, Howe said, by highlighting the question of legalizing marijuana, the White House's Online Town Hall focused attention on a matter that did not normally appear on opinion-poll lists of the top issues facing the Administration. By handling the issue with a joke—saying that legalizing the drug was not a good way to grow the economy—Obama passed up an opportunity to deal openly with a legitimate, if off-topic, question, Howe said in 2009. Reflecting on the matter in 2013, Howe observed that the White House

used Google Moderator to crowdsource the questions that he was going to address. They started out and it made a lot of sense. We'll have ten categories. We'll have veterans' affairs. We'll have health care. We'll have economy. Etc. And in every one the marijuana legalization folks shanghaied the forum and voted their question to the

top. In every single one. So it was like, "Don't you think that veterans would be better served if?" "Marijuana has been shown to help with PTSD [post-traumatic stress
disorder]," "Think of what marijuana could do to the agriculture and the economy
for farmers." So Obama made a joke about it and proceeded to completely ignore the
crowd's questions.[15]

Commenting on the interaction of technology and issue control in the Online
Town Hall, Micah Sifry, cofounder of the Personal Democracy Forum (PDF),
which covers the ways technology is changing politics, said, "Well, right at the
beginning, they knew there was a lot of enthusiasm with the campaign for a continuation with a genuine kind of engagement with the public at large and with
their supporters in particular, so they did these 'open for questions' experiments."
However, Sifry, who edits PDF's *techPresident* web log, also noted that the platform itself was compromised. He explained, "The problem is that they were using
a dead tool, Google Moderator, which was not designed to handle those sorts of
numbers, so you end up with a popularity contest. You know, whose question
will get the most upvotes?" He continued, adding that the problems with Google
Moderator had consequences on the discussion. "Sure enough," he said, "it was a
question about medical marijuana, and instead of treating it respectfully, they felt
they had to laugh, they had to make a joke about those Internet people and their
silly preoccupations, even though 40 percent of the public is interested in legalizing
marijuana or medical marijuana."[16]

For John Wonderlich, Policy Director for the Sunlight Foundation, which aims
to increase transparency and accountability in the US government, Obama's reaction to the marijuana question illustrated the challenges inherent in governmental
attempts to hold a real conversation with the public. The White House reached out
to the public for ideas and what came back was an opinion "that marijuana laws are
counter-productive, and that became a liability for them from a communication
perspective," Wonderlich said in an interview.[17]

David Stern, former Director of Online Engagement at America*Speaks*, which
seeks to enable citizens to shape policymaking using online tools, saw constructive qualities in the White House Online Town Hall. Although President Obama
addressed the marijuana question "very briefly and with a mocking attitude," he
"gave it at least that," said Stern. That "is about as much as you can ask for.... If you
are a representative of democracy, you can't commit to incorporating all the input
you receive."

Stern said the Administration's mistake was "they haven't thought enough about
who is participating and how they are going to hear about this project."[18] If the
presenters of the crowdsourcing projects had worked "with groups across the political spectrum, such as AARP, the Chamber of Commerce, MoveOn.org (a left-
oriented political advocacy group), and simultaneously said, 'here, go at it,' it would
have been impossible for any one of those groups to take over and dominate the
process."

He praised the Obama Administration for taking on "an inherent political risk."
They were "willing to essentially disagree with the public...simply to establish this
conversation," Stern said. The emergence of marijuana legalization as a major topic

was "somewhat meaningful," he said. "People were talking about it," after the event. "It's died down significantly since then, but it was still revelatory in that sense."[19]

Laurel Ruma, a Government 2.0 "evangelist" for book and website publisher and conference producer O'Reilly Media, said the communication challenges the marijuana question created for the government showed them that "this is the way the Internet works."

"That's the danger of people coming to the Internet and not understanding that people will pick over and hijack threads," Ruma said. "That's how mob rules on the Internet, and that's a price of doing business on the Internet. The hope is you can separate heated arguments that are off topic or off the goals that you are trying to achieve; because you can never close the Internet."[20]

She also saw positives in the Online Town Hall, particularly in the attention it drew to the marijuana-legalization question. "Marijuana legalization is actually a real issue," she said. "And the people it did motivate, even if they thought it was a funny thing to play with, at least they now know about it."

The Administration's Office of Public Engagement later characterized the event as a "trial run" and promised to "continue to look for new ways to engage with the public and get your input."[21] (Which they have done, as will be discussed later.)

THE PATTERN CONTINUES

The cat-and-mouse game between President Obama and the insistent advocates of marijuana legalization has continued since this electronic town hall. At other social media events, such as his Facebook and Twitter town halls, marijuana was inevitably very high on the agenda. At his 2011 YouTube question-and-answer session, a *CBS News* analysis found that the predominating question concerned marijuana: "More than 193,000 people have submitted questions for the President via the video website or cast votes, rating the questions positively or negatively," *CBS* reported, adding that all but two of the 200 most highly rated questions dealt with drug policy.[22]

Given that social media applications of the kind we have been discussing were designed to provide a forum for public input, and given that the President has frequently claimed that he wished to be guided by information thus gathered, the organized use of social media to press for policy changes presents a fascinating problem. President Obama is plainly not interested in seeking to legalize marijuana use and does little to engage those who advocate for it at social media events.

Yet, advocates take seriously his invitation to use the tools of social media to press for their viewpoints, and refuse to disappear. This is embarrassing for President Obama, not the least because he is, on the one hand, rhetorically and symbolically committed to respond to the "wisdom of crowds." On the other hand, the persistence of pro-marijuana groups and advocates demonstrates a profound weakness in the use of social media as a form of social steering. That is, a well-organized group can "game the system," using the levers of communication to press for its views over (and, presumably in this case, against) those of the mass of disinterested citizenry. ("Gaming the system" means that participants in a system use the rules and tools of that system in a way that thwarts, evades, or defeats the legitimate goals of the system, usually to the advantage of the manipulator. Although the process used by the "gamer" may not be specifically forbidden by the rules, it is nonetheless against the spirit of the process as envisioned by the system designers.) There is controversy over whether such actions are acts of bad faith—which they would be from the system designer's viewpoint. Users, however, often view the system as theirs to use in a way that fulfills their own objectives, caring little whether it fulfills the system designer's objectives. Not only may they not care about actions that conflict with the designer's objectives, in some cases they actively seek to thwart the designer's objectives.

The issue of the disproportionate prevalence of marijuana legalization advocates among those responding to the call for public input brings an important issue to the fore. Social media entail not only a technological dimension but also an ideological dimension with a strong rhetorical element concerning the political prospects of these media. Social media are seen as a means for breaking up the dominance of entrenched elites who have controlled policy partly through their privileged access to communication channels. In opening up the policy process to new voices with new perspectives, the outcome was expected to be not only more democratic but also of a higher quality. This obviously had an ideological dimension that viewed the social media as a tool for changing the power structure.

More generally, from an ideological perspective, proponents of social media thought the technology would level the playing field, and that all voices would have an opportunity to be heard. In social media's purest form, all voices would have, if not an equal weight, at least an equal opportunity to carry weight on the basis of the force of argument and empirical evidence rather than any extrinsic or historical advantage. Pure democracy and an unencumbered marketplace of ideas would reign free. However, in the proponents' enthusiasm to reduce the influence of elites, they may not have properly factored in the pressure of other groups who are not traditionally defined as elites. That is, from the viewpoint of the general public, while large corporations and conservative philanthropists are seen as having enormous influence, the voices of unions, environmental groups, and other organizations are seen as being muffled, if not muted. Thus, *from both the public's and the advocates' perspectives*, social media could be seen as leveling the playing field.

This sanguine view, however, ignores the unequal effect that these latter groups often have in specific policy contexts. Yet, social media advocates, in their enthusiastic pursuit of the technology's employment in public policy debates, underestimate a different class of problem, which is the outsized influence of committed minorities who press for their own preferred policy options. All such groups may be less well-endowed in terms of the financial resources of powerful labor unions or large corporations; they often have members with only a profound commitment to the cause and ample disposable time and personal energy. When such groups exploit social media—and the policy process does appear to be open to manipulation through these platforms—the system actually falls prey to precisely the same problem it is meant to solve: domination by a minority group or viewpoint.

In one sense, democracy is served by this new group becoming involved in the process: a new voice or set of voices enters the dialogue and has impact. Moreover, the process now advances the cause of splinter groups that would otherwise be frozen out or at least have their energy absorbed with precious little impact.

IDEOLOGIES OF ENGAGEMENT AND NONENGAGEMENT

At this juncture, another element of the ideology of social media enters. This is that the public should be more knowledgeable about issues due to the greater abundance of information and the ease with which it circulates. The line of argument here is that with new information and more engaged public analysts, novel problems can be identified and old ones can be analyzed from a more fruitful perspective, that is, one that is more amenable to just solutions. Following the logic of classical democratic liberalism (and neo-Marxism), it would be expected that information and social connection should lead to political mobilization of the masses. With better information, the public can throw off the chains of false consciousness and better protect its interests in the welfare of society. A vision invoked by the New Testament captures the sentiment concerning the promise of social media: "And ye shall know the truth, and the truth shall set you free" (John 8:32; Darby translation).

Sumit Agarwal,[23] a former Google executive who in 2010 was the Pentagon's social media chief, told us that although social media fueled his dream of someday being able to confer "some amount of voting rights or decision-making authority" to "groups of people large or small that are able to demonstrate expertise," the reality was that "a fundamental disconnect" complicated the issue. "If people want to have influence on complex issues, they have to become experts," Agarwal stated. "They have to be more than just passingly familiar with a complex issue.... Social media absolutely allows them to band together, educate themselves to a higher degree and then really weigh in once they've reached that level of expertise."

Certainly, millions of people have used social media to find out about government policies, receive government information and messages, and weigh in on policy directions. Yet, in terms of policy activism, the overwhelming bulk of Americans pay little attention to policy pronouncements, and even fewer offer their policy views to elected representatives. As Laurel Ruma has noted, social media are most effective at changing the way business is done at the local level of government. The technology, Ruma said, has prompted "a return to do-it-ourselves, where if you have a problem because the park is dirty and your kids play in the park every week, you're going to go clean up that park. And you're going to use the Internet to organize other moms and dads to clean up that park every week." Ruma also emphasized the localized relevance of such interactions. She explained, "Honestly, it does not matter what goes on in Washington to most people in America. What matters is if they can drive down their street, if there's not a pothole ruining their cars...And if you don't see that pothole being fixed, you feel that your tax money is not being used wisely."[24]

That is, even though social media are used by many people to get involved in political discussions and weigh in on political issues, and many of those so engaged find meaning and satisfaction in doing so, many more users have little to no interest in these issues and do not wish to become mobilized on behalf of any cause.

Given the absence of total mobilization of public sentiment, the precise problem that social media have targeted—the predominance of elites and the absence of widespread public input—seems, if anything, likely to remain the same (as we will argue at length, later in the book). Even with greater public input, however, it seems that new coalitions of special interests will form to press for their own issues. Put differently, rather than greater democracy, the result will be a greater number of factions involved in policy issues (much in the manner characterized by the *Federalist Papers* in the late 1700s). But despite the greater free-for-all of information and participation, the tendency for a minority to seek to control input will persist. This would appear to be the case with the advocates of marijuana legalization, not only as we have discussed above but also as we will demonstrate later. (We must emphasize that we are not taking a position here about the advisability of the legalization of marijuana; rather, we highlight the issue because, with only one exception, no scientific public opinion poll through mid-2011 showed even a plurality of support for such a measure,[25] compared with its overwhelming prominence on governmental websites that allow public-opinion inputs.)

So, an interesting possibility opens up in which a dedicated minority can exert a powerful influence over the agenda and even influence it in a direction that does not reflect the will of other members of the public. In policy-setting systems, such as those proposed by social media experts, a hugely significant, but largely unexplored, issue is how to ensure equal representation. Without equal representation, it is hard to say that any outcome of a socially-mediated system could be fair or possibly even just. (Some would consider a fair and desirable outcome arrived at in a process-violative or nonrepresentative way to be an unjust result.)

At this point, these are the radical issues that need to be addressed if social media are to fulfill the highest expectations in terms of ideological ambitions for political intervention. When we asked Agarwal how realistic it was to expect that meaningful citizen participation in governmental decision-making would be achieved through social media, he replied: "I think it will absolutely happen." But "I'm not going to be overly naïve about it. It isn't clear to me that we're yet at the point of policy being driven by large groups of people." He said he does believe that "we'll have a greater number of people participating in policy-making, year-over-year, than we had in the past."[26]

Agarwal's views on this point were echoed, to an extent, by Ruma, who argued that over time—possibly a very long time—citizens ultimately could participate more meaningfully in the way Washington does business. "The question," she asked, "is will people be able to sustain this effort, to not only be involved in technology, but also be interested in what the government is doing?"

The CBB experiment, Ruma said, demonstrated why the government would prefer to limit conversation with the crowd through specific questions rather than by asking open-ended ones. "When you ask—broadly—for a list of top issues deserving of the incoming Administration's attention," she said, "that's how you get people saying legalizing marijuana should be your most important issue. That's not the answer [the Administration] wanted." She continued, "They wanted answers that they had on the platform—health-care, education, etc." Consequently, she said, "agencies are now tailoring their questions and ideas and interactions much more specifically... It's never an open-ended question anymore. It's like: 'do you think we could improve roads by doing certain things?' It's a way to have a conversation that's just that much more germane to the mission of the agency." She noted that agencies will "still have their fact-finding mission[s], and think-tank reports, and everything else to rely on" but "they absolutely are not relying on the American people to tell them what's what."[27]

Micah Sifry echoed this sentiment when he spoke about why the Obama Administration has not institutionalized two-way interactive engagement. "My view is just that it comes down to partly Obama's own preference for control," the Personal Democracy Forum cofounder said. "He's shown he really dislikes it when leaks happen that are not authorized, so there's a desire for control. And secondly, the communications team is still led by people who are more old-school about this stuff and even though they've shown they're savvy about how to project the President's image or message through social media, that's all they really seem interested in."[28]

For policy crowdsourcing to work at the agency level, Ruma said, "What has to be hard-wired into your agency's personality is saying, 'I am going to ask people all the time what their opinion is, not do it once a year.' Not come out of the blue and try to do this enormous campaign for the Census and spend enormous amounts of money and then go away for ten years." That, she said, "is not what works. You need to be top of mind for everybody all the time, and that's difficult, because you have earthquakes, and hurricanes and things that need people's attention immediately that take priority...But the average American cannot process and should not be asked to give their opinions to every agency at every second."

At bottom, Ruma observed, "Policy-making is not done by the masses. Policy-making is not done by consensus—that's everyone involved. That's why we have elected officials, and I don't see that changing at all...Honestly, the most earth-shattering thing is basically someone in the government saying 'we don't know everything and we need help.'"

At this point, this discussion remains entirely theoretical, since the ideas to which Ruma refers are not being acted upon by the Obama Administration; that is, public policy is not yet being steered by social media. As cold comfort in light of the radical issue of representativeness in a social media policy setting, we have suggested up to this point that social media inputs to governmental policy have been limited largely to the first of three modalities—soliciting public input and opinion. To a lesser degree, though, social media inputs fit the second modality of governmental/social media—the opportunity to communicate Administration views to the public. But in terms of the third modality—allowing citizens to radically affect governmental policy—evidence is lacking for its existence under the Obama Administration.

As with the CBB, the eventual experience of the Online Town Hall corroborated the ability of applied communication technologies to further bolster the position of entrenched elites in the landscape of power relationships and communication pathways referenced earlier.[29] The executive personnel charged with running the Online Town Hall events were able to use issue selection, scheduling, and prioritization of debate topics in accordance with Administration interests. Additionally, the dynamics of the Online Town Hall is a concrete illustration of the unpredictable and incongruous volatility of online participation.[30] Reflecting on the Online Town Hall experience, Sifry said, "They've had the opportunity to reinvent the Fireside Chat for the Digital Age, but they haven't done it."[31]

The Sunlight Foundation's Wonderlich told us that he saw the Obama Administration's early attempts to tap the wisdom of the crowd, including the Online Town Hall, as "an effort to garner public support and to foster a certain kind of public image." There were "some fascinating things there," he said. "But I think some of those early experiences turned [members of the Administration] off to what they could be doing creatively online." The CBB and the Online Town Hall "tried to reach out to the crowd on what major issues it thought the government should tackle and heard a sizable number of voices demanding the legalization of marijuana, an issue the Administration was not willing to contemplate in any new way."

"I think that they got somewhat burned," Wonderlich said. "I think the marijuana thing was a very big deal for the White House to say 'we've tried to reach out to the public and it's become a liability because the Internet is unanimously saying that marijuana laws are counter-productive,' and that became a liability for them from a communications perspective."[32]

CONCLUSION

In sum, although these crowdsourcing projects were promoted as ways to give Americans unprecedented input to governmental decision-making, neither the CBB nor the White House Online Town Hall stimulated meaningful citizen participation in policy-making. In both projects, the questions selected and the method used to select them suggested that the experiments had underlying purposes: to help the Administration build support for its positions, to blunt critiques, or to strengthen the President's image in the eyes of the audience.

These exercises paved the way for the social media initiative on which we will focus next: the Expert Labs scientific and technological outreach.

CHAPTER 6

GRAND CHALLENGES: CROWDSOURCING A VISION FOR SCIENCE AND TECHNOLOGY

DESPITE THE JUSTIFIABLE SKEPTICISM ABOUT ITS CROWDSOURCING ATTEMPTS, IN April 2010, the Obama Administration advertised what appeared to be a desire for meaningful citizen participation on the website of the American Association for the Advancement of Science (AAAS). Across an image of the White House ran the words: "Join the conversation on the future of science." A smaller headline below the photo called out, "The White House wants to hear from you."[1]

"FULLY OPEN GOVERNMENT" GRAND CHALLENGE

The essence of the call for participation was that, as part of its effort to "introduce fully open government," the White House sought to "draw on the collective wisdom of scientists everywhere" in order to formulate policy for potential scientific and technological Grand Challenges. The scheme through which these new ideas were to be gathered was Expert Labs, a nonprofit, "nonpartisan" venture set up by AAAS, an organization designed to promote cooperation among scientists, following discussions with the White House Office of Science & Technology Policy.

Grand Challenges was positioned to be the Obama Administration's most ambitious crowdsourcing experiment yet. Unlike the Citizen's Briefing Book (CBB) and the White House Online Town Hall, the Grand Challenges campaign had a more specific task and audience: it sought to involve citizens in determining which scientific and technological challenges "should be the focus of policy initiatives" in the years ahead. Furthermore, it claimed to offer direct citizen input in policy-making, the dream of millions of Obama supporters.

The invitation to "join the conversation" came four months after the Obama Administration issued its memorandum to create more "open and transparent government" and to promote citizen participation in government decision-making. The

Administration began to expand the availability of Internet tools and social media on government websites and sought to make available an array of new government information, through the recently created online Federal Register.[2] Now, anyone with a computer could go to the new public website, data.gov, and find such previously hard-to-locate government data as job-related deaths, flight delays, and government notices. These actions were part of an attempt to create what then-Chief Information Officer Vivek Kundra called a "culture of accountability."[3]

Although Expert Labs technically was not a government project, the White House nevertheless embraced the Grand Challenges initiative. The White House's posting on the AAAS website (and a similarly worded AAAS news release)[4] reflected how the Administration attempted to position the Grand Challenges campaign as part of its Open Government plan.

At the heart of Expert Labs was Anil Dash, cofounder of Six Apart Ltd., the maker of the popular blogging software program known as Movable Type. The Office of Science & Technology Policy reached out to Dash to direct Expert Labs after officials read his August 2009 blog naming the federal government as "the most interesting new tech startup of 2009."[5]

"To know that the White House read what I said and was actually listening, that in itself is much more motivating than a million other things—like money or building something really cool," Dash told the *New York Observer*.[6]

AAAS, publisher of the journal *Science*, set up Expert Labs in November 2009 to support "policy crowdsourcing efforts in the executive branch of the U.S. government." The initiative was backed by a $500,000 grant from the Chicago-based John D. and Catherine T. MacArthur Foundation, known for its "genius grants." When the Grand Challenges project was launched, AAAS Chief Executive Alan I. Leshner declared that "opening government up to a broad array of expertise" was no more than the "next logical step in improving American policy-making."[7] Dash put it more wryly, commenting, "All of us together are smarter than any one of us alone."[8]

Dash boasted to the *New York Observer* that "the government is already using technology to talk to citizens, but we're going to make technology that helps government listen to them." He said Expert Labs would "borrow developers from the hallways of Google in Silicon Valley or start-ups like Foursquare in New York to build government applications and social media tools in exchange for grants, and the chance to connect with some of the most powerful people in the country."[9]

Grand Challenges had an additional function: it allowed Expert Labs to conduct "alpha testing" of its new crowdsourcing tool, ThinkTank. In an interview with *techPresident* blogger Nancy Scola, Dash speculated on the potential benefits of using ThinkTank to collect ideas from the crowd via Twitter and Facebook. "Maybe instead of working from a set of a few hundred ideas, maybe 100,000 people will have a response...an answer," he said. "And Expert Labs can provide the technology to collect those answers, give policy-makers tools to filter them out, and we can publish the responses for anyone in the public to analyze."[10]

These words reinforced the idea that the collected submissions would be used to inform policy. Nevertheless, in a June 2011 interview, Dash disabused us of the notion that the purpose of Grand Challenges was to produce governmental policy.[11]

He said that the Grand Challenges outreach was only a test and that producing policy recommendations was not an expected end product. Expert Labs' goal was to develop a policy recommendation for the White House sometime in 2011, he explained. Expert Labs did forward the more than 2,000 Twitter and Facebook replies it had collected in just 48 hours from the Grand Challenges exercise to the Office of Science & Technology Policy, and included a public link to a Google spreadsheet containing 1,981 of the replies,[12] according to a Dash blog posted on the Expert Labs site in May 2010.[13] The decision to prioritize the ideas for policy purposes, however, rested with the White House. That no prioritized list of Grand Challenges ideas has been released to the public raises doubt about the crowdsourcing campaign's effectiveness in bringing citizen participation into policy-making.

Grand Challenges, however, had a significant impact on the ultimate look of Expert Labs. In the months after the Grand Challenges campaign, Expert Labs restyled itself into an entity that embraced a more structured concept of policy crowdsourcing. The revamped initiative also promoted the idea of using crowdsourcing to make the work of government employees easier while deemphasizing the notion of directly involving citizens in governmental decision-making.

Dash explained to us that the original concept for Expert Labs was to create an "expert network" from scratch, based on Vivo, a Cornell University-developed social network that allowed scientists in many disciplines to collaborate on projects. Soon, however, the plan changed from building a new network to tapping into existing networks, Dash said. The focus also was narrowed from wide-open idea generation and discussion to specific tasks. "There's a lot of noise around Government 2.0 and Open Government, and a lot of it wasn't really directed," he observed. "It sort of was a lot of enthusiasm without a lot of focus."[14]

According to the Expert Labs May 31, 2011, year-end report,[15] off-topic responses were a major problem for the initiative, along with participants' skepticism that their suggestions could actually catch the ear of a governmental policy-maker. Another concern was agencies' resistance to the idea of policy crowdsourcing, due to the perceived extra time involved, as well as a dearth of successful examples of government crowdsourcing. Agencies, the year-end report noted, sometimes saw transparency-focused efforts as "burdensome homework that must be done out of obligation."

Dash acknowledged in our interview that off-topic responses influenced the decision to back off emphasizing broad citizen participation. He invoked the lessons of the Grand Challenges experiment and also alluded to the Administration's experience with the CBB and the White House Online Town Hall, when he noted that if the Department of Justice were to invite public feedback on important policy questions, "no matter what they ask, some percentage of the public are going to respond around decriminalization of marijuana. That's the nature of conversation on the web and that community is very effective at mobilizing their voices. I don't have an opinion on that but I know that it's not on topic for a lot of policy questions."

NEW CROWDSOURCING TOOL

In September 2010, five months after the Grand Challenges campaign, Expert Labs released a beta version of its crowdsourcing tool, now renamed ThinkUp. Developed by Gina Trapani, founder of mega-blog Lifehacker, ThinkUp was a web-based installation that could archive, curate, and thread tweets and Facebook postings and the responses to them. As the ThinkUp website said: "With ThinkUp, you can store your social activity in a database that you control, making it easy to search, sort, analyze, publish and display activity from your network. All you need is a web server that can run a PHP application."[16]

The thinking behind the tool, *techPresident's* Nancy Scola reported, was that "at some point in your social media evolution, your ability to manage your engagement doesn't scale. Attract enough followers, tweet enough times, and you'll need some help making sense of what ripples out from your activity—especially if you've got a big footprint in those spaces, like, say, the White House."[17]

In short, the reworked and more structured application aimed to make agencies feel that they could manage an outreach to a crowd, while deemphasizing the ideal of citizen participation in policy-making that the agencies regarded as burdensome. ThinkUp's curating and storage feature—which helped to keep the discussion coherent by permitting the user to park off-topic responses on the sidelines—also made crowdsourcing more palatable to agency officials who were skeptical of the credibility of outsourced ideas.

"What it's trying to do is give a layer of understanding on top of the inherently chaotic nature of social media," Dash explained. "So we're still saying, by all means, let everything be as open and unfettered as it is across Twitter and Facebook and all these networks: you couldn't rein them in if you tried, and we aren't trying to. But can you put a thin layer on top of that that lets you tease out meaning, from amongst the noise?"

Dash said Expert Labs' goal is to "increase the raw number of respondents that are saying something valuable." Using ThinkUp's ability to isolate and break out the good, on-topic responses, Dash said, "will naturally feed a good feedback cycle of people saying, 'well, I want to be here on this list of the on-topic responses.'" ThinkUp's ability to "bucket" and filter off-topic responses simply was not available in most other applications, including "most email systems that the government is using," Dash said.

Yet, even with all these plans and modifications, Expert Labs still faced significant challenges in persuading governmental agencies to buy into the notion of policy crowdsourcing. According to the Expert Labs progress report, agencies and their policy-makers needed to be educated in "detail" about the "benefits" of the exercise.

In particular, crowdsourcing agencies needed to be taught how to write prompts to minimize off-topic responses. To ensure success, they needed to strictly observe such guidelines as declaring the intentions of the policy discussion being conducted, addressing the public's motivations to respond, appealing to experts by using phrasing and language that seemed "credible and germane to their interests," and formulating questions to avoid yes/no answers, according to the Expert Labs progress report.

Moreover, "successful" campaigns also needed to rely on "stakeholders to control the outreach"—a "community of peers, often comprised both of other staff in the same agency as well as staffers who are attempting similar efforts in other agencies."

As of May 31, 2011, Expert Labs had pursued or received indications of interest in policy feedback campaigns with such agencies as the Federal Communication Commission, Consumer Financial Protection Bureau, Department of Education, and the Department of Health and Human Services.

But even with these efforts, Expert Labs' long-term work was expected to be treated with continuing skepticism, the progress report said. Ultimately, Expert Labs' major challenge was convincing a well-entrenched governmental system to accept what amounted to major "cultural change... on top of people's normal every-day reluctance to embrace new technologies."

The changes in Expert Labs' focus reflected a conflict between the institutional realities of government and the character traits of the crowd. Other forces, however, may have been at work as well. Alexander Howard, O'Reilly Media's Government 2.0 reporter, speculated in an interview[18] that a "political roadblock" went up in 2010 to prevent Expert Labs from doing the kind of policy consultation originally envisioned. "I was watching when Gina Trapani (who developed the original source code for ThinkUp) joined....And that was all about 'how can we do structured crowdsourcing using social media?'" Howard said. "The transition accelerated once Gina came on."

The refocusing of Expert Labs' mission mirrored developments at an Obama Administration "citizen-consultation" open government blueprint called Expert Net. Expert Net (a working title) was a joint effort of the General Services Administration and the White House Open Government Initiative that proposed using "expert public participation" to "provide useful, relevant, and manageable feedback... to government officials."[19] The project was to complement the federal government's traditional methods of obtaining expertise for decision-making, such as through Federal Advisory Committees and announcing public comment opportunities in the Federal Register.

Howard said the Expert Net proposal, which was announced on the White House blog,[20] "was in the same bailiwick" as Expert Labs, in terms of "having the same specific focus on consulting experts in a given area." But "from what I can tell," he said, "they had one junior level program person in the White House Office of Science & Technology Policy guiding the community. So it's not clear to me that there was a top-level [official saying] this is something we really are going to pursue for the purposes of making policy." Howard speculated that the Administration's social media plan "ran into someone who had the ability to say, 'We're not going to go in that direction.'"

DISCONNECTION BETWEEN CROWDSOURCING AND POLICY INNOVATIONS

The utterances and writings of Obama's campaign manager, David Plouffe, have suggested that a disconnect did indeed exist—and that it stemmed from a view within the Administration that the digital strategy that helped propel Obama to power was no longer viewed as urgent once the new president took power; moreover (and more pertinent to our inquiry), grassroots empowerment was not viewed as a priority by Obama's Chief of Staff, Rahm Emanuel.

Micah Sifry, co-founder and Executive Editor of the Personal Democracy Forum, observes that insider "tell-all" books support the claim that it was useful during the 2008 presidential contest for Obama to appear driven by grassroots support to set himself apart from Hillary Clinton, initially the heir-apparent of the Democratic political establishment.[21] Plouffe's book, *The Audacity to Win: The Inside Story and Lessons of Barack Obama's Historic Victory*,[22] held that having a large volunteer base was "inherently valuable in its own right." Volunteers' efforts translated into a delegate edge for Obama in the February 2008 primary and caucus states, and a victory over Clinton in June. But once victory in the November presidential contest was at hand, Plouffe resorted to what Sifry described as the "dusty old playbook used by White House insiders for decades."

CONTROL OF THE NEW ADMINISTRATION'S AGENDA

In March 2012, Expert Labs officially ended and in a blog post Anil Dash cited the success of protests against the Stop Online Piracy Act (SOPA) as proof that crowd-sourced citizen engagement was effective at changing policy and that the program was now outdated. "Simply put, the effective public use of social networks to influence policy isn't something that needs to be proven feasible now, it has shifted into a reality that needs to be improved upon and promoted."[23] However, while citizen backlash against SOPA clearly influenced congressional action, this post is somewhat misleading. Rather than working with the government to influence policy decisions through official channels provided for citizen engagement and voices, activists expressed a need to combat the government through alternative channels. Anonymous, a group of activist hackers, responded to SOPA and crackdowns on file sharing sites by taking down the website for the United States Department of Justice and the Federal Bureau of Investigation as well as websites for SOPA supporters such as Universal Music Group and the Motion Picture Association of America.[24] Alexis Ohanian, the co-founder of the popular social networking site Reddit, also organized boycotts, in-person protests at Senators' offices, and letter and email campaigns. In an article in *Wired* magazine, he suggested that the American people felt Congress was more interested in lobbyist money than citizen concerns or even political party agendas and therefore these mass protests were necessary. He wrote, "On that day—Jan. 18, 2012—America reminded Congress that it's beholden to the electorate, not lobbyists."[25] Thus, citizens unhappy with SOPA resorted to heavy-handed and at times illegal tactics to force the government's decisions about policy rather than relying upon just the official citizen engagement platforms available to them. This suggests that despite the Administration's efforts and rhetoric, citizens neither feel these methods are very effective nor that their concerns are well represented within the Administration.

"Why wasn't more done to extend that sense of ownership meaningfully into the life of the Administration?" Sifry asked in a *techPresident* blog. "If you could trust your volunteers to carry the campaign in all sorts of important ways, why not also give them a real say in how they could shake up Washington?" The answer, he said, ultimately was that Plouffe and the rest of Obama's leadership team were not "really interested in grassroots empowerment." For Plouffe, the bulging Obama email list, its scores of donors, and its thriving online social network were "essentially a new kind of top-down broadcast system, one even better than the old TV-dominated system."

Plouffe declared that "we had essentially created our own television network, only better, because we communicated with no filter to what would amount to about 20 percent of the total number of votes we would need to win.... And those supporters would share our positive message or response to an attack, whether through orchestrated campaign activity like door-knocking or phone calling or just in conversations they had each day with friends, family, and colleagues."[26]

Sifry noted that Plouffe's sentiments regarding Obama's base were captured in a December 2008 campaign discussion he had held with other top officials from the Obama organization as well as McCain's. "We wanted to control all aspects of our campaign," Plouffe declared. "We wanted control of our advertising, and most important, we wanted control of our field operation. We did not want to outsource these millions of people, and these hundreds of thousands of full-time volunteers to the DNC or any other entity."[27]

Sifry suggested that Plouffe's and David Axelrod's selection of the politically "relentless" Rep. Rahm Emanuel (D-IL) as Obama's chief of staff was an incongruous one, considering that Emanuel lacked "any sense of how to work with the largest volunteer base" any presidential campaign had developed. Emanuel, Sifry noted, came up in politics the "old-fashioned way; organizing and empowering ordinary people" were "the least of his skills."

With the election safely won, the digital strategy became less urgent, according to Sifry. In an interview with Ari Melber of *The Nation*, Plouffe explained that the White House did not need to be putting its digital media operation on the same high level that the campaign did. "In the White House, obviously you're not really raising money and you're not really doing organizing," Plouffe told Melber.[28] "The main focus is to help deliver message." Hence, the digital media team, Sifry concluded, "belongs as a subset of White House communications, as opposed to 'digital strategy.'" In the interview with Melber, Plouffe admitted that staffing for Organizing for America had been slashed to "a fraction of the size" of the election campaign's more than 6,000 members. "Is it the same intensity as the campaign? Of course not," Plouffe acknowledged.

DRY POLITICS VERSUS HUMAN INTEREST

But this was not the only troubling sign to surface for citizen participation via social media in the White House. O'Reilly Media's Alexander Howard interpreted remarks from Macon Phillips, the White House New Media Director at that time, about struggles to interest the public in its "White Board" policy videos as an ill omen for the Administration's social media initiatives. In June 2011, as a panelist at the Brookings Institution's Governance Studies and Center for Technology Innovation event, Phillips said that a series of government videos showing an official discussing a policy in front of a whiteboard and available on YouTube rarely won the kind of wide, rapidly spreading viewership typical of items that "go viral" on the Internet, such as a clip of President Obama soothing a crying baby.

"A lot" of the policy videos attracted "tens of thousands of views," and some even broke 100,000 views, Phillips said. "It's frustrating," he declared, "to see these [other, nonpolicy] videos go viral and get a lot of views, when in fact our policy [videos] don't get as many views." Phillips said the "problem" remained unsolved, "but if there's a way to connect the two, it's a very powerful opportunity to get stuff out there that they want to see but also understand the policy positions."[29]

That it was Phillips, a mainstay of Obama's election campaign and the person with oversight responsibility for WhiteHouse.gov, acknowledging that it was difficult for the White House to engage the public in policy issues, suggested a disconnect concerning the effort to use social media to inform policy decisions, Howard said. "Either the President or someone else in the policy shop has decided that they're not looking at using" the technology that way. "They have not been willing or able to take the risk for more open deliberation."

GRAND CHALLENGES EVOLVE

The evolution of the Administration's Grand Challenges program reflects the change in tone. In April 2013, the President launched the 21st Century Grand Challenges initiative and called on companies, research universities, foundations, and philanthropists to join him in "identifying and pursuing the Grand Challenges of the twenty-first century."

Most prominent among the Grand Challenges promoted on the Office of Science and Technology Policy's website was the BRAIN Initiative, which included approximately $110 million in funding to conduct research across a host of neuroscience research areas. That the designated funding was channeled through the National Institutes of Health (NIH), the Defense Advanced Research Projects Agency (DARPA), and the National Science Foundation (NSF) reflected how the Grand Challenges had moved away from featuring crowdsourced inputs for surveying research objectives to go down predictable pathways associated with established, reputable institutions.

Social media engagement in Grand Challenges does live on in "We the Geeks." An ongoing series of Google+ Hangouts featuring scientists and industry leaders discussing their scientific work with the public, We the Geeks was launched in May 2013 with a blog post on WhiteHouse.gov stating the first installment of the project would focus on Grand Challenges—"ambitious goals on a national or global scale that capture the imagination and demand advances in innovation and breakthroughs in science and technology." Subsequent Hangouts have focused on super heroes, robots, asteroids, and other topics related to scientific research funded at least partially by the federal government. The public is able to take part by posting comments with a #WeTheGeeks Twitter hashtag and commenting on Google+ while watching the video chat in real time. This is a shadow of the former architecture deployed by the White House, and prompts questions about the ultimate change of course. Rather than asking for input regarding the direction of scientific research and funding, the White House has shifted to presenting already funded projects and participating scientists answering questions of their own choosing.

The choice of institutions and research initiatives that receive funding also suggests a conservative approach that does not stray from already established relationships between the federal government and scientific research. At a projected cost of $300 million per year, the BRAIN Initiative is a large investment but researching the brain is neither a controversial focus nor a new direction for scientific inquiry. It is also modeled upon the highly successful Human Genome Project, which, from a federal funding perspective, was a worthwhile investment, a point that President Obama discussed in his 2013 State of the Union Address, saying, "every dollar we invested to map the human genome returned $140 to our economy."[30] Considering the huge amount of money invested, however, the ethical concerns regarding medical research, and the rigorous standards necessary for reputable scientific work, we argue that established organizations and projects already supported by the scientific community may be the more prudent path. Arguably, with respect to the BRAIN Initiative, the historically reliable institutional expertise and competence associated with agencies such as the NIH and DARPA are preferable to the risks associated with crowdsourced neuroscience. When considering the measured constraints on collaborative populism in implementing scientific policy, it is easy to extrapolate outwards towards other areas of governance where the need for effective, knowledgeable management trumps the desire for broader procedural inclusivity.

CONCLUSION

As with the CBB and the Online Town Hall, the Grand Challenges/Expert Labs project represented another ambitious attempt to use social media to inform policy-making. However, the problem of aligning the reality of government with the nature of conversations mediated through the tools of the Internet created complications that cast doubt about the project's effectiveness in stimulating citizen participation. The White House has been adept at using crowdsourced suggestions to promote an image of inclusivity and participation, yet it has often failed to clearly communicate what the results of these efforts have been. If ideas gathered through the CBB, the Online Town Hall, and Grand Challenges/Expert Labs project were implemented or even seriously considered after the public relations moment ended, this was not reflected in press releases regarding initiatives that were pushed forward by the Administration. Presumably many citizens who chose to engage with these projects spent considerable time and effort crafting their pitches and garnering support for their suggestions. The initial excitement at participating and feeling heard may not survive the lack of response. Without a clear link between crowdsourced proposals and government action, interest in future citizen engagement projects may diminish.

In the next chapter, we will look more closely at the Administration's effort to use social media messages to garner support for decisions already taken, contrary to its stated initiatives to use the tools to prompt public participation in policy changes.

THE SUPREME COURT VACANCIES AND THE HEALTHCARE DEBATE

IN THIS CHAPTER WE LOOK AT THE COUNTERFACTUAL: HOW SOCIAL MEDIA COULD have been used, but were not. We also look at how social media were used by the White House to counter opposition to Administration programs, and some of the difficulties the attempts encountered. The two cases we consider are the Supreme Court nominations and the healthcare debate. While these paired counterfactuals might seem incongruously placed together in one chapter, they appear here because they represent instances where social media were used to push messages, but where there were no efforts to solicit public recommendations despite the easy opportunity to do so. Rather, social media were deployed solely to support predetermined presidential objectives. Thus we argue that the President pursued the modality of using social media to mobilize public support, but not to break new ground by using social media to engage the American people in addressing a problem. In addition, we include an insider's report about what some aimed for in terms of using social media for citizen engagement on healthcare legislation, and how this was an opportunity foregone.

SUPREME COURT VACANCIES: WHY WAS SOCIAL MEDIA VOTING NOT USED?

Given that President Obama was elected on a platform of change, it was almost fitting that he was confronted with not just one, but two major personnel changes in the nation's highest judicial body within less than a year. In May 2009, Justice David Souter, a liberal-minded judge appointed by President George H. W. Bush, announced he would resign from the Supreme Court. Just 11 months later, in April 2010, Justice John Paul Stevens, a liberal-leaning appointee of President Gerald Ford, and the oldest member of the court, announced that he would step down.

The pending retirements left the Obama Administration having to determine whether it could nominate candidates who could deliver votes as reliably liberal on major ideological issues as Souter and Stevens did in an era of increasingly hostile political confirmation battles.[1]

But the vacancies also seemed to present an opportunity for an innovative use of crowdsourcing via social media: the identification of overlooked but worthy candidates for important governmental posts. One might have expected that, given the publicly declared Obama Administration's intention to seek public input, and draw on previously underrepresented demographic groupings, the floodgates for social media applications at the White House would have been opened. The White House could have enthusiastically invited people to use social media to identify potential candidates. After all, this is akin to a system that the White House in fact did choose to put into place in terms of nominations for the Presidential Citizens Medal (and which is discussed in chapter 8). In this way, promising candidates who might not be known to the White House could be considered, greatly democratizing the process. It would also have advanced its agenda of widening inclusive and civic participation. Moreover, the White House would not have to accept any of "the people's choice" suggestions.

But even without necessarily having citizen nominations, the White House could have found other ways to gain public engagement. For instance, social media forums might have been staged so that the public could debate the respective merits of the candidates. Instead, the White House made its own selections, and did so in ways that were entirely out of public view.

SONIA SOTOMAYOR

Maneuvering around Supreme Court appointments is a perennial dimension to political party strategies. Immediately upon Obama's election, there was speculation that Judge Sonia Sotomayor of New York could be a leading candidate for a Supreme Court seat. The prospect of seeing Sotomayor become the first Hispanic, and third woman, to serve on the Supreme Court stirred excitement throughout much of the country, although Sotomayor's own public discussions of ethnicity and gender issues fueled claims that she was a judicial activist, a prospect of concern to traditionalists.[2] Obama, however, found her to be an attractive candidate due to both her demographic background and her justiciary philosophy. On May 26, 2009, a day after informing her of his choice, President Obama nominated Sotomayor to the Supreme Court.

On June 4, 2009, as the confirmation process got underway, the *New York Times*, citing documents made public by the Senate Judiciary Committee, reported that the White House had contacted Sotomayor about a possible Supreme Court nomination on April 27, three days before Justice Souter's plan to retire was publicly reported. From that point on, Sotomayor wrote, she had "near daily phone calls" with White House officials, indicating "how serious Obama was about her as a candidate from the beginning," the *Times* reported.

Once the White House had picked Sotomayor as the nominee, the social media outlets closely affiliated with the Obama Administration went into high gear. Their goal: to rally support from among Obama's virtual supporters. From "the Office of Barack Obama," Organizing for America director Mitch Stewart wrote, "We've just launched our action center, an online hub where you can find all the tools you need to help spread the word about Judge Sotomayor, engage in the public debate about her nomination, and make sure decision-makers in the Senate know where you stand. With only a few minutes, you can make a huge difference."[3]

Visitors were urged to use "our easy online tool" to download images, contact senators, write letters to the editor, and send electronic voice messages from President Obama to friends and family. This one-way conversation assumed an audience bound together by support for Sotomayor (and Obama's selection of the nominee): "You can send a letter to your local newspaper about why you support Judge Sotomayor's nomination," the posting said, "highlighting her extraordinary life story, her tremendous judicial experience, the historic nature of her nomination, or anything else that's important to you. It's extremely effective and only takes a few minutes." The blog posting contained a button for accessing the "action center" beneath the heading "Help Confirm Sotomayor." These examples showed how, instead of using social media tools to gather citizen input, the Administration used the technology to mobilize supporters to generate post-hoc support for a decision already made by insiders. Sotomayor's nomination ultimately was confirmed by the Senate in August 2009 by a vote of 68 to 31.

ELENA KAGAN

On May 10, 2010, President Obama nominated Solicitor General Elena Kagan as the nation's 112th justice following a month-long search for a successor to the retiring Justice Stevens. The nomination set up a "battle over whether it takes a judge to serve on the court," since Kagan was a top legal scholar, but not a judge.[4] Ten days later, the Organizing for America website went into action, as an attempt was made to mobilize support for Kagan as had been done for Sotomayor. This time, however, in addition to the tools used in the Sotomayor nomination, Organizing for America rolled out a new one called "On the Air" that equipped supporters with call-in numbers for political-talk radio shows and also offered "discussion points" if they got to engage a talk-show host on-air in support of the Kagan nomination. If the caller could not get through, he or she could click "Give me another show," to find another from the database of numbers for call-in shows that Organizing for America had compiled.

Nancy Scola, political commentator and journalist, noted that "Stand with Sotomayor" had "morphed into a rather more sedate statement of the obvious, Kagan for Justice," partly "because the former's nomination hasn't given rise to a battle atmosphere against Republicans in the same way the latter's did—at least not yet."[5] Nevertheless, the effort to mobilize support for the nomination via social media also included a YouTube video of President Obama explaining his selection of Kagan for the high court. Turning up his populist rhetoric, Obama noted that Kagan's confirmation for the Supreme Court would mean "three women taking their seats on the court for the first time in history—a court that will be more inclusive, more representative, and more reflective of us, as a people, than ever before." An unsigned posting accompanying the video extolled Kagan's achievements as the first female dean of Harvard Law and as solicitor general, noted that she and Obama were colleagues at the University of Chicago Law School, that she was the granddaughter of immigrants, and promoted the importance of adding a third woman to the Supreme Court. The note concluded by stating that "as the debate over her nomination takes shape, it's crucial that we show support from every corner of this country. Your signature will be part of a public display of support for this historic nomination in these crucial early weeks. Please add your name today to show you stand with Elena Kagan."[6]

On August 7, after a short, traditional ceremony, Elena Kagan was sworn in as the newest Supreme Court justice. Just as it could have done in connection with Justice Souter's impending resignation, the nomination could have provided an opportunity for the Administration to employ its social media tools to identify and even help choose a candidate to succeed Justice Stevens. But the White House made its own decision, obscured from public view, despite its general statements to involve citizens in "the real business of government."

As we saw with the White House Online Town Hall, the Supreme Court nominations demonstrated how political motives could push aside the notion of using crowdsourcing to set a new direction for the government. Rather than using the tools to generate useful ideas or to make meaningful personnel appointments, the social media were used only to invite people to support decisions already taken. The fact that Kagan was not a judge, and that this did not prevent her from being Obama's choice, demonstrated that there is a much larger pool of talented people who might be considered as a Supreme Court justice. That he reached outside a standard group to find his nominee suggests that decision-making could be improved by having a larger pool of potential incumbents. Certainly that is the hiring strategy of many organizations that seek to have a more diverse set of members. Neither is it necessary that there be a certain career trajectory for people to follow to be considered for Supreme Court nomination. According to Boston attorney William S. Strong, "some of the greatest justices we've had were not obvious candidates. They were not on the normal paths one would have taken to the Supreme Court."[7] Given the performance of some Supreme Court justices, one would be hard-pressed to say that the nation would have been better served had the net of possibilities been cast wider. There is also the question of legitimacy: it may be the case that if a citizen engagement process for nominees had been used, the ultimate choice would have been more palatable to the full spectrum of political opinion, reducing the need to invoke social media campaigns after the fact. Had Obama's choice appeared to come from public sentiment, it would have been much harder for other power centers in Washington to oppose him.

THE TOWN HALL ON HEALTHCARE THAT NEVER WAS

President Obama's healthcare initiative, something he campaigned hard for in 2008, became a controversial and unpopular undertaking. Although he had promised to make the discussions open and transparent, including having them broadcast on *C-Span*, and that all segments of the population would be included in the discussions, it did not transpire that way. They were conducted behind closed doors by lobbyists and special-interest groups. The trail of broken promises surrounding healthcare embittered many. Continuing with the counterfactual exploration, the behind-the-scenes report of Kate Albright-Hanna is revealing. In 2009, she was consultant to White House Office of Health Reform and the Department of Health and Human Services after having been Director of Video for New Media for Obama's first campaign.

"During the transition I was approached by Tom Daschle because he said he wanted me to do for healthcare reform what we did for the campaign in terms of building a grassroots movement of people to support healthcare reform. That was really exciting. We took a road trip to Durbin, Indiana and he went to a firehouse in this small town and did a listening session. One of the guys came up afterwards and said, 'This was why we voted for Obama. We were hoping that you would listen to us and our concerns and take that back.' Daschle was supposed to be the head of the White House office of health reform and the Department of Health and Human Services. But Tom Daschle had some problems with—I don't even remember what it was now. Lobbyists or taxes or something [*Interviewer's note: it was taxes*] and he didn't get confirmed. So there was a void there. A leadership void. Especially in the beginning of healthcare reform. They were trying to hit the ground during the transition. So the fact that he did not get confirmed meant that people were just a little bit at sea. So I was going to the meetings and it was, 'What can we learn from the first time around in 1993 when we tried to do healthcare reform?' There were some Clinton people in the room. The people who had been working with Tom Daschle were saying that the takeaway for them was that the first time was too secretive and closed off. It was really important to open up this process and be transparent. And really bring regular people into the process to build this movement. So there was a summit on healthcare reform that was scheduled for April of 2009. They asked me to do a video and to head up the social media strategy that would include bringing in satellite feeds from different communities, they put together this huge survey of what people wanted to see in terms of healthcare reform (a lot of people talked about single payer and public options) and they had actually one of the firefighters from Durbin, Indiana present this briefing to the President at the healthcare summit. But as it got closer to the summit new players came into the room and now they are waiting for a new secretary to be announced. And the conversation switched from, 'We need to be less secretive and less transparent' to 'We need to bring more of the stakeholders into the process. We need to bring in more message men' and it became much more of an insider strategy versus an outsider strategy. So what was going to be my job, which was to head up creating this kind of grassroots movement using social media techniques—video, Twitter, everything else—really shifted focus. I stayed with them up until the summit... and ended up in the back row of the breakout session. Before it was all going to be real people in the audience and then that plan was scrapped. I felt like obviously I wasn't going to be able to make a real impact. So I resigned my position after the summit in April of 2009."[8]

SOCIAL MEDIA TO COMBAT OPPOSITION TO HEALTHCARE

THE CASE OF THE FISHY EMAILS

Social media also were used to deflect destructive feedback about government policies. On August 4, 2009, in a blog on the White House website, Macon Phillips, the official responsible for the site, urged citizens to report "fishy" web postings about the Administration's health insurance reform plan to a White House email address. "Scary chain emails and videos are starting to percolate on the Internet, breathlessly claiming, for example, to 'uncover' the truth about the President's health insurance reform positions," Phillips wrote. In his posting, the New Media Director added that there is "a lot of disinformation about health insurance reform out there, spanning from control of personal finances to end of life care."[9]

Phillips wrote that "these rumors often travel just below the surface via chain emails or through casual conversation. Since we can't keep track of all of them here at the White House, we're asking for your help. If you get an email or see something on the web about health insurance reform that seems fishy, send it to flag@whitehouse.gov."

The apparent appeal to citizens to take on the role of informants raised accusations of privacy invasion. Fox News, known for its support of conservative political positions, claimed the White House was "turning supporters into snitches."[10] Judge Andrew Napolitano, a Fox analyst, said the White House had stepped into a legal "conundrum" owing to a statute prohibiting federal agencies from maintaining records on individuals exercising their right to free speech. (The statute, the Privacy Act of 1974, was passed after the Nixon Administration used federal agencies to illegally investigate individuals for political purposes.)

Fox also quoted Jay Sekulow, Chief Counsel of the American Center for Law and Justice, as calling the posting on WhiteHouse.gov "a very troubling attempt to stifle the free speech of Americans who have the constitutional right to express their opinion and concerns about health care." Fox also cited critical comments by Texas Sen. John Cornyn, chairman of the National Republican Senatorial Committee, and White House spokesman Robert Gibbs' denial of accusations that the White House was "collecting names," rather than trying to clarify misinformation.[11]

By contrast, the liberal-minded *New York Times*, in an August 5 piece less critical of the Administration, noted that Cornyn accused the White House of building an "enemies list" of people who opposed its efforts at overhauling the healthcare system, but also gave far more prominent play to the White House's denial of the accusations and its claim that it wanted to keep track of disinformation about the healthcare effort so that it could set the record straight.[12] Linda Douglass, Communications Director for the White House Office of Health Reform, was quoted as saying the government was "not compiling lists or sources of information," but allowed that it "may post fact checks from time to time to be sure Americans know the truth about health insurance reform."

Amid the controversy, the White House soon stopped using its website to target "fishy" emails. On August 17, the *Times* reported that the White House had deactivated the flag@whitehouse.gov email address. The article noted that emails sent to the address now bounced back, with the reply reading, "The e-mail address you just sent a message to is no longer in service. We are now accepting your feedback about health insurance reform via: http://www.whitehouse.gov/realitycheck."

Fox chronicled the deactivation of the email address as part of the implementation of "several new changes" to the White House's website, "apparently aimed at reducing the number of people who receive unsolicited e-mails from the Administration and at battling charges that it's collecting personal information on critics."[13] The article noted that through the "Reality Check" site, set up a week earlier to address what the White House said were healthcare reform rumors, the White House was "still asking people to send in their 'myths' on health care. But that site now included a warning that said, 'Please refrain from submitting any individual's personal information, including their e-mail address, without their permission.'"

SOCIAL MEDIA IN COUNTERMESSAGING DURING THE HEALTHCARE DEBATE

The Obama Administration's social media tools also were used to try to counteract protests over the healthcare reform plan by the Tea Party, a conservative political movement whose ranks included such Republican figures as Sarah Palin, the party's 2008 vice presidential nominee. The Tea Party had attacked the healthcare plan and President Obama in public meetings throughout the country.[14]

On August 10, 2009, toward the end of a summer of protests that began with opposition to a healthcare overhaul and grew into a broader dissatisfaction with government, the *Wall Street Journal* reported that "President Obama's political [Organizing for America] arm sent an e-mail to supporters over the weekend urging supporters to visit local congressional offices over the break in favor of the health care overhaul." The *Journal* noted that Organizing for America Director Mitch Stewart wrote that "as you've probably seen in the news, special interest attack groups are stirring up partisan mobs with lies about health reform, and it's getting ugly. Across the country, members of Congress who support reform are being shouted down, physically assaulted, hung in effigy, and receiving death threats. We can't let extremists hijack this debate, or confuse Congress about where the people stand."[15]

The article noted that Stewart's email directed supporters to "sign up for an office visit through the group's website," and, based on their voter database records, directed supporters to their local congressman. "Don't worry if you've never done anything like this before," Stewart wrote. "The congressional staff is there to listen, and your opinion as a constituent matters a lot. And if you bring a friend, you'll have more fun and make an even greater impact."

The article also noted the launch of a new White House website to "promote" the Administration's legislation and "combat what they say is misinformation about the bill." The site featured Reality Check videos of Obama aides discussing what the healthcare overhaul would or would not do.

The Reality Check website carried a logo with the heading "health insurance reform" and the caduceus symbol of medicine. A button on the website invited readers to "share this page."[16] This example shows how, in the face of a challenge to its policies, the Obama Administration used social media to step up its messaging effort in support of a policy position it had taken—namely the healthcare debate.

The idea of using social media to source democratic ideas through public participation had been pushed aside.

The Administration also tried to mobilize support for its healthcare plan through such events as a question-and-answer session on Yahoo.com's news website. A posting on the Yahoo site on September 9, 2009, informed visitors that "the Director of the White House Office of Health Reform, Nancy Ann DeParle, would answer questions from Yahoo users on President Obama's health care goals," which he would lay out that night in a speech before a joint session of Congress. "We've already received hundreds of questions and will submit a representative sample, which will be answered Thursday in a live video stream at 3 p.m. EST, 12 p.m. PST on this page," the website said. "However, users can also Twitter questions during the chat to @whitehouse. A YouTube video of the Q&A will be posted afterward."

On September 10, as advertised, the Yahoo site carried a sampling "from hundreds of submissions" made to the Q&A following President Obama's congressional address. Although the exercise provided a forum for the public to ask questions about a major proposed government social policy, its use of social media included nothing new or novel. The answers could have been found easily in other outlets on the Internet, or in conventional sources of information. Indeed, many of DeParle's answers referred the questioner to President Obama's well-covered address to Congress the prior evening, suggesting a major purpose of the exercise was, once again, to build support for decisions already made.

For example, in response to a citizen's question about when and how the health reform proposal would take effect, DeParle replied that the Administration was "committed to getting this done this year. We have waited so long." Then DeParle connected Obama's remarks from the evening before the discussion. "You heard the President talk last night about how the efforts to get comprehensive health reform date back to at least President Teddy Roosevelt," she said. "So we have been at this for decades."[17]

"If the bill gets enacted in the next few months," DeParle said, "then the exchange wouldn't become operational until 2013, because it takes a while to get that set up. But immediately, some changes could start to occur." She noted that "one thing the President talked about last night is that if you're an American who's been unable to get coverage because of a pre-existing condition, which happens to a lot of people, if they lose their job, or let's say they go off on their own to start a company, and then they would like to buy insurance, and if you have a pre-existing condition, it can be almost impossible, or prohibitively expensive." She continued, "So if you're uninsured because you have a pre-existing condition, you'll be able, a year from now, assuming this bill passes this year, you'll be able to be part of a new high-risk pool that we are going to establish to enable you to purchase coverage much earlier."

Aside from the fact that this explanation contains no more detail than could be found in many other media sources, this limited, purely informational use of social media fails to align with the idea of using the tools to put government in the people's hands. Ultimately, it is another example of how the Obama Administration used social media to build support for already-established positions.

ASSESSMENTS OF HEALTHCARE INITIATIVES AND
SOCIAL MEDIA

The "reality" of the Obama Administration's use of social media, according to journalist Alexander Howard, is "if you are going to try to run government, especially the U.S. government, you have to pay attention to politics."[18]

"A lot of these technologies have been focused on transparency," he said. "Yet, the harder thing to do is to get to participation and collaboration.... Congress is going to have to act at some level, and the agencies themselves are, I think, going to have to address long-standing cultural issues around openness and engagement."

Despite the political obstacles, Howard gave the Administration "credit for taking risks by trying experiments" with its early social media initiatives. The complexity of governance, he said, is "probably greater than any given executive can deal with." The challenge of getting things through Congress, the sheer size of the federal government and its different programs is "mind-boggling," he said.

Social media, however, have the potential to make government work "better," he said. "Social media platforms would enable collective knowledge and decision-making that would reduce the cost of governing itself—and empower the voices and the perspectives of people whose voices, frankly, haven't been heard," he added. "Much of the time, it's the wealthy and those who have access to lobbyists or government whose perspectives are met... Social media have the potential to enable 'a more complete and far-ranging diversity of perspectives—particularly from the young, from minorities, and from the poor.'"

He cautioned, however, that "even if the technology is new... people's inherent predispositions and their habits of mind... are going to persist. Human nature is not going to disappear because we have the ability to constantly be talking and be connected to our smartphones or to upload video and engage in policy-making online."

"The tendencies towards power, wealth, fame or other self-interested goals... are going to be around as long as there are people," Howard added. "And the digital technologies are going to have to find ways to moderate, recognize those tendencies, if they are going to really realize some of the vision for open government that's been articulated by Beth Noveck [Obama's first deputy chief technology officer] and others."

John Wonderlich, Policy Director for the Sunlight Foundation, found several negative implications for social media and policy-making in the political coopting of the public discussion on President Obama's healthcare bill. "Obama made promises about health-care negotiations being public," Wonderlich said, recalling a few. "The best that we ended up with was a public forum about healthcare negotiations, which seemed to end up becoming politically useful." During the campaign, Obama claimed he would broadcast the healthcare negotiations on C-Span, putting the process out in the open. By January 2010, however, the President was declaring that he wanted the final negotiations on healthcare reform—a reconciliation of the House and Senate versions of the bill—put on a fast track, even if it meant abandoning campaign ambitions for full transparency, and finalizing behind closed doors an enormously significant piece of social policy legislation. Republicans' angry complaints about secret backroom deals reversed past behavior, when George W. Bush was in the White House and the Democrats criticized covert talks.

"The negotiations are obviously being done in secret and the American people really just want to know what they are trying to hide," complained Rep. Tom Price (R-Ga.).[19] The resort to secrecy came on the heels of the stormy summer of 2009, when, at the height of the healthcare debate, astroturfing—a form of synthetic advocacy designed to look like a natural grassroots movement, but actually supporting a previously mapped out political agenda—was in full swing during public meetings on the proposed reforms. *Politico* reported on how "well-financed conservative groups" battled "well-financed unions to get their members to the head of the line at the town halls of hapless members of Congress." Also, "the pharmaceutical industry and the health insurance industry" pushed "various talking points through giant megaphones," and a public relations firm was accused of organizing "vaguely named new coalitions" that changed "their messages, and even their names, to match the latest White House messages."[20]

Politico's Josh Gerstein noted that just before the healthcare bill passed, in March 2010, President Obama said that in retrospect it was a "mistake" that short-term expediency led him to abandon his campaign promise to work out the legislation in public, in front of *C-Span* cameras.[21] "Part of what I had campaigned on was changing how Washington works, opening up, transparency," Obama told *ABC* in January 2010. "The process didn't run the way I ideally would like it to.... We have to move forward in a way that recaptures that sense of opening things up more."[22]

Like the Online Town Hall, the events surrounding the Patient Protection and Affordable Care Act, hereafter called the Affordable Care Act, revisit notions we discussed earlier addressing disproportionate influence which stem from the skewed access to digital participation platforms. Though the Citizen's Briefing Book (CBB) and Town Hall projects were far more open and transparent in comparison to the Administration's pursuit of the Affordable Care Act and the installment of Supreme Court justices, these activities nonetheless still managed to fall short of the demands of supporters who expected more in terms of collaborative inclusion.[23] Both detractors and supporters of the President expressed disappointment when relatively lower-stakes issues such as marijuana policy were not engaged in the CBB and Town Hall with the collaborative inclusion that they had hoped for. It can be argued that many such critics had preemptively formulated expectations that were unreasonable to begin with, envisioned in the transient post-electoral euphoria with inadequate attention to the combative realities of actual governance that would lie ahead.[24] The net effect of these initial dissonant experiences may well have made clear to the Administration that, with respect to the issues of health care and High Court composition, the resentment over limited transparency and engagement would be outweighed by the benefits of more efficient policy control and message management, especially given that even earnest efforts at transparency and collaboration would still invite criticism.

In essence, the White House is amenable to soliciting supportive stories about how one is benefiting from Administration initiatives, but not substantive, creative ideas about Supreme Court nominees. "Tell us your story" (an invitation that is often extended from the White House as a way to support one of its policies that seems to be having difficulty making headway) is quite different from "tell us your idea." They both fit under the rubric, "We want to hear from you," but are prompted by quite different reasons.

An important observation fits at this juncture, with reference to our earlier discussion of the CBB and the virtual town hall meetings. Kate Albright-Hanna, the 2008 campaign's Director of Video for New Media, and who was involved in early Obama initiatives, saw very clearly how some people within the Administration responded to the CBB and virtual town halls. With reference to the marijuana issue she told us, "The top question [about marijuana] led people who were in the communications department to say, 'See? All this social media communication is just a bunch of hippie stuff and if we open it up we will look ridiculous. What is really important right now is to make him look presidential.'" Albright-Hanna then explained her own vision for an engagement portal. "I had wanted to create this idea of a public town square on the White House website. A place where we would document WPA-style, when they sent out documentary photographers out about what life really was like. Conversations starting from where people lived and what they were actually going through. Republican or Democrat—just bringing Americans together to talk about what was going on in their lives." However, this idea was quashed. She explained, "I was told, 'We don't want to do stories about people with problems. We want to tell stories about people inside the White House solving those problems.' So for me that shift was very symbolic of, 'We're going to show you what we're doing instead of what is happening with you.' It is a subtle narrative shift that changed the whole tone of everything."[25]

Decisions about what kind of stories should appear on the White House website, and to what purpose, go to the heart of the way in which social media interface with citizen engagement. Albright-Hanna has highlighted the fact that ideas of post-partisan building of a national culture, or similar projects, are unlikely to be adopted. Instead, the distinct preference, according to her, is to use them to show the White House to good advantage, and succeeding in solving people's problems. Control over production and exposure is not democratically decided; it becomes an extension of the politics of citizen engagement. The topic of White House social media storytelling, and the purposes it serves, is taken up again in chapter 8.

CONCLUSION

In summation, this chapter has addressed counterfactuals of where the White House could have solicited citizen input at the policy level but chose not to. Yet the Obama Administration has also ignored even passive opportunities to create a platform that would allow citizens to aggregate their own opinions and assessments under a White House umbrella. As pointed out in chapter 4, a popular proposal arising from the CBB exercise was to establish an opinion registration system that would allow citizens to register their views of bills before Congress and their responses to how their representatives voted. The White House has chosen to ignore this low-cost, easy-to-create, and nonbinding policy guidance system. The reasons for this are easy to appreciate: it would constrain the President's maneuverability and complicate the White House's relationship with Congress members (to say the least).

One more point needs to be addressed before leaving the topic of the non-to-low use of social media for tackling presidential priorities. It could be argued that President Obama made healthcare a central part of his 2008 campaign, and paid quite a bit less attention to social media for citizen engagement. Hence, it is unsurprising that he would give up a lower priority goal (social media for citizen engagement) for one of the heavily stressed centerpieces of his campaign (the previously mentioned Affordable Care Act). This makes sense from the vantage point of expediency. But the choice to not go the high road, that is, to follow the democratic principles of governance that he espoused, and instead pursue a policy route that would accomplish programmatic objectives, says much about how quickly one will abandon means to achieve ends and the difficulty of governance by democracy. But, as the above quote from Kate Albright-Hanna shows, there were initial attempts to do both at the same time. However, the pressure of immediate needs means that ideals are sometimes shelved, to be retrieved only if needed for moral suasion. The story is an old one of idealists who accompanied a leader on a long campaign, but upon its successful culmination, find themselves being quickly shuffled out of the picture by pragmatists.

The next chapter will look at some additional uses of social media in federal policy beyond directly interacting with the White House in terms of national policy questions. In particular, questions of transparency, public service, and social media impact of the Obama Administration's first term will be considered.

CHAPTER 8

SOCIAL MEDIA MODALITIES: EXAMPLES AND PATTERNS FROM THE OBAMA WHITE HOUSE

IN THIS CHAPTER, WE CONSIDER ADDITIONAL EXAMPLES OF OBAMA ADMINISTRATION initiatives that illustrate the tripartite modalities concerning social media and governmental decision-making. This revisits the modalities in the second chapter, when we laid out three predominant ways social media can be used for digital engagement (the acquisition of information by the Administration, the broadcasting of White House prerogatives, and the engagement of public opinion for collaborative policy formulation). These explorations are brief, but they help by offering a more broadly encompassing survey of the landscape of Administration outreach programs. More importantly, these additional examples emphasize that the deeper case study examinations in chapters 4 through 7 are not unique forms or instances and lend further evidence to our themes. The examples in this chapter—an array of contests, awards, question forums, and event overtures—demonstrate that the crucial dynamic observed in the case studies permeates the spectrum of White House social media initiatives; this is particularly relevant since they provide additional evidence that these engagement initiatives do not ascend to the level of collaborative policy deliberation. Yet, interestingly, in a few instances, the public used social media to push back, demanding a greater role in the policy process. The White House, as noted above, is willing to accept a lot of rough commentary and ill will to get its message out via social media, yet it must exercise care not to create blowback when using social media, such as with petitions, if engaged citizens try to turn social media around to direct policy in opposition to presidential wishes.

THREE MODALITIES OF SOCIAL MEDIA FOR GOVERNMENT POLICY

Earlier, we described the three modalities for social media and governmental decision-making as: problem identification and fixes, power augmentation, and solicitation of mass opinion to determine public policy. Only the third category qualifies for meaningful popular empowerment via social media, and we have found that this form of social media, though pursued to a minor extent, has not yielded meaningful results. The other two categories are not an authentic form of engagement but rather business as usual, carried out with a new set of tools. Though from a distance they may appear to be a form of meaningful engagement of the citizenry for policy, upon further inspection they must be considered chimerical. We hasten to add, though, that simply because they are not a form of policy-making, does not mean that they are without value. Quite the contrary.

In the sections that follow, the discussion moves across the three forms of social media engagement. Though the tripartite division is valuable for analyzing the ideology and impact behind White House social media initiatives, many elements are seamlessly blended in the programs we discuss, and so cannot be treated entirely discretely. Still, each format is analyzed as appropriate within the examples.

SUGGESTION BOX SUBMISSIONS AND VOTING

The "suggestion box" is a hoary but effective way for superiors to get money-saving or process-improving ideas from those involved in the front line of operations. This perspective has been long recognized in all sectors. Airports around the world, for example, solicit suggestions from the public. In private organizations, it is not uncommon to offer monetary rewards for good ideas. When combined with social media, the wisdom of the crowd can be harnessed to refine and select among problems and proposed solutions.

The Obama Administration moved forward on this notion and, according to Beth Noveck, the US Deputy Chief Technology Officer for Open Government, speaking at Princeton University in 2009, one agency even substituted a physical suggestion box with a virtual one.[1] The White House has encouraged this kind of crowdsourcing. The White House Office of Public Engagement, which bills itself as "the open front door to the White House," has responsibility for this program, as it does for other social media-input programs of the White House.

Predicated on President Obama's belief that "the best ideas usually come from the front lines," in 2009 the White House launched the "SAVE Award," with SAVE standing for "Securing Americans Value and Efficiency." The award's purpose was to solicit ideas from federal employees about how to make the government operate with greater efficiency and effectiveness, or with less waste. In the two years following its creation, more than 56,000 ideas were submitted. From these many suggestions, which were voted on by federal employees, the Office of Management and Budget winnowed the number down to four, and these final four were then made available for online voting by the public. Thus, the American people were able to choose the winner, who was then invited to Washington to present the idea to President Obama. Observe that there was no commitment on the part of the President to accept the idea, only to have it presented to him; so, despite all the frenetic activity of selecting, commenting, and voting, at the end of the day there was no guarantee that the public's voice would necessarily be expressed in any action or policy change.

A wide variety of ideas were suggested under this program (including that government-office renovations or consolidations be undertaken only when needed). One of the final four suggested moving a glossy quarterly publication that was sent to nearly 90,000 Social Security Administration employees from print to online only. This move would have saved the government substantial printing and mailing costs (besides reducing demand on natural resources and energy). After 40,000 votes were cast, the 2011 top idea was to institute a tracking system for tools and equipment at the National Aeronautics and Space Administration (NASA) Goddard Space Flight Center, so that when a project was completed, the tools and equipment would be available for other uses.

It is hard to believe that some of the submitted ideas needed to be subjected to a "crowdsourcing" evaluation to determine whether they were worthwhile. For example, a top idea in 2010 was to stop using "next-day express" rates to ship empty sample boxes to FDA inspectors. Another was to allow any of the 8,000 federal employees who were shipped daily bulky paper copies of the Federal Register to opt to receive electronic copies instead.

Other ideas were simply comical. As an illustration, a proposal was tendered to pay off the $15 trillion US national debt by having the federal government hold a telethon conducted by celebrities and big-name athletes. The expectation would be that enough people would call in to retire the national debt. (In order for this plan to succeed in 2013, each man, woman, and child in the United States would have to donate about $48,000, when the national median income per *household* was only about $52,000 per year.)

The idea of a virtual suggestion box is a good one, and every organization should have a channel for gathering potentially useful ideas about how to improve its performance or better serve its clientele. Numerous money-saving and beneficent ideas have been forthcoming from these systems. Still, there were some oddities about the marriage of the White House suggestion box and social media-style voting. First, it invited generalists to weigh in on matters that sometimes required expertise or contextual knowledge that would have affected the appropriateness of an idea. Second, as then embodied, it allowed participants only to vote "thumbs up" for an idea, or to choose not to vote, but there was no opportunity to give a "thumbs down" vote. This set-up, of course, biased the relative position of an idea, and could have led to poorer ideas receiving a larger number of votes. The consequence of both of these factors—that is, the absence of specialized knowledge by voters and no possibility of negative votes—meant that more attention was given to high-ranking bad ideas by additional visitors. This result, in turn, raised the question about what constituted a good use of resources. As one petitioner pointed out, the idea-evaluation system and the voting itself carried financial costs. An informal estimate by one SAVE participant indicated that the program was costing the taxpayer about $120 million to run.[2] Though in our view, this estimate was much too high, even if it were a small fraction of that number, the cost was still substantial. Hence, it would be useful to see that the savings generated by the program offset its cost. Any such cost-benefit analysis should include the cost of an alternative to the voting system, such as one that would simply use the already-established panels of experts within each department to sort through the ideas.

As noted above, it was not clear that even if a suggestion received the winning number of votes, and its originator had a meeting with President Obama, the suggestion would have been adopted. So once again, we were confronted with a complicated voting scheme that would bring some poor ideas forward, with no assurance that valuable ideas would actually be receiving adequate notice.

A HOOK TO FURTHER ENGAGE PEOPLE AND PROPAGATE ADMINISTRATION VIEWS

Heads of state and other high officials use social media, such as Twitter, for many reasons. These include having an opportunity to (1) improve their image by appearing responsive to the public and social media savvy, (2) use the visibility of novel social media tools to attract public attention and engage thought leaders and potential voters, (3) assert Administration viewpoints, (4) galvanize supporters to take action, and (5) blunt criticism.

There is also the symbolic level to consider. Social interaction can often create a bond, a feeling that there is a relationship. Thus, social media can be a means to engage people, creating a sense of reciprocal caring and engendering feelings of commitment to the Administration and its leader, Barack Obama. For effective exercise of political power, the value of having the masses committed at a personal level to a strong, charismatic leader has long been recognized. A governmental goal of creating a personal connection is as ancient as minting a leader's profile on a coin. Roman emperors recognized the power of a flattering image every bit as much as the successful poster designers of the 2008 presidential election.

Such an example may be seen from the "Engage" page that is prominently placed on the White House Facebook homepage (as of July 2013). It offers visitors the opportunity to "stay connected & engage." It offers email "updates from President Obama and other senior officials" and signups for Flickr, LinkedIn, Foursquare, Twitter, and YouTube. The only engagement opportunity offered, though, is to visit the White House blog and see more photos on Flickr. Though the meaningful opportunities for engagement may be hard to discern, the connection opportunity for one-way communication is not.

Yet there have been plenty of potential opportunities to engage with the President via short questions moderated through Facebook, Google+, and Twitter sessions. Though the probabilities of actually interacting with President Obama, even under these circumscribed conditions, are remote, they are thrilling for his media-savvy supporters. (This is discussed more fully later in the chapter.)

Not only was President Obama involved with these constrained interaction opportunities (as described earlier) but so too were a parade of top Administration officials, ranging from Vice President Biden on down. One fairly typical instance was a January 2012 "White House office hours" program during which Obama Administration officials were "taking your questions" on a report the Administration had produced to increase spending ("investment for") projects to spur innovation.

With only 149 characters with which to query officials, it would seem that the major purpose of this initiative was to generate public interest in a new White House report on fostering innovation (box below). But while this activity was fulfilling the letter of President Obama's call for increased interaction between top officials

EXAMPLE OF WHITE HOUSE SOCIAL MEDIA "OFFICE HOURS" VIA TWITTER

January 9, 2012 at 10:38 AM EST

We're holding a special session of "Office Hours" on Twitter with Rebecca Blank, Acting Deputy Secretary of Commerce and Under Secretary for Economic Affairs (@commercegov), and Aneesh Chopra, United States Chief Technology Officer (@aneeshchopra), to answer your questions about the new report.[3]

and the public, one might be reserved about how searching and meaningful public inquiry can be when even the short questions are carefully screened.

In early 2012, the top feature on the White House homepage was an "engage" hotlink. The invitation read as follows:

WHITE HOUSE ENGAGEMENT INVITATION

HOW TO ENGAGE WITH THE WHITE HOUSE

We want to hear from you. Learn how you can get involved, share your stories, and add your voice to help address the challenges of the twenty-first century.[4]

This invitation had two dimensions that connected with recurring tropes of the social media mirage. First, it claimed that the White House wanted to hear from ordinary people, echoing similar declarations from politicians who claim to want to "listen to the voice of the people" but then go ahead and do what they had already planned to do, using the "listening" exercise as a rationale.

HILLARY CLINTON'S LISTENING TOUR

A classic example of artificial solicitation of public input was Hillary Clinton's 1999 multi-month "listening tour" of New York State, during which the former First Lady "learned" from listening to the problems of the people of New York that they would benefit from her serving in the US Senate, and thus she decided to run for Sen. Moynihan's seat upon his retirement.[5] A wag quipped that if Clinton's "Listening Tour had been any further scripted, it would have to have been registered with the Writers Guild."[6]

Second, it also asked people to "add their voice[s]" to help address the challenges of the twenty-first century. However, this "adding of voices" was operationalized far differently than the original 2009 White House webpage that invited people to send a question or comment to the White House via electronic interface, extending the impression that a response would be received.

The greeting screen was headlined, "President Obama believes that change starts with you," followed by this declaration: "The President has always believed that the best ideas don't just come from Washington. They come from individuals and communities all across the country. They come from people like you. To bring about real, lasting change, the President needs you to stay engaged, share your stories, and add your voice to help address the challenges of the 21st century so we can win the future."[7] This commitment was operationalized by several measures, including a series of "immigration roundtables."

LIMITED INPUTS ON GOVERNMENTAL DECISION-MAKING VIA SOCIAL MEDIA

As we pointed out in the case of the Citizen's Briefing Book, the social media sources came up with plenty of recommendations that the Administration embraced. Insofar as we have been able to determine, however, all of them were already supported by the Administration during the campaign, or, in a few instances, were arrived at without any apparent reference to guidance by the social media inputs. In other words, from among the various justifications available to it related to social media, the Administration selected those that would bolster its case for policies it wanted to pursue in the first place. We also have identified examples where the public came forward with ideas (marijuana legalization among the most prominent) that the Administration chose not to endorse, despite the expressed will of (a large segment of) the public, biased though it may have been. If our conclusions to this point are valid, this examination would suggest that no matter the motivation, the social media uses of the Obama Administration, in terms of guiding policy, have not been implemented in a meaningful way. A skeptic might conclude that, instead, social media was used as a form of manipulation and pseudo-engagement, a topic to which we will turn next.

THE "WE THE PEOPLE" CAMPAIGN

"We the People" was an online tool that allowed a person to sign or initiate a petition. If the petition garnered sufficient support, the White House staff agreed to review it, send it to the appropriate policy experts, and provide an official response. Anyone wishing to use the system had to begin by registering with the White House. It was then up to the petitioner to generate enough additional signatures to meet the threshold for a response. The White House altered the parameters for petitions. For example, when the system was launched in September 2011, petitions required only 5,000 signatures to merit a response. The White House, however, found that it was getting more petitions than anticipated. Hence in October of 2011, the White House raised the threshold for a petition to be considered successful to 25,000 signatures within 30 days.[8] (Reflecting the initiative's ballooning success, this standard was raised on January 15, 2013, to a dual level process. First a petition needed to get 150 signatures within 30 days in order for it to be searchable within WhiteHouse.gov. A second threshold was levied of 100,000 signatures within 30 days in order to merit a White House response. Also, the range of issues qualifying for a response was restricted to those relevant to the White House's remit.[9]) What is the definition of success? According to the White House website, the "petition" will be sent to the appropriate agency for an "official response." An official response, though, is not what was originally offered, namely (according to the video on the White House website) to "petition your government to take action on a range of issues."

A conundrum here is that from the White House's perspective, having to be too responsive to the public's interest—even to the extent of providing an "official response" concerning a matter of policy versus actually taking any action on the policy itself—was seen as a "problem," albeit a good one.[10] That is to say, the White House deemed it to be a problem to get an executive branch response about a governmental issue that was of concern to at least 5,000 people. (Moreover, a "response" is a standard far below a serious evaluation of policy alternatives, a substantially higher burden, but one that is nonetheless implicit in the notion of a petition.) One might draw a conclusion that the White House wanted to respond to the public's concerns, if it could, and was happy to reap the benefits both of knowing what was on the mind of some segments of the public as well as providing an opportunity for concerned citizens to express their concerns and wishes for changes in policy. The White House also had to be willing to take the anger of frustrated petitioners who found that their concerns did not lead to a meaningful response, let alone change in policy.

Registration is required, for understandable reasons. Yet privacy concerns surrounding such registration on the petitioning system are also understandable; these include the potential loss of anonymity, fear of reprisal or even of being "spammed" by future White House entreaties and messages. Privacy concerns arising from the registration requirement are partly allayed by the fact that despite a signer's name being publicly displayed, it only included a first name and last initial plus city and state, thus offering a degree of anonymity. Once affixed, however, the signature would be publicly displayed along with this information, and could not be removed. Though John P. from New York might have little to fear from exposure in this manner, those with unusual names in small towns may have. This dilemma raised a variety of concerns regarding privacy, personal security, and traceability that are touched on elsewhere in this book. Moreover, a record is created that may be subject to unexpected uses, as noted both in this book and elsewhere.[11] Beyond the question of registration is the use of third-party cookies. Even though the White House may not track a visitor to its website, other parties may be able to do so. In the senior author's experience, a visit to the White House website meant that numerous ads from the Obama campaign began appearing on the pages of news service websites that he subsequently visited. Together with other user-generated behavior and third-party monitoring, quite a bit of valuable information can be gathered about White House website visitors, if not collected directly by the White House, that can be harnessed to serve the interests of the political party in power. That is, even assuming that the White House itself is not directly involved, its political interests can be advanced by those who are allied with it as they collect and exploit such data.

Turning to the contents of the petitions themselves and their policy relevance in the summer of 2013, marijuana legalization was among the top-ranking issues, as would be expected, but signatures were also being sought for numerous other issues. These included demanding a rise in the cap on the amount of earnings subject to Social Security taxes, ensuring that every American child had access to adequate library resources, and banning the use of gas chambers for euthanizing animals. These were all policy measures that could have become laws, if the Administration had backed them and Congress had accepted them. There was no compact, however, that these suggestions would become Obama Administration initiatives. There was only the agreement that the government's position would be explained to the public, if these "petitions" received a minimum number of votes within a given amount of time.[12]

Many other wide-ranging topics have been raised. One was that the government should have revealed whatever information it had about extraterrestrials living among us. Two successful petitions read as follows, and may have been among the reasons that the threshold of petition signatures was raised to 100,000 (i.e., to save effort addressing seemingly frivolous petitions):

SAMPLE PETITIONS ON INTERACTIONS WITH EXTRATERRESTRIALS

Immediately disclose the government's knowledge of and communications with extraterrestrial beings. (5,387 signatures).

Formally acknowledge an extraterrestrial presence engaging the human race-Disclosure (12,078 signatures).

The response is worth quoting for its inoffensive "no evidence" tone.

"SEARCHING FOR ET, BUT NO EVIDENCE YET" WHITE HOUSE RESPONSE TO PETITIONS, WRITTEN BY PHIL LARSON

Thank you for signing the petition asking the Obama Administration to acknowledge an extraterrestrial presence here on earth.

The U.S. government has no evidence that any life exists outside our planet, or that an extraterrestrial presence has contacted or engaged any member of the human race. In addition, there is no credible information to suggest that any evidence is being hidden from the public's eye. However, that doesn't mean the subject of life outside our planet is not being discussed or explored. In fact there are a number of projects working toward the goal of understanding if life can or does exist off Earth.[13]

It could be argued, in light of overwhelming scientific evidence bearing on the topic, that the petition did not require a serious response. On the other hand, if it was being answered, and many thousands of people wanted to know about this question, a more authoritative response would have been appropriate. In fact, considerable rifling through governmental files by past Administrations to determine whether any information had been withheld from the public had come up empty every time.

So, at the end of the day, the public was left with many brush-off answers for uncomfortable questions, and petitions for policy change were not actually petitions at all. This situation did not escape the notice of social media advocates. As a result, there was demand for "truth in advertising," that is, to have the process labeled as "explanations" rather than "petitions."

The fundamentally misleading aspect of this social media initiative became a target of attack. Not the least of the reasons for the attack was the initiative's use of the term "petition." One Tim B. of Astoria, New York, submitted the following petition:

SAMPLE PETITION SUBMISSION CRITIQUING PETITION PROCESS

WE PETITION THE OBAMA ADMINISTRATION TO:

Remove the word "petition" from this website as it is misleading and untruthful. Instead, use, "Request an Explanation."

Petition; noun
"A petition is a request to do something, most commonly addressed to a government official or public entity."

Explanation; noun
"An explanation is a set of statements constructed to describe a set of facts which clarifies the causes, context, and consequences of those facts."

This website has helped in making zero changes and has failed to carry out its purpose according to the clear definitions it was created by. Therefore, I believe the word, "Petition," should be completely removed from this site. It is untruthful to all who vote and support commonly agreed upon causes. It is misleading and provides false hope, making people feel like their government is listening and willing to make changes based on the simple rules of, "Enough Votes = Change," when it will not.[14]

As of January 16, 2012, this petition had a mere 848 signatures, more than 24,000 short to elicit a response. Despite the lack of a widespread upwelling of public support for this position, the petitioners did have a point about wanting to see that votes would equal change. This sentiment had already been reflected in a successful petition late in 2011, which asked that the White House take seriously the petitioning function and respond substantively to the content of the petition. That petition declared:

SAMPLE PETITION ON PETITIONS

We petition the Obama Administration to: actually take these petitions seriously instead of just using them as an excuse to pretend you are listening Although the ability to submit petitions directly to the White House is a noble and welcome new feature of the current Administration, the first round of responses makes blatantly clear the White House intends to just support its current stances and explain them with responses everyone who has done any research article knows. An online petition is not meant as a replacement for using a search box in a web browser. We the People, those who grant you the power to govern in the first place, are requesting changes in policy directly, circumventing legislators who already do not listen to us. We the People request you govern FOR us, which means actually listening to us and actually acting in our interests instead of special interests.[15]

By garnering enough signatures to merit a response, it became clear that at least 30,000 other people wanted to have meaningful social media inputs into the governmental process. Clearly, many felt that once a promise was made, it should have been kept. As well, a good many petitioners tried to reverse the spin put on the White House's interpretation of a "petition." Disgruntled citizens seeking to be engaged have continued to express their resentment over the limited influence even 100,000 signatories can have over White House policy. A further dyspeptic take on the process was demonstrated by a June 30, 2013 petition asking that the petition website be entirely closed. A "Shutdown petitions.WhiteHouse.gov" petition stated: "This is not participation in the political process. This is a way for you to cherry pick a few popular issues and make a statement to get some quick press coverage."[16]

It would be unfair to say that the petitions have had no effect on Obama Administration policy. Macon Phillips, an architect of Obama Administration social media activities, observed that: "We've also used the platform to announce new directions in policy or to continue a dialogue with people who have an interest in this issue." He gave an example from March 3, 2013 in which "the White House responded to a petition that argued that individuals ought to have a right to unlock their cell phones. This was not an issue on which the White House had previously taken a policy position. But after more than 114,000 people spoke out using We the People, [Administration officials] ... decided that the petitioners were exactly right: Consumers needed a strong statement of support from the White House."

Nonetheless, in looking at this widely reported success story,[17] it appears that the petition was already in harmony with a previously stated Administration position as expressed by the National Telecommunications and Information Administration (NTIA)[18] even though the NTIA position had not been officially endorsed by the White House. The argument could be made that the petition helped energize policy change in this area, and certainly the declaration of White House endorsement did generate publicity. And it may have been that the NTIA document would have languished without White House intervention. However, it does not appear that the petition itself had any effect on the *content* of the policy toward unlocking cell-phones. Still, this instance can be seen as a success story for the petition movement, albeit one in which the Obama administration chose to intervene rather than felt that it had to take an action in light of the social media-expressed will of the people. In that sense, we would also judge that this example would fit more in form 1 (problem identification) rather than form 3 (citizen empowerment) of citizen digital engagement.

From his vantage point, Alexander Howard, the Government 2.0 Washington Correspondent for O'Reilly Media, commented that the lack of binding power on the petitions tends to vitiate their policy import. "The trick with WethePeople is that they're not bound by it." And even as to a response at all, there is no particular timeline imposed, and petitions can remain unanswered for a quite a while. Says Howard, "So you've got that Westboro Baptist petition [urging the White House to categorize Kansas's Westboro Baptist Church as a hate group] that's been up there for months and months and months and months and months, on top of the most popular petitions, but they choose not to respond." And even when they do respond, it is sometimes after the fact. Still they deserve some credit, noted Howard: "They responded to the open access one [i.e., a petition to expand federal policies requiring free access to scientific research papers that are taxpayer-funded], but that could be fairly argued, after the election, after the rest of the public proceedings around that had come to their own conclusion."[19]

Despite the lack of direct impact on policy, there appears to be a collateral benefit from exercises such as the "We the People" e-petition. This includes that many participants in the process find fulfillment in "just being involved" or "being heard" by someone in authority. Getting to vent one's concerns was gratifying for many. And this satisfaction occurred despite the seeming absence of impact on policy, and notwithstanding if they were even heard. We return to this topic in a later chapter.

Other Efforts to Gain Engagement

Obviously there are severe pressures on, and sharp competition for, the President's time and attention. How does the White House select topics and venues for engaging citizens via social media? Macon Phillips explained to us how the process unfolds at a high level:

> Yeah well we first think about the audience we're trying to reach. And then we think about where those people are going. And there are tools for that. It is interesting. In some ways it's the sort of marketing aspect of this. If you were going to try to make sure that people knew about a new product that you had one of the things you would do is probably buy advertising. Right? That's how the world works. And you wouldn't just say, "I'm going to buy 100,000 newspaper ads. Let's do it." You would say, "Well do my customers even read newspapers? What geographies are they in? What section of the newspaper should I be in?" So forth and so on. And so when you apply that model to the Internet you actually find a lot of these sites actually try really hard to show potential advertisers their demos. And you can look at that information and understand even though we're not buying advertising we know what demos certain types are in.[20]

To give a sense as to how that thesis has played out in practice, we examine a few more instances of the range of social media initiatives by the Obama White House. These will help fill in the picture concerning the wide array of uses and how they populate the three modalities of citizen engagement. The examples discussed here are social media-guided outreach efforts, including interaction opportunities, contests and prizes, and also social-network tapping initiatives for people who propagate presidential messages or commentary on them. As these are presented as examples to illustrate principles and practices, rather than nuanced mini-case studies as per the above, they will not be treated in depth. Yet even this brief review may suggest parallels between White House initiatives to build social media relationships with those of marketers, religious leaders, and formal organizations.

Before our brief tour begins, it should also be borne in mind that social media initiatives not only can arrive on the scene, they can quickly disappear as well. While the White House is constantly experimenting with new ways to connect with the public via social media, as exemplified below, some experiments are quietly discarded after a short time. For instance, White House "Office Hours" was unveiled in the summer of 2011. Senior White House staff would hold regular office hours during which questions could be tweeted to them, and they would answer back via Twitter. This experiment lasted about one month.[21]

GOOGLE+ HANGOUTS

On January 30, 2012, President Obama held his first Google+ Hangout interview, which, the White House declared, was the first completely virtual interview from the White House of a president.[22] The President keyed off his State of the Union address to answer questions from a handful of live people who participated via video and recorded questions. (In preparation for the Hangout, more than 227,000 people submitted or voted in support of specific questions for the President to address.) As the event got underway, the moderator told the President, "Mr. President, we're going to put you in the hot seat." Just how hot were the questions? In the prolegomenon, a young man asked, "How do you plan on getting anything done in this election year with this Congress?" (These are the kinds of questions that politicians love as it allows them to outline their goals, encourage their supporters, and confound their opponents.)

A range of questions, dealing with jobs to drone strikes was posed to President Obama who nimbly explained how concerned/effective his Administration was in trying to respond to the questioner's concerns. One of the guest questioners, "Jennifer," whose engineer husband had been unemployed for over a year, was dubious as to the advisability of allowing more foreign workers to seek US engineering jobs under the President's loosened visa program proposal. Though dealing more broadly with her question, saying that jobs in the high-tech sector were going wanting, he responded to Jennifer's concern about her unemployed husband by extending an offer: "We should get his résumé and I'll forward it to some of these high tech companies."[23]

What was the reaction to this "first of its kind" social media event? Inevitably, there was a range. Here are a few plucked from among the numerous YouTube comments: "It is cool that the President did this" ("OlderThanTime09"). "Communication through the Internet can be very relieving and positively influential for anyone who knows about this opportunity" (London Phillips). (This comment, by the way, speaks to the "relief" or pleasure some social media users report experiencing by participating in digital engagement with the White House, even though no action may be taken—just the experience of expressing oneself is a positive, a point to which we return later.) "He always speaks so well. But the questions weren't hard or pressed at all" (Gerry Stevens). "I am not Obama's biggest fan, and I probably won't be voting for him this year either, but this man is very classy and thoughtful and I really appreciate that" ("Webpaycheck"). "FloridaBoyyyyy" commented, "Wow, Jennifer [the question-asking wife of the unemployed engineer] used the hangout for a personal agenda...I don't think this was the purpose."[24]

The White House, obviously pleased with this experience, has repeated it in a subsequent State of the Union address, not only with the President but with a cavalcade of Administration officials, as well. The format not only attracts lots of interest, but creates the image that the White House is seeking, of a president authentically engaged with the people's concerns.

Kori Schulman, Director of Online Engagement at the White House's Office of Public Engagement, said in a web publication interview that during an online chat President Obama "was responding to a question and noticed that the Twitter user had blue hair in her profile picture. In the response tweet, the President noted that he liked her hair. It was this *wonderful, authentic, dialogue* on Twitter between the President and someone in their living room. From the *President all the way down, this Administration is committed to public engagement and participation*" (emphasis added).[25]

Her comment nicely contextualizes the Administration's view of public engagement and participation as articulated by the Office of Public Engagement. Concerning progress in social media engagement terms over the years the President has been in office, Schulman noted, "In fighting to preserve tax cuts for the middle class last month [January 2013], President Obama called on people to speak out and share what $2,000 meant to them on Twitter, Facebook and WhiteHouse.gov." She continued, adding, "Hundreds of thousands of people participated (135,000+ people shared their stories on WhiteHouse.gov with more than 350,000+ tweets with the hashtag #my2k on Twitter)." Schulman also emphasized the White House's responses, explaining, "But it didn't end there—the President stopped by the home of someone that shared their My2k story on WH.gov, the Vice President had lunch with a few folks that were concerned about the issue and spoke out online, and others were invited to the White House to join a discussion." In summarizing, she stated, "We're using social as a way for people to participate in their government, we're reading their stories, and we're following up."[26]

REDDIT AND "ASK ME ANYTHING (AMA)": EXTENDING SOCIAL MEDIA INTERACTION TO A CRITICAL AUDIENCE DURING A CAMPAIGN STOP

The line between Commander-in-Chief and campaigner-in-chief can be blurry. We earlier referred to the permanent campaign concept, so this blurry line can run through the entire length of a presidency. But it is especially blurry during election season, whether one is listening to a stump speech at a county fair or participating in an online social media forum. Yet when a candidate visits a forum such as Reddit, which is a bumptious social news site, the audience expects an original and open engagement, even if is already predisposed to like that candidate. This situation is exemplified by the reaction to President Obama's 2012 social media exchange on Reddit. Reddit allows users to post discussions, links, photos or video in bulletin board conversation threads. The relative visibility of individual discussion threads rises or falls in accordance with viewers' "up" or "down" votes. In contrast with Facebook and Twitter, whose administrators and design logic place prominent emphasis on the verification of individual user identities, Reddit does not actively seek, nor does it enforce, any norms of verified user identification. While preserving anonymity and egalitarian crowdsourcing dynamics, the absence of verification makes the site more prone to volatility and misinformation.

In August 2012 the Republicans were having their national convention in Tampa, and most political and media eyes were focused there. However, President/candidate Obama was able to draw some attention to himself by having a surprise question-and-answer session on Reddit. During a campaign stop in Charlottesville, Virginia, on August 29, 2012, he went online to field questions as part of a Reddit "Ask Me Anything" (AMA) session, in which candidates field queries from Reddit users. Unlike many more structured forums, the AMA is open to verified and unverified users, who could theoretically be participating from any location. During the 2012 election cycle, presidential candidates Ron Paul, Buddy Roemer, and Gary Johnson participated in AMAs—as did Barack Obama, who holds the distinction of being the first head of state to participate in an AMA. Over the course of 30 minutes, he answered ten questions. His surprise visit stimulated so much traffic that it crashed servers.

Teddy Goff, the Digital Director for President Obama's 2012 campaign, observed, Reddit "is a place that doesn't get the mainstream attention of Facebook or Twitter but had millions and millions of users." Noting the demographics, he added, "A lot of them [are] the very people we want to reach. A lot of younger people, mainly male, who may feel a little disaffected from politics. It was the perfect audience for us." In addition to this specific outreach, he spoke of general interest, explaining, "We thought there would be interest just in the fact that he was doing it. And we thought it would be attractive to sort of the younger and tech savvy community and that he is a guy who is willing to put himself out there and take questions from wherever they come in the sort of Wild Wild West that is the crowdsourced platform." Importantly, Goff also noted the personal dimension that the Reddit initiative could highlight. "We thought that could be a good show of the sort of person he is. So there were a lot of factors that went into that particular decision." When asked about monitoring of Reddit afterwards, he replied, "Well, you know that was a case where we knew we were only going to do it ... So I wouldn't say that we put a huge amount of time into that sort of thing as distinct from Facebook, Twitter, Email which we worked with every day and we were trying to get better at and were much, much more concerned with monitoring."[27]

Stephen Muller, Vice President of Strategy at media strategy and technology firm Blue State Digital, and the Online Video Director for Obama for America in 2011–2012, described the authenticity of the experience. He explained, "He's sitting there on the computer, reading these questions as they get pushed up on the AMA and he is deciding how he wants to answer them based on what he feels is the right answer."[28]

Kate Albright-Hanna, Obama's 2008 Director of Video for New Media, commented about the Reddit Ask Me Anything experience. "On the Reddit discussion he only answered a few questions, but he came off as very approachable. For example, he discussed his home brewed beer like a guy who just enjoys a normal hobby."[29]

However, the editorial reviews were negative. *The Atlantic Wire* said that "it seems that the President's Reddit visit was another carefully scripted campaign stop" and *Slate* headlined: "Obama Joins Reddit, Invites Tough Questions, Leaves Without Answering Them."[30] Online commentators at *The Atlantic Wire* captured both the thrill of potential presidential attention and the agony of being exposed to another set of lifeless answers to easy questions rather than a serious or insightful analysis.

> *Musik Wayman*: Is everyone grumbling because their question did not receive an answer, or because..what??! It would be cool to say I asked the POTUS a question on Reddit and he answered ME....wow!! Ppl.
> *Skinny Chicken*: No, mostly people are grumbling because he gave canned, expected responses instead of candid, personal responses.[31]

Likewise, some Reddit denizens were disappointed by the lack of continuing attention paid to Reddit, compared to other social media sites such as Facebook. (The President has largely bypassed Reddit since then, though he did make his final appeal of the 2012 campaign to voters via Reddit.) This reflects the concern that presidential exposure via social media carries not just benefits but also risks, such as growing cynicism or disappointment among followers. As to this point, Peter DiSilvio, a Redditor who participated in the event (and is also head of new media projects for Nassau County's Executive), commented:

> People are already angry that Obama is not doing another AMA...He could be thinking about doing another one. But people are just ticked off. "He'll never come back. He'll never come back." People remember. People remember that someone was on a social media...They are going to feel used. They are going to feel that you only need them when you need them.[32]

There is a significant corollary to the symbolism of President Obama's participation in Reddit. First, it demonstrated he is tech savvy, which, as described above in the elections chapter, is important to his image. Alexander Howard captured this dimension of the Reddit experience, telling us, "When Barack Obama logged on to start answering Twitter questions himself at the keyboard, he put the period in front of the post so his reply went to everybody—that's a level of understanding that absolutely came from...making Macon sit next to him going 'holy crap, don't screw up.'" He added, "Obama is a smart guy. 'Okay, so this is how that works, so I type in that name, or now that I'm on Google+, I type in a +, or now that I'm on Reddit, put in a rage comic because that's funny.'" Howard explained the benefits of the President's attentiveness. "That kind of stuff demonstrates understanding that goes a long way with those communities. It carries risk for the person but the reward is to get people to feel like you have actually answered the darn question."

But the size and reach of the activity must also be considered. Alan Rosenblatt, Founder and Executive Director of the Internet Advocacy Center, noted, "Reddit's a big community—there's a lot more voters on Reddit than there are in New Hampshire, and I think that people should recognize that that's reality. There's way more voters on Facebook and Twitter than there are in any state in this country, and that's a big deal." Concerning elite awareness, he added, "For them to take that seriously is really key. I think that whenever you have a Twitter town hall or any social media town hall and you make yourself accessible to the questions that you will answer from the public, you increase both internal efficacy (that person feels like you are more responsive to them) and you increase external efficacy (people who are watching, seeing the conversation of the President interacting with other people, with ordinary citizens)." The net effect, he said, is that participants "start to feel that the government truly is more responsive to the people in general."

Speaking of the issue of vicarious connection between asking a question and its gratifications even if not answered, Rosenblatt offered, "You see other people being answered and you see other people asking the same question and the question being answered, even if it wasn't yours. So, I think even if they're answering someone else's question on another topic, you just see a responsive government, and I think that's the key—restoring the connection between government and the people, and social media is a great tool for doing that."[33]

The Reddit experience was less about determining presidential positions, and more about the experience of interacting with Obama in conjunction with a community that led to a feeling of connection; it came from participating in a communal process. This is far different than a model of one individual obtaining a particular piece of requested information from a decision-maker. The collective engagement with the person who represented the power and importance of the office, combined with demonstrating an understanding of shared community codes, made the experience especially meaningful for many Reddit denizens. There is another difference too: unlike some linear aggregation systems, such as "Ask the White House" (discussed above), Reddit encourages horizontal engagement among participants, especially as collectivities within the subcommunities. It also allows participants to see and comment upon the questions that are left unanswered.

THE FIRST PRESIDENTIAL TEXTING EVENT: YOUTH TEXT OBAMA ABOUT STUDENT DEBT

When in spring 2013, President Obama's efforts to keep student loan rates low stalled in Congress, he turned to social media to try to influence Congress to act on his recommendations. A good match was found between the interests of the White House staff and a leading not-for-profit service for young people that led to the first presidential texting event.

The not-for-profit is DoSomething.org, which describes itself as using "text messaging to connect teens with volunteer opportunities that don't require money, a parent or a car."[34] DoSomething.org has 2.1 million members, 1.3 million of whom are connected to the organization via their mobile devices.

The event was borne out of a concern that in 2013, "The President was not able to be out there as much as he wanted to. So [White House staff] were looking for other ways to make sure that the public knew that the President was on the student's side."[35] The way in which the White House and a volunteer organization hooked up yields some insight into the process by which social media events are born. Muneer Panjawani, DoSomething.org's Business Development Manager, was the lead for bringing the texting event into being. The connection grew serendipitously when he was attending the 2013 South by Southwest (SXSW) festival and conference in Austin and met someone from New York City who shared his activist interest in immigration issues. While exploring trying to put an activity in motion with his

New York contact, that individual put him in touch with the White House in an attempt to see if there was "alignment" of interests on immigration issues between DoSomething.org and the White House. According to Panjawani, no alignment was initially found but, eventually, Macon Phillips learned of his interest and made contact with him, paving the way for the project.[36]

Marah Lidey, DoSomething.org's Digital Engagement Manager, said that the White House's initial interest arose from their prior experiences on Reddit, LinkedIn, Facebook, and Twitter. She explained, "What they found was that they weren't getting the momentum for the audience that they really wanted to reach." Lidey described the process for helping the White House reach out on the specific issue of student loans. She said, "Essentially we came up with this idea of just making Obama the very first president ever to text with young people. Because young people have a very strong voice in these things, a lot of people think they don't care or they're lazy but you just got to reach them where they are." Describing the reasoning, she added, "You have to put yourself on their level. I think the White House was really looking for that: How do we put ourselves on their level? Not talking down or sending out to a huge group or a general statement." Ultimately, this led to the texting strategy. Lidey continued, "And so we came up with this idea that young people could text him their questions about student loans. And every day of the week for a week they would hear responses from the President. We were really excited because we were giving our members access to something this big and this influential."[37]

Beginning June 24, 2013, President Obama (and then Vice President Joe Biden when the President departed for Africa) promised to respond daily for one week to one member's text selected by DoSomething.org in conjunction with the White House. In terms of the young audience's reaction, the event fully met expectations: 70,902 mobile members submitted 54,503 questions for consideration. DoSomething.org staff personally reviewed each incoming text and sent the most popular ones to the White House for the President to answer. President Obama himself personally reviewed and approved a text prepared by his staff, and he then texted an answer to the one question that the White House selected. The President's response was then sent to DoSomething.org, which broadcast it to everyone who opted in to the event.[38]

In keeping with the rather staid nature of presidential interactions, and the limited bandwidth, the first text message was informative but not dynamic. For example, the first exchange (on Monday, June 24) was:

What have you done and plan to do to lower student debt & tuition? *Dan*—Ann Arbor, MI

We've expanded grants & tax credits, provided new options to manage debt and proposed incentives for colleges to keep costs down. More here: http://at.wh.gov/mlnUx. *President Obama*

Considering the lively nature of texting, this answer, though purely informational and "disciplined" on message, was also rather staid. After this information-heavy beginning, a note of informality more typical of teen text messaging became discernible in Obama's responses. The President typed out the colloquial "gotta" instead of "got to" when responding to his Wednesday interlocutor, to wit, "We gotta make sure higher education isn't a luxury."[39] The DoSomething.org teens especially liked invocations of personal experiences by the President. (On Tuesday of that week, President Obama texted that his Financial Aid Scorecard & Financial Aid Shopping Sheet, which he took credit for launching, was "something Michelle and I wish we had had when we were in your shoes"[40]). Overall, the DoSomething. org members reported being thrilled with the idea that they were texting the President, and even more so that there was some possibility that he would respond to their question. The personal connection that they felt via text was something that impressed the White House, according to DoSomething.org.[41] When arranging for the event, the White House told Panjawani that they wanted to "make sure that the experience is authentic."[42] Authenticity, as noted earlier, is an important quality for successful social media outreach campaigns, and compared to other modes its absence is particularly objectionable to the audience.

The extent to which these efforts were effective in stimulating support, or generating an outpouring of messages to Congress from teens, is unknown. Though Congress failed to act on the measure that President Obama had been promoting through this initiative by the July 1 deadline he had set, the student loan rate reduction bill was subsequently passed and signed into law later that summer. However, this effort further demonstrated President Obama's continuing interest in and use of social media to reach out to the public. Among young people, at least in this instance, the use of social media created a sense of a personal if transient bond between the apex of national leadership and idealistic young citizens.

Although it can be risky to generalize from a single case, Briana Veal, whose Wednesday question was cited above, was interviewed by DoSomething.org. Her responses capture the thrill she experienced:

> DS: How does it feel knowing that you texted with the President of the United States?
> BV: It feels really awesome! I still can't believe it. I couldn't stop smiling the whole day after I found out he'd answer my question. I'll always remember that feeling and his answer. It just really means a lot to know that he cares this much to stop whatever he's doing and answer a young student's question that could help us in our future endeavors.[43]

The vicarious anticipation of possibly having an experience like that of Brianna could be a good motivator for participation in social media activities; certainly it is pleasant to imagine sharing one's thoughts with someone of great power.

CITIZEN ENGAGEMENT VIA AWARD NOMINATIONS: THE CASE OF THE PRESIDENTIAL CITIZENS MEDAL

We noted earlier that the White House could have launched a citizen nomination process (including polling and crowdsourced recommendations) for important posts and highlighted the Supreme Court justice nominations in particular. Certainly, these actions could have also included a host of other positions, such as ambassadors and program administrators. But as we pointed out, the White House made no move in this direction. Nonetheless, a mechanism along these lines for public input has by no means been entirely forgone. One such instance was the launch in 2012 of an online submission form for nominating people for the Presidential Citizens Medal. This prestigious award, established by President Nixon, recognizes "citizens of the United States of America who have performed exemplary deeds of service for their country or their fellow citizens."[44] Despite the medal's general recognition as the federal government's second highest civilian award, there had been no official channel for people to nominate candidates. But in April 2012 the Obama Administration opened an online form so that individuals could do so electronically. While this was an important step forward in terms of creating an image of openness (anyone could be readily nominated by anyone) the power over the decision remained entirely in the hands of the White House. As there was no allowance for gaining online support or petitions for this award, this initiative did not fit the richer sense of the term, "social media." It could at least theoretically bring some hitherto unknown people to the attention of the White House, and could certainly give a good feeling to those who could now know that they had been nominated. Also, it could allow groups to organize on behalf of a candidate, though that was not encouraged by the system. Yet, though a step toward citizen empowerment, it did not fundamentally, or even significantly, alter the power balance: the system remained "we decide." That said, it could also be a useful talking point for how President Obama worked to fulfill his promise of citizen engagement.

FREE MORAL LABOR: ENGAGED CITIZENS AS PROPAGATORS OF PRESIDENTIAL VIEWPOINTS

Another central theme of social media presidency, as practiced during the Obama Administration, is the recruitment of citizens on behalf of presidential initiatives. Although we have explored this theme earlier in the book, and see it developing out of the "hook" discussion earlier in this chapter, we want to address here its flowering in the more mature phase of social media for citizen engagement during the Obama Administration, namely the period that followed the crowdsourcing activities that characterized the Administration's transition and early months. Engagement of citizens in the Obama Administration social media network means attracting their attention and moving them up the commitment scale from merely being passive recipients of White House information to transmitters of that information to others with whom they have personal contact. It also involves the creation and sharing of pro-Administration content. One advantage of having engaged citizens create their own pro-Administration material is that it has the precious ring of authenticity. (This was mentioned in the "text Obama about student debt" example.)

Illustrations of this process are given below. In each of them, citizens are expected to be conduits of Administration messages to the public or to others in their social circle. In most cases, they are expected to act as value-added participants, contributing their own personal story or creative twist to the Administration's message. Yet, in the examples it must be borne in mind that participants are seldom hapless individuals who stumbled upon the White House social media initiative and are passively following orders. Rather they are likely supporters of President Obama who are seeking to help him and his policies, and thus are gratified by the opportunity to foster a cause in which they believe. In fact, it could be argued that these initiatives are doing these particular engaged citizens a favor by providing them with the tools to do what they want to do, and to do it more effectively. A second set of people who participate in these social media initiatives are likely to be interested in the affective or entertainment aspects, or in seeking additional information. They would plausibly be able to move up the ladder of commitment. As discussed in chapter 3, social media can be useful in gaining a foothold in a citizen's mind, and once established, used to build greater involvement and commitment.

WHITE HOUSE SOCIAL SERIES

The White House Social series bridges the virtual and physical worlds by arranging for

> in-person meetings of people who engage with the White House through social media, including Twitter, Facebook and Google+ and Pinterest. Building off of the White House Tweetup series, we're inviting people that engage with us online on a range of social sites to participate in face-to-face meetings.[45]

(Obviously, those who don't choose, or are unable, to participate in social media cannot be considered for these events. In this, the incentive structure has similarities to "discount club cards" at supermarkets or retailers; gets benefits, but also gives up some privacy and exposes oneself to the sponsor's targeted messaging and behind-the-scenes tracking. And like these clubs, how the information is used after it is collected and into whose hands it may pass remains opaque to the individual from whom it has been collected.) You have to be politically engaged with the White House in order to be included among those to whom the White House will open its doors. This is an extension of politics, using visits to the White House as a tool of political enticement. One cannot help being reminded of President Clinton's use of the Lincoln Bedroom to reward big donors.[46]

Past White House Social events have included "a Twitter Town Hall with the President, a Tweetup Briefing with Press Secretary Jay Carney, a Let's Move! Tweetup for the First Lady's garden harvest…a Pinterest Holiday Social and most recently a White House State of the Union Social."[47]

The invitation can certainly be thrilling. In January 2012, a Vermont school teacher was among 100 or so people who were chosen to participate in a White House-sponsored Twitter "Tweetup" event in Washington around the President's State of the Union address. It included an opportunity to ask senior White House staff questions following the SOU. His reaction to the experience: "I feel really awesome to be here and chosen. This is a highlight of my political involvement in my life…It's just really, really amazing."[48] Interestingly, part of the participants' responsibility was to stimulate discussion via Twitter during the speech, which presumably was intended to help stimulate audience interest. (The White House posting announcing the contest said, "After you sign up, spread the word! Let your followers know that you signed up for the #WHTweetup and tell us @WhiteHouse."[49] This request to notify the tweeters' followers about the White House Tweetup under-scores the citizen-propagation element of social media engagement.)

The attraction of a White House invitation, or even an exquisitely rare treat—a surprise visit to one's home by the President himself—can be a powerful magnet that directly encourages social media participation. It also encourages a chain of interest, as those around the participant are also affected by the participation. One is reminded of radio stations that make a practice of giving out bumper stickers adver-tising their station; they incentivize people to put the stickers on their car by giving them a chance to win a prize occasionally given out to the occupants of a car bear-ing the sticker. While the attraction of the program is obvious—the tiny chance of winning something is of great psychological value—it is difficult to discern how at a cognitive level the above listed garden harvest and holiday social activities are mean-ingfully related to the business of citizen engagement at the policy level. Certainly it is relevant at the level of keeping the Administration's name in the people's mind in a happy or beneficent way (just as in addition to debates and position papers, during campaigns it is important to shake people's hands and kiss babies). Also, for many, policy is not important, but an imagined association with a person of great status is. Finally, vast numbers of people value entertainment and vicarious enjoy-ment, even sentimental connections that border on the mawkish. This was a lesson learned as early as the Barney Cam experiment that took place during the Bush Administration; presumably the lesson will be applied in future administrations.

$40 PER YEAR CONTEST

Contests are inherently interesting, as demonstrated by the enduring popularity of gambling, spectator sports, and TV game shows. This lesson is by no means lost on the White House. One such contest held by it has been the opportunity to tell the President what one might do with an additional $40 per year. Those with the winning story get invited to the White House. This was designed to pressure Republicans to extend a payroll tax reduction.[50] The overall contest proved to be an effective way to stimulate people to exercise their intelligence and creativity on a topic in order to win a prize. By influencing an individual to do this, the con-test sponsors expect new ideas to become engrained in the contestant's mind, and change attitudes and behaviors. In this sense, the activity is no different from the risible contests in the 1950s in which kids would be offered some prize if they could write a winning essay about why they liked a cereal or some other commercial prod-uct. This is comparable to YouTube contests in which sponsors encourage people to submit their self-produced videos promoting a product and become a winner of some prize, usually of a monetary nature.

STATE OF THE UNION

President Obama is no exception to the tradition of using the constitutionally man-dated State of the Union address to marshal support for his program and vision, but he does deserve credit for being the first to add a social media twist to enliven and enrich the experience. Following on the heels of his 2012 social media engagement (noted above), in 2013, his staff used the SOU address to offer an opportunity to "take ownership" (our term) for its content. (Offering "ownership" of material has been shown in educational settings to be an effective way to engage learners and to make lessons meaningful to students.[51]) Visitors to the White House website section on the SOU were invited to "share your citizen response" and "get involved" and were given an opportunity to do both. (The invitation remained on the site more than nine months after the address; how much longer it may remain as a functionality is unknown.) The site said:

YOUR RESPONSE TO THE STATE OF OUR UNION

President Obama's State of the Union address is just the beginning; now we want to hear from you. Highlight a passage of the speech that was meaningful to you and tell the President how you're connected to that issue. Then share that part of the speech with your friends.[52]

By moving a cursor over the speech's text, highlighting would appear over it. Clicking on it led a response box to appear. The box solicited the site visitor's name and role and offered the writing prompt, "this matters to me because" with 400 characters available in which to formulate a response. (Brevity is required here; no deep disquisitions could be formulated in 400 characters.) An email was solicited. Visitors were informed that "The White House will use this info [sic] for follow ups and general updates." (Visitors had to provide an email in order to be able to submit the reaction to the White House.)

Upon submission, a message box appeared, saying, "You've told President Obama why this part of the speech matters to you. Now share it with your friends," with share buttons for Twitter and Facebook. (The construction of the sentence "You've told President Obama…" seems puzzling in the sense that it strains the bounds of credulity to think that the message was actually "told" to the President.) Note that by participating in this form of citizen engagement, one is being invited to reflect upon and respond to the words of the President. Once that task is completed, one is then recruited to work on behalf of propagating President Obama's message to one's friends (interestingly, one is not asked to forward it to one's family members). Further, as stated in the messaging tool template, one is also opened up to receiving updates from the White House. Yet, it is unclear how the sharing of one's reaction to the SOU speech is in any way a form of reciprocal citizen engagement.

TELL US YOUR STORY

The value of using stories to convey a message has been recognized since ancient times, as witnessed by the enduring popularity of biblical parables and Aesop's Fables. The testimonial, too, has a longstanding role in the history and practice of persuasion. A characteristic of social media is the easy creation and sharing of digital materials, especially those involving images and sound, such as short video clips. Bringing these three strands together, the White House has created an opportunity for citizens to create and share their stories in support of White House policies and initiatives. Participation is induced through the invitation to share one's story with the White House (associated with the power of the President himself) and the possibility of seeing it on the White House website. Several different White House webpages encourage citizen engagement via story sharing. On a generic page, a pull-down menu offers topics ranging from veterans affairs to foreign policy.[53] Visitors can offer comments and sign up for updates from the White House. For pivotal Administration issues, such as healthcare, even more options are provided, as well as prompts to help guide citizen input. These prompts outline the many benefits that are included in the Affordable Care Act. Citizen contributors not only can write a brief comment or vignette, but can upload photos and add links to YouTube or Flickr to help illustrate their story.[54] For this (and many other such pages), story contributors are notified that "stories submitted through this web form, along with your name, may be featured on WhiteHouse.gov and posted on White House social media channels."[55]

In an effort to understand the purpose of the Affordable Care Act story-sharing site, it is notable that it highlights many of its claimed benefits. Yet none of the criticisms or drawbacks of the Act are enumerated or intimated, which is understandable if the White House "share your stories" engagement effort is intended not as a policy discussion form or an educational effort, but rather a weapon in a battle over public opinion and political support. It would be less understandable if the site's purpose were to find stories that would uncover problems or difficulties with the Act so that improvements could be made. If there were a desire to hear about the concerns and difficulties people might encounter, this might serve as a good complaint or suggestion box. The fact that no such purpose is included in the website (though visitors are not explicitly told they cannot use it to offer stories of complaint), prompts one to think of this citizen engagement forum, in light of our three modalities, as a form of message push or propaganda.

MOTHER'S DAY AND SUBORDINATION OF SENTIMENT TO POLITICS

In yet another form of social media as propaganda push, for Mother's Day in 2012, the White House offered the opportunity to share an electronic Mother's Day card celebrating the Affordable Care Act.[56] In fact, the e-card was explicitly sent from the Affordable Care Act, and contained a message attacking insurance companies (and celebrating the fact that women will be paying lower rates for insurance, with no acknowledgment of the reciprocal result that men would be paying higher rates). A pro-Obama campaigner could see this as a wonderful way to further celebrate the Administration's achievements and perhaps use it to garner support from others for the President's position. But a skeptic might see a Mother's Day card from the Affordable Care Act as a form of using the White House resources, and thus the public purse, to advocate for a partisan and hotly contested cause. A labor justice activist might criticize the move as an opportunity to exploit free (i.e., unpaid political advertising efforts stealthily camouflaged as family sentiment) labor on behalf of a political battle. A social policy expert could go even further, and criticize this as an attempt to harness a formerly apolitical event in the service of a controversial policy decision or even decry the diminishment of the sphere of the family to the benefit of an overarching political mobilization. This endeavor would thereby erode the status and sanctity of motherhood, the very institution that it is purporting to celebrate. Thus, the critical argument would continue, loyalty to the political leader is purchased by the diminishment of the family, leading to the weakening of one of the counterbalances to centralized political authority in society.[57]

CONCLUSION

These examples show that the White House has been frequently engaged in social media outreach to the public. President Obama in particular has taken the lead in having his name associated with social media engagement efforts. There is ample evidence to indicate that social media tools have been used in novel ways in efforts to mobilize public support and to give the impression of responsiveness. However, the White House continues to use a strategy that creates opportunities for input but that also avoids putting itself in a position that necessarily requires anything more than a nominal reaction.

There was an important irony associated with the use of social media by the Obama Administration, and that would apply to any other government that operated along the same lines. Specifically, the very use of social media to call forth The People's Opinion allowed the Administration to claim greater legitimacy for any actions that it took in light of the call. That is, by structuring an invitation for a town hall meeting, asking people to vote on issues, and invoking other forms of social media intervention, the Administration was given a perfect platform to claim that it was in touch with the people's will, and was responding to it. So, the irony was that rather than enhancing public control over the direction of policy, social media actually were manipulated in such a way that, in an attempt to get involved and have impact, the public was only further exposing itself to manipulation by White House political staff. With large user-generated datasets that result from the public's participation, the White House now had additional information and responses to targeted initiatives that were far beyond the ken of their predecessors in the eras when letters and telephone calls were mainstays of gathering information about the public. And the data was generated far more cheaply than if it had been collected via focus groups, surveys, or other opinion-assessment techniques.

Of course, the strategy was not entirely risk-free when a degree of unscripted interaction was permitted, such as with the Online White House Town Hall's allowing the public to vote on issues: a special interest group, in this case the pro-legalization of marijuana group, was able to game the system and make sure its issues were prominently listed in any set of concerns. On the other hand, the Administration had little trouble batting these matters aside. As well, the Administration appeared to be ever more effective in using moderators and question selectors, not to mention selecting audience participants, in order to stage-manage the process.

In chapter 9, we will examine some of the possible reasons for these mixed results, as well as some broader arguments about the merits of direct mass engagement.

PROPAGATION OF SOCIAL MEDIA MODALITIES IN THE FEDERAL GOVERNMENT

TO GIVE A BROADER SUPERSTRUCTURAL VIEW OF WHAT IS ENTAILED IN A SOCIAL media presidency during the Obama Administration, we next discuss several larger examples and trends regarding the use of social media in federal policy. Though our focus in this book is mainly on the White House, in this chapter we give greater emphasis to how the social media initiatives of the Obama Administration intersected not only with the public at large but also with the federal bureaucracy and other branches of government. (Again, we will not be addressing the topic of federal e-rule-making, but rather how White House initiatives toward social media may have affected policy practices.) This inquiry helps reveal a more comprehensive account of the collision between a heterogeneous technocratic agenda—the ambitious goals and projects geared toward greater collaboration with citizens—and the complex topography of political realities, namely the internal, bureaucratic, and interbranch limits on implementing such projects. This subject goes to the heart of citizen engagement and interrogates how it may have affected administrative practices, which is a major theme of the book. And again, the subject is so broad that it cannot be tackled here in its entirety. (In fact, it seems that, at least as of mid-2013, "no complete official government list of federal agencies and programs currently exists."[1])

Looking over the record, which we do in a selective manner in this chapter, we find many exciting and valuable social media-based initiatives emanating from the federal government, some of which were inspired or promoted by the Obama Administration. Yet, despite the admirable aims of information delivery and service assistance of these initiatives, as before, the record is quite sparse in terms of initiatives in accordance with collaborative objectives and policy codetermination. To understand the reasons for the particular ways in which social media engagement unfolded in the federal bureaucracy under President Obama, we will continue to draw on the statements of both officials and outside observers.

RESONANCE AND LIMITS WITHIN THE ADMINISTRATION

In May 2008, the Obama-Biden campaign declared, "We must use all available technologies and methods to open up the federal government, creating a new level of transparency to change the way business is conducted in Washington and *giving Americans the chance to participate in government deliberations and decision-making* in ways that were not possible only a few years ago" (italics added). This declaration was repeated on multiple sites, stimulating enthusiastic support across many parts of the Internet. It was also used as a conversation framer for federal officials in early 2009 as they participated in an internal government blog, the MAX OMB Wiki.[2] Discussants on the Wiki proposed numerous ways to involve citizens in formulating policy. Many spoke openly of getting public engagement in drafting policy. One official suggested creating a "Wikipedia for public draft directive sections...You would have a mass collaboration crowdsourced approach towards crafting very specific language. At a minimum you'd get some terrific ideas." Unsurprisingly, contests were also among the ideas: One unnamed agency was planning a "'Data Visualization Contest' to promote use of our data and our future APIs." (APIs are application program interfaces.) We were unable to determine whether any of the suggestions in this Wiki were acted upon.

Barack Obama sought to "integrate citizens into the actual business of government" by, among other things, "establishing pilot programs to open up government decision-making and involve the public in the work of agencies, not simply by soliciting opinions, but by tapping into the vast and distributed expertise of the American citizenry to help government make more informed decisions."[3]

Considering the MAX OMB Wiki, it would seem reasonable to conclude Obama planned to use technology to gather wisdom from the crowd, not merely to help make the machinery of government operate more effectively, but to involve citizens in meaningful participation to facilitate better decision-making by government officials.

Following the 2008 election, however, Obama's populist social media promises faded as governmental staff began laying practical plans to use Internet technology to achieve operational goals. In November 2008, shortly after the election, the Federal Web Managers Council, a group of about 40 senior web managers from every cabinet-level agency, several independent agencies, and representatives from the judicial and legislative branches, submitted to the president-elect's Transition Team a white paper entitled, "Putting Citizens First: Transforming Online Government."[4] The report contained recommendations for "revolutionizing" the delivery of online services to Americans. The white paper emphasized three words that would become the Obama Administration's mantra for its social media initiatives: transparency, accountability, and participation.

"We need to build on the groundswell of citizen participation in the presidential campaign and make people's everyday interactions with their government easier and more transparent," the report said. President Obama, it added, "should be able to promise the American people that when they need government information and services online, they will be able to 'provide feedback and ideas and hear what the government will do with them.'"

The report said its recommendations were "designed to help the new Administration increase the efficiency, transparency, accountability, and participation between government and the American people."

But rather than stimulating citizen participation in decision-making, the Federal Web Managers Council report prioritized helping governmental agencies to more effectively manage content and deliver business services to visitors of their websites. The foremost goals of the government's use of the tools of the Internet, according to the report, were "establishing web communications as a core government business function," "ensuring underserved populations [could] access critical information online," "helping the public complete common government tasks efficiently," and "cleaning up the clutter so people can find what they need online." The report also identified engaging the public in "a dialogue to improve our customer service,"[5] as an important goal, but "dialogue" in this case implied a user-centered design approach to making the web-based services more useful to visitors and agency clients rather than engaging them in terms of policy preferences and direction.

The key to understanding the government's view of how it would use social media was contained in the white paper's conclusion. It invoked the Obama-inspired paean to social media as tools for citizen participation in what, technology enthusiasts hoped, would be meaningful decision-making: "By harnessing the collaborative nature of the web," the white paper said, "the new Administration has the potential to engage the public like never before. The web can foster better communication and allow people to participate in improving the operations of their government."[6] But just when the report seemed to suggest that a significant role for citizens in governmental administration was in the offing, it quickly shifted its stance, speaking of citizens as "customers" for whom the government's priority was providing "better services," focusing on "their most pressing needs," and spending "their tax dollars efficiently."

Notwithstanding its commendable interest in spending the public's money efficiently, this position fixed the government and the public in roles as providers and consumers of services, not as potential collaborators, except in terms of bettering the delivery of services (an entirely laudable goal, we hasten to add). This controlled relationship effectively precluded an opportunity for meaningful citizen contributions to government decision-making per se. Nor did it align with the view of participation as espoused by President Obama in terms of gaining citizen participation in setting directions for the government through deliberative engagement.

Did these differing approaches to using social media in government point to a gap in communication between the President and the civil service? Or was there some other explanation for these divergent views?

Beth Noveck, the US Deputy Chief Technology Officer for Open Government who led President Obama's Open Government Initiative, clarified to us that the two perspectives were "not meant to be conflicting explanations of the same thing, but rather to parallel unrelated efforts." Which is why, she said, "there was an 'open government' initiative separate from the White House effort."[7] Noveck emphasized that Macon Phillips, the White House Director of New Media, oversaw White House digital media. "They do social media for these populist efforts, whereas the stuff that I did was more focused on this issue of the operations of government," she said. "They're related obviously, but I never describe what I did as a social media effort…although social media tools obviously play a role in helping government to be more effective and to work better in what it does."

PUTTING THE BALL IN MOTION: TRANSPARENCY AND THE OPEN GOVERNMENT INITIATIVE, 2009

On January 21, 2009, a day after being sworn into office, President Obama participated in a ritual considered highly symbolic—taking his first executive action; in this case, issuing a memorandum on "Transparency and Open Government."[8] In addition to telling the heads of executive departments and agencies that they all should "work together to ensure the public trust and establish a system of transparency, *public participation, and collaboration*," (emphasis added) the new president emphasized the need for creating a climate of openness. "Openness," Obama declared, would "strengthen our democracy and promote efficiency and effectiveness in government." One section of the memorandum gave social media enthusiasts reason to believe that a new era of citizen participation in governmental decisions and policy-making was at hand. It stated: "Executive departments and agencies should offer Americans increased opportunities to participate in policymaking and to provide their Government with the benefits of their collective expertise and information. Executive departments and agencies should also solicit public input on how we can increase and improve opportunities for public participation in Government." All this should have given hope to those who wanted to encourage electronically enabled citizen engagement.

In December 2009 the Administration's Open Government Directive was issued by the Office of Management and Budget. In some areas, such as availability of federal data, it showed remarkable progress toward citizen empowerment by making the raw materials of independent analysis available. The document, a blueprint for publishing government information online and expanding the availability of Internet tools and social media on government websites, spoke of collaboration primarily in relation to the release of data rather than encouraging direct citizen participation in policy-making.[9]

The Directive noted that "the three principles of transparency, participation, and collaboration form the cornerstone of an open government." Transparency, the Directive said, "promotes accountability by providing the public with information about what the Government is doing. Participation allows members of the public to contribute ideas and expertise so that their government can make policies with the benefit of information that is widely dispersed in society. Collaboration improves the effectiveness of Government by encouraging partnerships and cooperation within the Federal Government, across levels of government, and between the Government and private institutions."

In a move that attracted widespread media attention, the Directive said the Administration would make available to the public government information that was restricted during the Bush Administration. It also said it would post on a new public website, www.data.gov, previously hard-to-find government data through the readily available online Federal Register. The Directive also announced, within

60 days, the creation by each agency of an Open Government webpage located at http://www.[agency].gov/open to "incorporate a mechanism for the public to give feedback on and assessment of the quality of published information; provide input about which information to prioritize for publication; and provide input on the agency's Open Government Plan." Raising hopes for citizen participation, it said, "Each agency shall respond to public input received on its Open Government webpage on a regular basis."

The release of data described above seemed designed to be especially beneficial to activist groups and good government watchdogs—people who would be strongly motivated to use their research skills and knowledge to challenge the government on certain issues. Such relationships existed long before President Obama's decision to seek the presidency; adding the tools of the Internet merely made the activist's and watchdog's jobs easier. The possibility of creating new analyses and tools that would aid in holding public figures and institutions accountable is an objective worthy of praise.

On the other hand, the Directive did little to boost direct public participation in the policy-making process. Thus, references in the document to measures that seemed designed to stimulate citizen participation were open to a variety of interpretations. For example, under the heading of "participation," the Directive said: "To create more informed and effective policies, the Federal Government should promote opportunities for the public to participate throughout the decision-making process. Your agency's Open Government Plan should explain in detail how your agency will improve participation, including steps your agency will take to revise its current practices to increase opportunities for public participation in and feedback on the agency's core mission activities." The plan also should include "proposals for new feedback mechanisms, including innovative tools and practices that create new and easier methods for public engagement."[10] Though clearly stated, these lofty pronouncements seem when parsed to not necessarily connect the actual use of the social media tools (helping agencies to achieve operational targets) to giving the public the opportunity to influence policy.

IMPLEMENTATION AND BUREAUCRACY: PUTTING THE FEDERAL DATA SHARING/TRANSPARENCY DIRECTIVE INTO ACTION

To give a sense of how the Directive was put into action, we draw on the July 2010 congressional testimony of Dave McClure of the General Services Administration's Office of Citizen Services and Innovative Technologies. McClure highlighted a few of the "literally hundreds of examples" of agencies using Web 2.0 tools. We excerpt the following from his testimony:

- *NASA's Use of Twitter as a Communications Platform*: On June 19, 2009, NASA used Twitter to announce that the Mars Phoenix spacecraft had discovered water on the Red Planet, proclaiming: "Are you ready to celebrate? Well, get ready: We have ICE!!!!! Yes, ICE, *WATER ICE* on Mars! w00t!!! Best day ever!!"...On May 12, 2009, Astronaut Mike Massimino made history by sending the first tweet from space while onboard the space shuttle *Atlantis*...NASA created a Buzzroom to aggregate online conversations about NASA.[11]

- *U.S. Geological Survey Earthquake Monitoring Through Twitter*: In 2009, the U.S. Geological Survey recognized that many citizens were using Twitter to share information about earthquakes, and that "for felt earthquakes in populated regions, Twitter reports often precede[d] the USGS's publically-released [sic], scientifically-verified earthquake alerts." Drawing on this observation, McClure said, the USGS created the Twitter Earthquake Detector, or TED, to draw on citizens' updates as an "early warning system" of seismic activity and, potentially, to enable a more rapid and well-equipped response to these events than was previously possible.

- *State Department Haiti Response*: Following the January 2010 earthquake in Haiti, the State Department used SMS text messaging—a mobile technology available even to those without computers—to create a system that allowed mobile users to donate to an earthquake relief fund simply by texting a short code to a specified number. The campaign generated $1.7 million in its first 24 hours, and as of August 2010 had raised more than $40 million from about four million donors, making it the largest mobile donation campaign to that point.

- *Environmental Protection Agency Puget Sound Mashup*: This application of social media allowed the EPA to draw on the wisdom of state and local governments, nongovernmental organizations, stakeholders, and citizens who are directly impacted by the Sound and its surrounding environment. Using a basic wiki— a tool that allows anyone to contribute or edit content on a single website in real time—the EPA called on these groups to share their best information resources, tools, ideas, and contacts to protect Puget Sound. In just 48 hours, they received over 175 contributions, and the site's pages were viewed over 18,000 times.[12]

All of the instances McClure presented of federal agency uses of social media had appeal and in many cases substantive benefits as well as tangible opportunities for citizens to engage with governmental views and activities. His examples provided clear demonstrations that transparency was intended to make government information "useful" to the public. Yet the notion of being useful, as may be detected in the examples he cited, did not actually involve sharing policy-making power with the public. Despite many useful steps at the level of transparency and citizen engagement with federal activities, a wide gap remains between how Obama Administration officials have used social media versus the commitments made during Obama's 2008 campaign and the early days of his Administration. In fact, as of 2013, the Obama Administration stands accused by both right and left leaning media outlets as likely being "the least transparent in American history."[13]

ANOTHER VIEW FROM AN ANONYMOUS OFFICIAL: SOCIAL MEDIA FOR INFORMATION AND PROGRAM IMPROVEMENT MODALITIES

Social media can be used for purposes other than influencing policy. In our three modality divisions, we have highlighted their utility in serving as a source of information for governmental agencies and for citizens. One highly-placed and well-informed government official shared her/his perspectives on this, but part way through our interview for this book asked not to be identified.[14] This official dismissed our suggestion that a major point of the Administration's social media initiatives was to put government more directly in the people's hands. This official asserted that the government was not set up to let go of control, or to share power with citizens to the degree envisaged by Facebook cofounder Chris Hughes and other technology enthusiasts. But even for social media venues of the government that were open to the public, this official acknowledged that handling off-topic responses was challenging, explaining that while off-topic responses occasionally contain enlightening feedback, they often disrupt coherent discussion.

In this official's view, social media allow citizens to "engage" around the idea of better performance: "It's not that the citizens are making policy; it's just more input into policy, another piece of the government." The official argued that the Open Government webpages represented a major shift by inviting citizens to work with agencies to improve service.

The official cited numerous contests in which the public could offer ideas or inventions to help the government solve problems. For instance, in 2008, the Department of Energy solicited energy-efficient designs for 60-watt lightbulbs. The eventual winner was Phillips Lighting North America. The celebratory announcement noted that if every 60-watt incandescent bulb in the United States were replaced with the 10-watt prizewinner, the nation would save about 35 terawatt-hours of electricity, or $3.9 billion in one year, and avoid 20 million metric tons of carbon emissions.[15] Thus, the government successfully crowdsourced a new lightbulb design that would save energy and money—but it did not use social media to tap the crowd for potential new energy policies.

Also cited was Apps for Healthy Kids, a competition that was a part of First Lady Michelle Obama's *Let's Move!* campaign against childhood obesity. Apps for Healthy Kids offered $60,000 in prizes to "software developers, game designers, students, and other innovators to develop fun and engaging software tools and games" to drive children, especially "tweens" (ages 9–12)—directly or through their parents— "to eat better and be more physically active."[16] The tools and games had to be built using the Department of Agriculture's nutrition dataset that had recently been made available to the public through the Open Government Initiative. The challenge ultimately created $5 million in software, and thus was an example of a "huge return on investment on how the public is helping government meet its mission."

In another instance, Health and Human Services Secretary Kathleen Sebelius announced a video public service announcement contest on getting vaccinated against the H1N1 influenza virus.[17] Participants could go to the Health and Human Services YouTube channel and cast their votes for the best video from among the top ten entries as chosen by Sebelius and a panel of experts. The winning video was awarded a $2,500 cash prize and broadcast on national television. (We note that the finalists for whom the public could vote had been picked by the Secretary and her experts.)

In yet another example, USA.gov ran a video contest in early 2010, asking people to submit videos showing how the website made their lives easier. Peter Sullivan of

Nashville, Tennessee, won the $2,500 cash prize with his video, "Get Your Voice Heard," featuring a song he wrote himself. (Reflecting the self-serving aspect of the contest event, the winning entry was described as using "a catchy song to bring attention to the many ways USA.gov is of service to the public.")[18]

All of these contests may have been useful in helping an agency to meet an operational target. But they also promoted themselves as products every bit as much as manufacturer-sponsored contests for consumers to submit original commercial jingles (which of course are designed to implant positive sentiments about the products in the minds of the contestants). This observation is not intended to deprecate the value of contests run via social media any more than we would deprecate suggestion boxes or other modes of input to garner suggestions or report problems. Social media are helpful in their automation and optimization of processes. However, contests, especially when the finalists are selected via closed panels, are not seeking public collaboration. They are giving policy-makers an opportunity to influence the public.

BROADER OPERATIONAL GOALS AND TRANSPARENCY

On December 10, 2009, shortly after the Open Government Directive was issued, Vivek Kundra, the federal government's Chief Information Officer, told a Senate budget committee hearing that the Administration was "committed to creating an unprecedented level of openness in government" and "firmly (believed that) having an engaged and informed public is the foundation for a government that works for the people."[19] He emphasized that President Obama's appointment of a team of senior leaders aimed to "drive improvements in performance tools and capabilities," to "make sure that we are executing at the highest standard."

Rather than encouraging the rise of "an engaged and informed public," Kundra's statement implied that the government sought to use social media to apply pressure on others in the government in order to achieve operational targets. For example, he talked about the Information Technology (IT) Dashboard—a platform that "enables anyone with a web browser to track federal IT investments and hold the government accountable for progress and results." The Dashboard, Kundra explained, "allows the public to see which IT projects are performing well (and which are not), offer alternative approaches and provide direct feedback to the chief information officers (CIOs) at federal agencies—in effect, keeping tabs on the people responsible for taxpayer dollars." The Dashboard, he said, "represents a shift from a closed, secretive and opaque approach to management to one that is open, transparent and participatory."

"In our everyday lives, we can track our packages, monitor flight status and evaluate the health of our personal investment portfolio on a real-time basis," he added. "Similarly, the federal government must aggressively embrace technologies that help improve performance and deliver results." Through initiatives like the IT Dashboard and Data.gov, Kundra said, the Administration was "changing the default setting of the federal government from that of being closed, opaque and secretive, to one that is open, transparent and participatory." The Open Government Directive, he concluded, "demonstrates the Administration's commitment to hardwire accountability and drive performance to restore the American people's confidence in their government."

These initiatives, to the extent they could be realized, would allow people to share in knowledge about governmental activities and find ways to improve them, making them more equitable and efficient. However, this is not the same as having them involved in setting policy directly. Nonetheless, it does give them an indirect voice in policy if they can find ways that the process of governance needs to be changed in certain directions.

PROGRESS IN THE EARLY OBAMA ADMINISTRATION

Transparency can be a pivotal component to public involvement in changing policy, but it may not be a sufficient one. Governmental entities can be quite effective in protecting their prerogatives.

In an interview published prior to the release of the Open Government Directive, Beth Noveck agreed that creating a permanent climate of openness was "core to the president's vision of government." A key member of the Technology, Innovation and Government Reform team that was focused on thinking about "how to actually bring about open government" after Obama won the election, Noveck (who is also a law professor) pointed to "the ability to use new technology to hardwire this kind of reform and accountability into the culture of government so that it can't be undone in the next Administration." When one uses technology to put information up online, she wryly observed, "it becomes very hard to take it offline without people noticing it."[20]

In this regard, the Obama Administration's goal was to separate itself from its predecessors by installing Internet-based tools that would preserve the idea of "openness" for posterity and become part of its permanent legacy. This grand plan and the Directive's suggestion of citizen impact and input notwithstanding, the government actually seemed to back away from encouraging real citizen participation while continuing to use its Internet tools chiefly to help it meet operational and administrative goals.

In the published interview, Noveck gave her vision for how a government could engage the public through social media. "Previously, you had only a few ways in which you could engage with government.... Now what we see is the opportunity to do things like get involved in a policy forum, not just by writing a comment that you have to mail to a federal agency in Washington, but by much more easily and quickly responding to a discussion about information technology in health care, and electronic health care records on a Health and Human Services Department blog."

In her interview for this book,[21] Noveck touted the Administration's use of social media. "When you consider that the first blog didn't exist in the federal government until 2008 in the Transportation Security Administration, the adoption of social media has really been extraordinarily accelerated," she said. "I started a Twitter account that now has over 300,000 followers. I can't think of an agency right now that doesn't have Twitter and Facebook, that doesn't have a blog, that isn't using social media in some way to communicate better and to begin to create a two-way channel for communication....I think there's been a tremendously accelerated adoption of social media."

Asked to describe "open government" and the Administration's goals for it, Noveck replied, "Open government is the effort to create government institutions that are more transparent—that work more in the open and that provide information more readily online and in real time—and that are also more participatory, engaging people in how government makes decisions and policies, earlier in the process, and with the benefit of input from more and more widespread stakeholders, not just people in Washington." She added that the government's role "becomes more collaborative, working together across government institutions, and then across levels of government."

Technology, Noveck stated, "is making available this kind of open collaboration that we've never had before. Now we can get more information up as close to real time as possible and make it available, not just on the Internet, but make it available so people can download it, look at that data, mash up that data, and derive greater meaning from it, and hopefully also, hold government more accountable as a result."

Noveck's down-to-earth view of collaboration—giving citizens data they can use to hold the government accountable—did not align with Obama's loftier notion of stimulating direct public participation in policy-making. These words suggested the Administration wanted the rhetoric of participation, but not the reality.

In our interview, she contrasted the Obama Administration's actual social media achievements with the more elevated ideas espoused during the campaign. "There was a real sense that this would be 'We Government' and that we would all play a role, that we would be the government because the campaign engaged so many people and gave so many a role in the campaign and ownership of the campaign," she said. "There was a real disappointment and disconnect when it came to government, which stems from a lot of reasons. But...the reason was not some sort of malice or bad intentions on the part of the Obama Administration. Lack of tools, lack of experience, lack of legal framework, lack of knowledge, lack of experience with civil society, as well." She added, "You don't have interest (groups) or a civil society sector that is really experienced or positioned or always interested in helping to foster direct engagement between people and the government. So, this is a larger ecosystem problem that, I think, created that disconnect and disappointment."

Noveck was asked for her thoughts on the Obama Administration's use of social media, in light of the campaign promise to use the technology for informed policy-making. "First, social media tools like Facebook and Twitter are really ideally suited to this process of better broadcasting of information or short input backhands," she said. "The tools aren't well designed or...are not well suited to the processes that you are talking about, which is potentially thoughtful participation in the policy-making activities before the fact."

The first priority, Noveck said, was to "look at the tools and what they're suited to do." A "brainstorming platform is great to get quick ideas from people, and I do think there has been successful use (of that technology) across agencies," she said. For example, the Department of Veterans Affairs used a brainstorming platform to "get ideas from its employees about how to reduce backlogs on veterans' benefits claims," Noveck said.

On developing policy, however, Noveck was less upbeat. "Tools aren't really well suited to that," she said. "As much as these tools have become prevalent and we use Facebook and Twitter, there's very much a culture in which television still matters and traditional media are still predominant in their importance and those media cover the wrangling between the White House and Congress. Most of the bandwidth, if you will... is taken up with the politics rather than with government." Finally, she said:

> there really isn't culture or experience with getting to the polic[ies] before they are created—it's still a very new idea. We did it when I was in the government. We said "okay, we're going to develop our Open Government policy with citizen input before we write the policy." We're going to ask people how to craft that policy and we ran a three-stage process where we did brainstorming, blogging, and then drafting collaboratively before we ever came up with a policy. Then when we drafted and published the policy, we made links to all the places that we took ideas from, and where their suggestions came in the policy.

Besides crafting "this idea of inside-out, of getting the input before we actually wrote the policy, rather than the other way around," Noveck tackled a longstanding legal framework within government of "getting citizen input on regulations, draft regulations after those rules are drafted, rather than before. That's what's been in trend in law since 1946 so that has been the practice—an agency crafts a draft rule and then gets citizen input. And that has been how it's done for 60 years."

Noveck praised the Obama Administration for its efforts to "break away from that tradition and that cultural practice and norm." But, she asked rhetorically, "have they done as much as they could do? No. Have they done more than anybody else and do they stand [as of September 2011] with the potential over the next five years to do more? Absolutely."

INTERBRANCH REALITIES: A CHANGED LANDSCAPE

In the spring of 2011, the prospects for using social media to stir citizen participation in the US government suffered a major setback. Amid a political climate much changed by the Democrats' bruising losses in the 2010 midterm elections, Congress was knotted in a drawn-out budget wrangle. One target of Republicans was the Obama Administration's electronic government initiatives, which were chopped 75 percent, to $8 million for fiscal 2011 from $34 million a year earlier.[22] Consequently, Vivek Kundra declared that the White House would terminate the FedSpace social media network for federal employees and scale back or stop further improvements to other high-profile online programs.

The Administration said that though it would continue operating transparency websites—including USAspending.gov, Data.gov, Performance.gov, and the IT Dashboard—it would not improve or further develop them.[23] Yet Data.gov, the IT Dashboard, and Performance.gov were at the core of the Administration's open-government efforts. Plans for a Citizen Services Dashboard were also canceled.[24] After a little more than two years, an entire cadre of IT professionals departed government service, including Vivek Kundra and Beth Noveck. Reasons offered from various sources for the departures included not only budget cutbacks but burn-out, frustration, and the realization of the glacial pace of technological change in Washington. Also, it is not uncommon for people to leave after a few years in top federal positions.[25]

As a coda to the early efforts in IT and open government of the Obama Administration, Alexander Howard, O'Reilly Media's Gov. 2.0 reporter, said, "If you look back at Change.gov/content/home, there's a record of what was there back in 2009, and this idea of share ideas and write submissions and a citizen's briefing book. Or to get connected with the Administration as it comes in, there's so much there—the tiger team that talked about what we want to do to change Washington and its institutions, and so much hope. [But by] the end of 2010, the arc of disap-pointment that had fallen after so many of these pretty ambitious projects ran into the piece of interest opposition, the polarized electorate, [and] the hyper-kinetic media."[26]

DEMOCRACY WATCHDOGS REVIEW PRESIDENT OBAMA'S EARLY SOCIAL MEDIA STRATEGY

UNIDIRECTIONALITY

Certainly no other president has been as engaged in using social media as Barack Obama. President Obama's many initiatives have included Facebook town halls, Google+ hangouts, intensive blogging from the White House, and calls from the President himself asking citizens to use social media to bombard Congress in sup-port of his initiatives. Yet, after years in office, there is scant evidence that the Obama Administration has employed social media to generate consequential policy initiatives or guide public policy at the national level, despite prior overtures. As Alan Rosenblatt, speaking to us in 2011, and at the time serving as the Associate Director for Online Advocacy at the liberal Center for American Progress, said, the Administration's attempts to communicate with citizens through social media largely have been "one-way" affairs, where the technology has mostly been used as a "broadcast" tool. "They have not interacted at all," Rosenblatt claimed. The Administration's use of social media, to put it simply, is "not very social."[27]

Likewise, also speaking in 2011, John Wonderlich,[28] serving at the time as Policy Director of the pro-transparency Sunlight Foundation, commented that the Administration's social media initiatives such as the White House Online Town Hall and the Citizen's Briefing Book were "more like broadcast communications than...collaborative or meaningful policy-making." At the Administration's out-set, "there were some goals or poorly interpreted policies that stood in the way of people being able to do creative things online, so I don't interpret that time cyni-cally," Wonderlich said. "But I do interpret a lot of what has happened since that time cynically."[29] (This raises some questions as to whether the initiatives were cynical from the outset, a topic to which we will return later.)

David Stern, Director of Online Engagement at America*Speaks*, which aims to increase Americans' voice in policy-making, told us in 2011 that he had found "very few examples" where "you can say that this policy was created because of an explicit feedback mechanism that the Obama Administration has built." In the beginning, the Administration "did a fair bit of experimenting and that seemed to trail off as their political circumstances have changed...Probably like most administrations, they've been a little less experimental as time has gone on," Stern said.[30]

Although some democracy watchdogs see positive accomplishments in the Obama Administration's social media initiatives, particularly in the placing of social media tools across government websites, their reviews of the overall social media effort often turn negative. Wonderlich said the social media initiative's most meaningful action was "the effort that went into the Open Government Directive" aimed at putting more government data into citizens' hands.

"That's the one place where they did really put in a lot of effort and make a broad, systematic public dialogue about what the White House should do," Wonderlich said. "A lot of the things" that ended up in the Open Government Directive can be traced to "specific comments either from the public or specific commenting" on blogs, he added. "They had an interior dialogue for government officials that said, 'what should we do for the Open Government Directive?' and they got tons and tons of valuable comments there that they ended up releasing. Some of those comments certainly ended up changing what the Open Government Directive looked like."

Wonderlich said the sharp 2011 social media budget cuts that Congress imposed represented "a sort of walking away from social media experimentation." On the other hand, he said, "we also have a growing set of expectations about what they should be able to do with social media." Wonderlich warned of an impending collision "soon" between those two developments. "Specifications about having legitimate, authentic interactions online with government officials (will crash against)...the Obama Administration's feeling, for the most part, that this is a liability to engage in too seriously because the marijuana people might show up," he said. "Those things are in opposition, so I guess it depends on which force wins out or how they combine, to see what the legacy will really look like."

In the final analysis, Wonderlich said, "It's really hard for the White House to engage publicly in good faith in a dialogue. There's a lot of things that they can never say and that makes it hard to host any dialogue, let alone a broad-scale public dialogue where they don't have any tradition."

ASSESSMENT OF PROGRESS IN THE EARLY YEARS
ACROSS THE THREE MODALITIES

A good number of observers have dismissed the Obama Administration's use of social media as a broadcast tool for one-way communication rather than as a collaborative outlet for dialogue with citizens. Although we have had reported to us that Obama's key strategists eased the Administration away from closer social media engagement with the public once the Obama Administration entered office, Alan Rosenblatt thinks the sheer difficulty of renovating an antiquated bureaucracy for the digital age—reinterpreting the Paperwork Reduction Act, for example—and keeping up with events, knocked the idea of using citizen participation to inform policy-making from its high perch on the Administration's agenda.

"They've been overwhelmed," said Rosenblatt in a 2011 interview.[31] Echoing the points made earlier by Dan McSwain and others about the backward state of information technology in the White House, Rosenblatt commented that upon taking office, the available technology was itself an obstacle to developing social media initiatives:

> They got into the White House and all the desks were equipped with 486 computers and so they weren't even capable of running Facebook or Twitter on the operating systems, on the chips that they had in the computers on their desks. There were all sorts of legal issues. The social media sites were essentially blocked. For a long time, they were working off of their own personal laptops to access social media. It took a good year to get the technology up to speed in the building so they could incorporate social media into it. And by that point, they were smack dab into the healthcare debate and very much swamped with financial reforms, and I just think it got out of hand.

The Obama Administration's first years in office, Rosenblatt said, fell short of expectations lifted high by the promise of the 2008 campaign. "One of the big, really cool things about the [2008] Obama campaign was that it was incredibly interactive," said Rosenblatt. "There was a feedback loop, there were citizens to message back and they were excited to respond." Once they got into office, "they sort of backed off on it. They focused on promoting community service. A single issue focused on was health care, which really didn't appeal to the vast majority of the 13 million people who were on the [Obama campaign's collected email] list because they weren't all single-issue health-care people."

Rosenblatt continued, "And the one thing that they did that was more along the lines of a social engagement was they had a live-streaming video where you could watch the President in a strategy meeting. You couldn't even interact with it, but you could watch with sort of a bird's-eye-view, and it was the most popular thing they did."

Rosenblatt said if the Administration had "done more of that" in its first year, it might have been "more effective" in mobilizing supporters on other issues. "They wouldn't have alienated people," he said. "They would have given them exactly what they were looking for in the campaign. There was a very high expectation of social interaction."

But alienating many supporters is what they did. And President Obama's willingness to remain unengaged with his flock, after boosting expectations of interaction to the lofty level he did, carried a high price tag, Rosenblatt claimed. One effect was that it depressed "the performance of the [Administration's email] list for future emails," he said. "I think there's more sympathy and more forgiveness in an audience who is engaged with you if you don't deliver 100% than if you're not engaged with them," Rosenblatt offered. "I think there's more give and take allowed if you actually have this relation."

During our June 2011 interview, Rosenblatt said he was unsure whether citizen input collected via the government's social media tools shaped any governmental policy. "I haven't seen any specific evidence yet that a policy has been driven by social interaction," he said. "Administration aside, if you look at the Congress, there's a lot of examples of people using social media but not paying attention to what people say back. I think there's a predisposition across the government and with elected officials to think of it as another broadcast channel."

These critiques notwithstanding, Rosenblatt sees the use of social media in the Obama Administration as signifying an improvement in the degree to which the government is willing to listen to its citizens, at least compared with the era of Obama's predecessor, President George W. Bush. "If you are interacting and open to getting information back from the audience, even if you don't actually act on it, but the opportunity to be heard is there, that goes an awful long way to increasing political efficacy, even if it doesn't actually translate into policy implementation," Rosenblatt said. "There's a level of 'they're listening'" that is "better than it was before. The contrast I always give was, during the previous Administration when Bush was doing town halls, before you could even walk in the door, you had to sign a form saying you agreed with the President. So...just the willingness of the President to hear, to listen, goes a long way towards engaging in a social environment. You don't have to actually follow through with policy for it to be a benefit to your efforts."

Rosenblatt gave kudos to the Obama Administration for "pushing the envelope" on policy crowdsourcing "further...than anyone else has ever done." But, he said, "they became very touchy and very sensitive to message control and they saw social media as too unstable, too risky. And then the other side of it is that they didn't really have or set up the right work process and workflow to handle it."

Micah Sifry, co-founder of the Personal Democracy Forum, was also not satisfied. Commenting in the summer of 2013, he said, "I think Obama has a largely undeserved reputation for being tech-savvy, when he's not. He has people around him who are, and he will periodically allow them to use him, but I don't think he's pushed hard enough on the opportunities that were available." He added, "I don't know how fair it is to criticize him, given all of the other things he has to do, but the pattern that flows out of an administration flows out of the guy at the very top."[32]

RECENT PROGRESS

The mature phase of the Obama Administration has seen progress on many fronts in terms of its energetic efforts to connect with audiences via social media. We discussed some of these advances in greater depth in chapter 8. Here we return to the bigger picture of accomplishments. In terms of an overview, we asked Macon Phillips, White House New Media Director, about this. Phillips acknowledged that there were places for improvement but was proud of what the Administration had achieved thus far. But he recognized that "everyone can agree there is so much more possibility there." One question is whether forces inside the White House were antagonistic to the idea of Obama continuing or even intensifying his social media outreach activities. Philips gave no indication of this, but rather the contrary, saying that his office's activities have been carried out "not despite other people in this building [the White House] but because of them. And everyone wants to do more."[33] This accords with our perception: there is an energetic and creative team at the White House that is vigilantly looking for certain types of social media opportunities for citizen engagement at all levels of the Obama Administration and for the President in particular. Also, as reflected by Teddy Goff's comment in chapter 3 about Obama's interest in using the Internet, the President likewise wants to use these opportunities, and, as we have seen, even takes pleasure in communicating via various social media formats such as Twitter and Reddit.

When re-interviewed in 2013, Alexander Howard painted a mixed picture of success, finding some meaningful achievements but also many areas that needed improvement:[34] "The White House has done credibly well in some ways and struggled in others. Just as I think any administration would under those circumstances... To a significant extent I think they've shown how those channels can be used to get the Administration's message out. I think that has been pretty conclusively shown to work to their advantage." Still, making sense of input from citizens remains difficult, and progress has been slow. "The much bigger challenge," Howard said, is "around listening to the people and responding to those hundreds of millions of voices—particularly ones in a very sharply polarized moment."[35]

Howard sees that social media can provide a refreshing perspective. Obama's participation in two Google+ hangouts was described as "actually pretty interesting because he got asked questions that are not questions that the White House press corps asks. Despite people making fun of the media and the rest of it, it broke news. Somebody asked him about the drone program, which he respectfully acknowledged and he answered the question about it."[36] Additionally, some technically valuable topics were addressed, and the questions asked brought to the President's attention topics that ordinarily would never come to him. Said Howard, "We were free to ask him about patent trolls [firms that buy up patents and then seek money from companies that purportedly infringe on them].[37] The White House press corps doesn't ask Obama about patent trolls, and he gave a really strong answer, and not so long afterwards, they actually released a series of executive orders[38] that at least tried to address some of the issues."[39] This was presumably the staff acting on items that came up during the event, and certainly the President had been briefed on that topic, but nonetheless this example provides support for the idea that social media can be a valuable source of input concerning citizen interests and identifying issues in need of a policy review. It also suggests that an initiative can be catalyzed or even launched in response to citizen interrogatives.

The federal government, using social media, has undertaken some useful citizen engagement outreach efforts. So too the federal government has been able to learn via social media about the concerns of citizens. It has also taken steps in response to, or at least in accord with, issues that have been raised during social media question-and-answer forums. This even includes trying to find a job for the husband of a social media participant. In terms of the third modality, meaningful input into policy, there remains an absence of substantive steps. Yet, many of the successes, such as the patent troll example mentioned above by Howard, can be conceptualized as a modern-era suggestion box. Of course the suggestion box has been around a long time, both in the United States and in other countries. The role of social media as an automated suggestion box is discussed next.

GLASS SUGGESTION BOXES, DOMESTIC AND INTERNATIONAL

As touched on at several junctures, and especially in chapter 8, in many ways, much of the progress has been toward speeding up and automating two long-established practices. The first of these is the suggestion box. Social media allow the box to be transparent to all; thus we dub it the glass suggestion box. Information technology enables suggestions to be compiled, analyzed, and even acted on much more quickly. The second is voting. Technology and social media allow all kinds of sentiment collection and decision-making procedures to be implemented, quickly, cheaply, and even automatically. Do these constitute radical transformations in the governmental process? It would seem that they do. At the White House level, lots of innovative applications and forms of citizen engagement have been built on these ideas. Have millions of people engaged in these processes and seem to have either enjoyed or benefited from having done so? Again, the answer is affirmative. Have they made a difference? The answer in terms of finding solutions, such as cutting wasteful spending and improving processes, is also affirmative. In terms of the impact on policies—that is, engagement in the highest sense of the word—the answer is: not yet.

Other countries have tried similar systems and have, to a limited extent, attempted to incorporate more binding commitment to referendum processes. These include Iceland, Finland, and the United Kingdom. However, in each of these cases, despite the appearance of more contractual adoption, there is an escape clause: the official bodies are only agreeing to consider the petition winners and/or the social media outcome. They are not, in fact, bound to act on any of the endorsed actions. This held even in the case of Iceland, having a population of only 310,000, where due to its small scale and its ethnically homogeneous composition, direct representation via voting and social media made some sense. The 2012 claim that Icelanders "approved a crowdsourced Constitution,"[40] which attracted notice around the world, is misleading. Rather Icelanders had an opportunity to weigh in via Facebook, and their recommendations were screened by staff before being shared with the council that composed the actual document. (Even then, input was also permitted through non-Facebook sources.) The 25-member council's finished document was the proposed Constitution, which was then voted on by the island's population—and the popular vote was subject to final approval by Iceland's parliament.[41] It would therefore be more correct to say that a draft constitution was written by a council that received some feedback via screened social media. In fact, the constitutional initiative has been declared dead, in part because it was "not so clear that the public [was] very engaged on the issue." Though this particular initiative failed, to draw on the words of Chris Hughes regarding social media in the Obama Administration, the effort to crowdsource legislation "is not going away."[42]

Once again, the seeming opportunity to have citizen engagement via social media turns out to be an opportunity to give commentary that will be considered. The reins of power are not easily turned over to the vagaries of a crowd using social media. That said, we quite agree that "New England Town Meeting-style" discussions and voting are feasible for local decision-making. But what of a larger scale? The meaning of these varying initiatives, and their likely long-term trajectories, are taken up again in the concluding chapter.

CONCLUSION

Upon an examination of an array of White House social media engagements, a pattern becomes clear. First, social media initiatives are useful in serving the aims of two modalities of interactivity—the collection of information and the broadcasting of Administration perspectives. The operational definition of a social media president has been enacted by the President himself and his peripatetic staff. New ways for people to follow, contact, and vicariously interact with the President via social media have been put into place. Millions of citizens have used these tools to take part in a vast social media-supported conversation stretching over years, topics, and apps. Second, no matter the format, these engagements seldom approach, let alone traverse into, the territory of meaningful collaborative policy-making or serious reconsiderations of policy directions (in the sense of a forthright reappraisal). Irrespective of the goals or intentions of dedicated staff, auxiliary support structures (such as tech industry consultants), or the President himself, social media initiatives invariably stop short of the deliberative ambitions for social media in governance to which dedicated activists have aspired. Third, the role of internal, bureaucratic, and interbranch limitations should not be overlooked. As discussion of the interactive modalities illustrates, the precise engagement goals within the Administration itself are not always consistently embraced.

Collectively, these conflicts can combine with the effect of strengthening the model of the glass suggestion box—transparency of certain processes offers the perception of openness while simultaneously obscuring the more complex dynamics of bypassing meaningful citizen inclusion and collaboration.

In earlier chapters, we analyzed initiatives such as the petition system and Online Town Halls, and programs from creative competitions to user-generated testimonial projects. In this chapter, we probed documents and statements from the Administration and advisory bodies. We also presented outside experts' assessments of the President's statements and the extent to which the Administration fulfilled his lofty calls for a citizenry fully engaged via social media and information technology. We examined transparency, Web 2.0, and the continued unidirectionality of social media use for citizen engagement. The pattern continues: the social media modalities of gathering input and getting the presidential message out are aggressively pursued. The modality of engaging citizens, in the promised sense of a bidirectional, reciprocally influential dialogue, is almost entirely bypassed.

In the next chapter, we examine crosscutting issues and explanations about the Obama Administration's activities in social media and citizen engagement. We also extend our analysis to analytical frameworks that offer ways of interpreting the role of presidential leadership and mass civic engagement.

PART III

PERSPECTIVES AND OUTLOOK ON THE SOCIAL MEDIA PRESIDENT

CHAPTER 10

ANALYTICAL PERSPECTIVES

IN THIS CHAPTER, WE CONSIDER POSSIBLE REASONS WHY SOCIAL MEDIA INVOLVEMENT in setting governmental policy unfolded as it did under the Obama Administration from 2008 to 2013. While the Obama campaign and Administration stressed its intentions to use social media for guiding governmental policy, such initiatives have ultimately not materialized in any significantly consequential ways. There are several conceivable explanations for this outcome. One possibility is that there was, in fact, a sincere desire to pursue this objective and that the Administration was simply constrained by an unfavorable political environment. Another possibility is that the Administration, despite forthright intentions, was unable to proactively organize and execute its initiatives from within due to operational shortcomings within the White House. Or, perhaps, the Administration was strategically manipulative (either initially or as these initiatives unfolded), hoping to capitalize on the symbolic political value of rhetorical appeals concerning transparency and popular engagement, but without sacrificing any substantive control over its agenda. Alternately, absent any sort of deliberate manipulation, it could be that such ideas and initiatives were simply nonfeasible and, while an understanding of the practical limits of social media engagement has slowly been realized, the Administration remains trapped by its earlier rhetoric. Lastly, it is possible that there was no overarching vision for social media grounded in predetermined designs—the origin, progression, and denouement of the Administration's rhetoric and actions concerning social media engagement with the public may simply be the result of unplanned events and the trajectory of popular appeals at key moments. Each of these possibilities hold varying levels of probable explanatory power, and all offer nuanced insights into the complexity of overall questions of motivation, intent, and hazards of navigating the reality of the American political environment. We will now look at each explanation in more detail.

SINCERE MOTIVATIONS IN A CONSTRAINED LANDSCAPE

It could very well be that there was a sincere and powerful desire on the part of the Administration to undertake programs that employ citizen input to guide policy. There is little evidence, however, that such a desire was successfully translated into a program despite the fact, as our analytical narratives have sought to show, there have been ample opportunities to do so. Failure to carry out meaningful solicitation of public involvement could be due to a variety of factors. Our examination of these factors focuses on what Andrew Chadwick refers to as "internal institutional variables" (Chadwick notes that most analyses of social media for public engagement overlook this vital dimension).[1]

LEGAL OBSTACLES

One factor is that laws actually prevent the Administration from pursuing public input to policy—and there is no evidence of efforts to change the relevant laws and regulations. In an interview for this book, Micah Sifry, Executive Editor of the Personal Democracy Forum, was cautious in assessing the extent to which the Obama Administration's social media initiatives were translated into meaningful alterations to the traditional process of governance.[2] "It's still early in the implementation of these ideas," he said, and "you have to take baby steps before you can walk, and walk before you can run."

For instance, he said, in the Obama Administration's first year, "they just had to get over hurdles as basic as upgrading the hardware they were using." The first step, he said, was "redoing the participation of the third-party providers like YouTube, so that the government, from a legal standpoint, would be able to use their services."

Bureaucratic rules "blocked agencies from doing any kind of online survey or poll without the approval of the GSA," Sifry added. "Their rule was: it had to first be approved by the GSA to be sure it wasn't violating the government's Paperwork Reduction Act and Information Collection Policy (PRA). They were not even going to get to the starting gate for the first several months, until they cleared these obstacles out of the way."

In April 2011, the Obama Administration unveiled "a new fast-track process" for collecting service delivery feedback under the PRA, a statute first passed in 1980 and then revamped in 1995, which gave authority over the collection of certain information to the Office of Management and Budget (OMB). A memo from Cass Sunstein, Administrator of the White House Office of Information and Regulatory Affairs, explained "that under established principles," the PRA did "not apply to many uses" of social media and web-based interactive technologies.

Political writer Nancy Scola blogged for *techPresident* that, "boiled down, the result of the Sunstein memo is that federal agencies under the Obama Administration have been handed freedom to engage online without having to worry quite so much about collecting and archiving every blog comment, retweet, or Facebook wall post."[3] The OMB, she reported, considered interactive meeting tools such as public conference calls, webinars, blogs, discussion boards, forums, message boards, chat sessions, social networks, and online communities, "to be equivalent to in-person public meetings." The memo from the Obama White House, Scola observed, "knocks away one obstacle for agencies considering engaging the public through social media."

This seemingly upbeat finding notwithstanding, Sunstein suggested that agencies were not being freed to let social media write public policy. The OMB recommended "that agencies exercise good judgment and caution when using rankings,

ratings, or tagging," Sunstein said. "Specifically," he said, "agency use of the information generated by these tools should be limited to organizing, ranking, and
sorting comments. Because, in general, the results of online rankings, ratings, and
tagging [(e.g., number of votes or top rank)] are not statistically generalizable, they
should not be used as the basis for policy or planning."

Tony Romm, a writer for *The Hill*, a newspaper that covers events on Capitol
Hill, noted that while few would dispute Sunstein's assertion "that one Facebook poll
hardly doubles as a scientific sampling of the country," Sunstein's comments nevertheless "may shock some of the open government community's most vocal proponents, who regard social media as precisely the best source for public policy input."[4]

At any rate, movement on reinterpreting the PRA tended to lend credence to
some critics' arguments that the Administration's biggest achievements in social
media lay in its willingness to try to update existing practices that would impede any
potential effort to use social media to inform policy-making.

For instance, in a June 2009 White House blog, Chief Information Officer Vivek
Kundra and Michael Fitzpatrick, Associate Administrator of the OMB Office of
Information and Regulatory Affairs, talked about efforts to enhance online citizen
participation through policy changes and to open "more back-and-forth communication between the American people and the government."[5] A big goal, the blog
said, was updating "how these tools can be used to break down barriers to communication and information." The blog covered the following topics:

Paperwork Reduction Act and Information Collection Policy
As noted earlier, the PRA requires agencies to make public their reasons for levy-
ing paperwork requirements on the public or for requesting information and to
ask for public comments before actually taking the step in question. The Obama
Administration looked closely at the PRA with the aim of opening the door for "a
more direct back-and-forth between the agencies and the American people," the
blog said. The Sunlight Foundation's John Wonderlich commented that the Obama
Administration made an "initial push to reinterpret" the PRA "so that every online
interaction wouldn't potentially be considered an information collection subject to
approval."[6] The aim was to increase transparency and give members of the public
"a more direct role" in shaping the direction of their government's policies, according to the blog. During a "brainstorming" session with officials on how to increase
transparency, the blog continued, one federal employee commented that the PRA
imposed a "burden" on interactive web innovations and efforts to obtain "any user-
generated input." As a result, the employee added, "we often don't go to the trouble."
The Administration, according to the blog, hoped to turn the PRA into "a stronger
tool to promote stronger citizen participation in the digital age."

Federal Cookie Policy
Beginning in 2000, with the object of protecting the privacy of Americans, a federal
policy has limited government agencies' use of persistent "cookie" software to track
or authenticate web viewing activities by the user. "Since this was put in place,"
the blog said, "website cookies have become more mainstream, as users want sites
to recognize their preferences or keep track of the items in their online shopping

carts." The blog referred to one person's comments that "persistent cookies are very useful as an indirect feedback mechanism for measuring effectiveness of government websites…cookies allow a greater level of accuracy in measuring unique visitors.…Being able to look at returning visitors allows us to see what content is important to our citizens. We can use that data to improve the content and navigation of our sites." In light of the "fundamental change in technology in the past nine years, and the feedback that we've received so far," the blog said, "the Office of Management and Budget (OMB) is reexamining the cookie policy as part of this Open Government Initiative. There is a tough balance to find between citizen privacy and the benefits of persistent cookies, and we would welcome your thoughts on how best to strike it."

Records Management
Record management laws, defined across a number of federal statutes, protect transparency and accountability by ensuring that government preserves "records containing adequate and proper documentation of the organization, functions, policies, decisions, procedures, and essential transactions of the agency," the blog said. The National Archives and Records Administration (NARA), it said, developed detailed guidance to agencies on how to keep electronic records. "NARA is also working to develop guidance on managing records for new, collaborative, and social media environments and working on strategies to assist agencies on how to most effectively implement these new policies," the blog explained. "As we learn how to implement these policies for emerging media, are there ways to make the law easier to follow and more effective?"

Federal Advisory Committee Act (FACA)
FACA is intended to ensure that the "numerous committees, boards, commissions, councils, and similar groups which have been established to advise officers and agencies in the executive branch of the Federal Government" do so in the open, and that the membership of these advisory groups is balanced. The blog noted that although "new tools facilitate open and transparent participation in the spirit of FACA, we're hearing from some of you that there is a reluctance to embrace participatory innovations for fear of triggering the requirements of this law. That leads us to some questions: Does FACA safeguard transparency while enabling civic engagement? Is there room for any improvement in the law, policy or technology that will realize both the letter and the spirit of FACA? How can we enhance FACA through technology?"

The blog concluded by reaching out to its audience: "We want to hear from you, get your ideas, and learn from your suggestions," it said. "In some cases, laws or policies might eventually need to change or we might simply need to look at ways to apply them in the context of a changing technological environment. Let us know what you think about the policy context for Web 2.0 in the federal government."

This effort to ease the burden of bureaucracy led Micah Sifry to muse that the Obama Administration's social media initiatives were "more about process than results." Establishing the HealthCare.gov website, for example, provided "an important vehicle" for President Obama's prized legislation—his health-care reform package, he said.[7] The site, launched in July 2010, informed users about the

Affordable Care Act, which had been signed into law by the President three months earlier. In addition to allowing users to find out about available insurance coverage options, it included updates on the implementation of the regulatory overhaul of the US healthcare system, tips for healthy living customized for individual circumstances, and details on how changes triggered by the act might affect a person's particular health care situation.[8] It was, however, "not very interactive," Sifry said. "It was about the government delivering timely and valuable information," rather than stirring public participation in decision-making. The health-care debate, Sifry noted, showed that when something engulfs the White House and the president, "they want to control the methods...and limit the participation format."

Sifry pointed out in his blog that as of July 2010, every White House event had a Facebook presidential commentary alongside it, "but there's not engagement on it." This observation reflected the Administration's tendency to use social media "mostly to explain what they are doing," or to "justify what they are doing, instead of sharing power," he said.

In the final analysis, Sifry said that tapping crowd wisdom to make policy can improve the process of governmental administration. Whether the government considers every comment is unimportant, he said, responding to a question critics often raise about efforts to tap the wisdom of the crowd for ideas. "I don't know that you have to (consider every comment)," he said. "Does every letter that the White House gets, get responded to? No. Does the country stop working?" He acknowledged, however, that "so far, they don't have a lot of great successes to point to, because the pipes aren't designed well."

As we have documented above, there were numerous attempts by the Obama Administration to change the Paperwork Reduction Act as well as revise the Cookie Policy and the record management regulations. Yet, given Obama's electoral margin and the fact that the Democrats controlled both houses of Congress during the first two years of the Obama Administration, more progress might have been expected.

BUREAUCRATIC OPPOSITION

Another explanation for the failure of social media-driven policy-making to gain traction in the Obama Administration may be that it was thwarted by internal opposition. This opposition could have come from bureaucratic sources—administrative units who might fear losing power if these initiatives succeeded. To better examine these questions at the level of agency operations, federal government officials were interviewed concerning their respective agencies' use of social media to inform policy, as envisaged by the Obama campaign and Administration and implied in the government's Open Government Directive.

The thrust of the officials' responses was that the Open Government Directive aimed to create a climate of openness, not stir participation in policy-making. For instance, one official with the Defense Department said it was "unrealistic" to expect that a single individual, posting an idea on a government website, could attract the attention of a high-level official and significantly influence policy-making. The official stated that the overarching aim of the Open Government Initiative was to create "a broader, cultural, more qualitative openness to ideas and transparencies." He added, however, that gauging the success of this goal was "a bit hard" to do.[9]

A Department of Commerce official told us that department employees generally did not comment on the public's message-board postings; citizens often were asked to clarify, but the response from the Commerce Department would not go much farther, the official said.[10] An official with the Securities and Exchange Commission (SEC) told us that "all" online policy suggestions were viewed by staff, but little chance existed that one could make it to the highest levels of the agency.[11] He implied that it was rare to find publicly submitted ideas that would be useable.

The Defense Department official asserted that the government's relationship with the citizenry could block the effort to use public input to inform policy-making. "There are great ideas out there," the official said. "The nature of democracy is such that we set up a system where, on some level, there are experts and full-time people to do the governing, because that's their job and to execute it so not every single person is going to...be in the weeds of it all the time. But you know those people obviously have ideas and suggestions in addition to opinions that...are valuable and useful, without a doubt."

The SEC official held that social media tools can exclude the least capable users. However, he said the need to keep up with the rest of the pack in a world of high-speed securities transactions has led to an Internet-savvy culture flourishing within the agency's online community. The agency's practice of seeking comments on proposed rules has prepared this particular audience to use social media tools, the official added. In sum, then, we can observe how some of the government's social media initiatives create a feeling of engagement among citizens, but stop short of the power-sharing envisioned by many open-government advocates. These observations support our view that it is unrealistic, at least in the short term, to expect social media to be a major source of *meaningful* citizen participation in policy-making.

POLITICAL OPPOSITION

Top Obama Administration officials may have resisted meaningful social media initiatives because they saw politics as a zero-sum game in which social media would take policy in a direction inimical to their interests. Opposition may have come from those who wanted to control the direction of politics, and, seeing the threat, used their positions to thwart the social media initiatives.

Alexander Howard, the O'Reilly Media Gov. 2.0 correspondent, described the political tensions inherent in policy crowdsourcing as follows: "Politics is very difficult," he said in his interview with us. "There's a political side to this, in that if you can't get a clear political return, then will they spend political capital on this?"[12]

While these technologies are "profoundly lightweight" and becoming an integral part of American society, "the question is whether the politicians and the people in policy [making] are willing to be bound by what they see there—whether there's a true feedback loop and people are actually brought in to the process rather than consulted," Howard said.

"It's the difference between participatory budgeting, where people vote on something and that's actually where the money gets spent, versus a consultative process, which is 'what do you all think?' and then the [politicians and policy-makers] take that and do what they want," Howard said. "It's the difference between the direct democracy and the representative democracy—and there's a lot of good reasons to like the latter model."

Howard said that President Obama's Twitter Town Hall of July 6, 2011 underscored both the promise and the challenge inherent in using social media to communicate with the citizenry to make policy. The President used a laptop computer, set up in the East Room of the White House, to type from the White House Twitter account: "In order to reduce the deficit, what costs would you cut and what investments would you keep?" The President took 18 questions from the "Twitterverse" before Jack Dorsey, the Twitter cofounder and Town Hall moderator, turned the conversation around and read the President an array of people's responses to the live tweet from Obama that started the event.[13]

Howard acknowledged that "there is something important in the President asking a question [by Twitter] and people giving answers back." The rest of the Twitter Town Hall, however, consisted of "the same talking points the President has been delivering at events over the past year," Howard said. "There wasn't anything new there." In fact, Howard said, President Obama used the Twitter Town Hall as a vehicle for running plays from the standard Washington playbook: Obama criticized Republicans who fought with him over raising the nation's borrowing limit, saying they should not use their votes on that matter as "a gun against the heads of the American people" to retain the tax breaks they wanted for corporate jet owners and oil companies. The content of the President's responses illustrated the difficulties in divorcing engagement from partisan politicization, and that using social media for citizen participation in policy-making remains a distant possibility.[14]

DISTRACTIONS OR COMPETING OBJECTIVES

Another reason for lack of progress on social media is that staff members assigned to these activities have often become distracted by other commitments. Given the limitations on time and manpower resources, and the complicated nature of allocating these limited resources, it is plausible to think that, despite an interest in using social media for governmental policy setting, other projects took higher priority. This could be particularly true when considering how the Administration may weight the pursuit of various objectives owing to shifts in legislative balance (as after the 2010 midterm elections) or fluctuations in public opinion (as seen during the periodic debt ceiling debates, Supreme Court case reviews and major international events). That said, it can always be argued that other priorities can eclipse a commitment, but for those citizens who believed in the prospects of enhanced engagement opportunities (and voted, donated, or volunteered accordingly), the excuse of distractions or competing objectives would carry minimal explanatory power.

OPERATIONAL SHORTCOMINGS

Obstacles to public engagement initiatives may have arisen due to the Administration's difficulties in overcoming the hurdles of mechanical challenges or even its own internal operational culture. Just as they are for individual users, private enterprises and lesser public agencies, technical limits of scale, speed, efficiency, and access are potential bounding factors for information and communication technologies at the level of White House operations. Additionally, large-scale participatory initiatives are often fraught with personnel complications. Along with difficulties in delineating specific responsibilities and privileges across different organizational spheres, recruiting and retaining an effective talent base for managing the implementation of these ambitious projects is challenging in its own right. Also not to be ignored is the stark reality of financial hurdles—amid a challenging and highly scrutinized national economic picture, the Administration is certainly no exception to the difficulties of securing and disbursing funds for new programs. Lastly, in response to, and in concert with, the aforementioned difficulties and the constraints discussed earlier, it should be noted that there is no guarantee of permanence to project initiatives.

TECHNICAL DIFFICULTY

One possible operational reason for the underperformance of President Obama's social media initiatives is that it was too hard to achieve the objectives set forth for the technology. This rationale actually has two components: the nature of the task and the nature of the staff. In terms of the first, we have shown that the objective of having social media guide governmental policy is technically achievable. In fact, it was achievable in the pre-digital era, though it could have consumed enormous resources. This potential for stimulating citizen input to decision-making has been demonstrated, for instance, by public referendums used by many states to determine policy. Had there been an interest, local meetings could have been organized to identify the policies (or in the case of a nominating process for, say, Supreme Court justices) and the decisions could have been passed along in ever more competitive forums, analogous to the elimination process used for talent contests, spelling bees, debate tournaments, college admissions, or hiring decisions. Expert commentary could have been added along the way to provide depth to the proposals.

Rudimentary prototypes of mass citizen polling on particular policy issues were demonstrated in the cable TV era with systems such as Warner Cable's highly ambitious Qube, deployed in Ohio in the 1970s. The contemporaneous French Minitel, a Videotex service that used domestic telephone lines, provided another example where a national initiative put technology for citizen input into the hands of practically every household but without any meaningful attempt to use it for guiding national policy through democratic participation.

Alan Rosenblatt, then at the Center for American Progress, argued in a 2011 interview with us that stimulating citizen participation need not be an "overwhelming" task for government. "If you start to think strategically about organizing participation based on letting people sign up for certain issues to participate in and...let people sort out accordingly, you can...narrow down the participation," he said. "But there has to be a systemic sense of listening and making the public aware that you are listening to what is being said." Acknowledging the audience through "occasional retweets," is one way to provide "a general response" that will let people know they are being heard, Rosenblatt said. "I think that's really what needs to be done." Some of that, he said, "can be done without really extending the staff."[15] Alexander Howard put this more succinctly when he said, "Just demonstrating active listening goes a hell of a long way."

Regarding the collection of submissions, Rosenblatt said it would be feasible to put a hashtag (the # prefix, or hash symbol) on a government-monitored tweet. Tools such as DiscoverText, a human language tool for reviewing large numbers of public comments, could collect the participants' input, he said. DiscoverText, developed by University of Massachusetts political science professor Stuart Schulman, "can collect all this content data that's coming in, and then start to sort it out by topic area and then do some content analysis on what's being said," Rosenblatt explained. "So, if you could have a person or two in the White House manning this monitoring system and then collecting and analyzing and producing reports so that the White House is aware of what's being said on an issue-by-issue basis, then they could be responsive to what people are saying on the hashtag."

"Large chunks" of the collected input could be taken care of with "a couple of tweets back out," Rosenblatt said. For example: "'heard a lot about this topic, really appreciate the comments. We're looking at this idea and this idea.' Then people will say: 'oh, this was my idea,' or 'yeah, I support that idea.'" So, Rosenblatt said, "it actually doesn't have to be an overwhelming task to be able to do this stuff."

As the director of Online Engagement at America*Speaks*, an organization that helps citizens shape policy-making through democratic online tools, David Stern has observed that government websites typically struggle to build a community of followers. "There are very few examples of government initiatives and stand-alone websites that have been able to draw millions of participants because they're not able to build a community up over time," Stern told us in an interview.[16] "They're sort of these one-off events. . . . You're limited to the framework of Facebook and Twitter. In Twitter, you have 140 characters to work with, so obviously that's a huge limitation in terms of the number . . . [and in] the complexity of the idea that can be expressed. . . . On Facebook there're no nested comments . . . so people can't interact with each other. There's 'like-ing,' so you can sort of get a sense of what the community thinks by what's most popular, but that's also a function of who's the most popular to begin with. Whoever has the most followers on Twitter is going to be re-tweeted the most."

These observations set up Stern's next point: that it is extremely challenging to find examples of meaningful policy-making attributable to the Obama Administration's social media initiatives. "There are very few examples that you can point to and say, 'this policy was created because of an explicit feedback mechanism that the Obama Administration has built,'" Stern said. "But, I give them a lot of credit for experimenting. It's not entirely their fault. Maybe the right tools aren't out there. Maybe we users haven't quite learned how to stay on topic and provide meaningful input that's relevant, that can be used, that's realistic and that isn't just pie-in-the-sky venting and talking about whatever the hell they're interested in."

The Administration's efforts to use social media in policy-making also were hampered by a paucity of successful models to emulate, Stern stated. "There are lots of examples of engagement happening on a relatively small scale or a local level, but at a national level, there weren't great examples that they could learn from," he said. "So, they had to do their own experimenting and they did a fair amount of that which seemed to trail off a bit as their political circumstances have changed. Like most Administrations, they've become a little less experimental as time's gone on."

In the final analysis, the appealing ideal of citizen participation will transcend whatever party's individual candidate is elected to lead the government, Stern said. "We've worked with Republicans…we've worked with Democrats," he said. "The incentives are the same on both sides; both sides, in terms of the politicians, avoid controversy. There's no structural reason why Democrats and Republicans aren't equally willing to engage the public." Before joining America*Speaks*, Stern cofounded MixedInk, an online democratic collaborative writing platform that allowed large groups to express collective viewpoints by weaving their ideas and language together. MixedInk's tool has been used by a number of prominent government officials, agencies, and media outlets to incorporate citizen input, according to the America*Speaks* website. Stern managed democratic engagement projects for many of MixedInk's clients, including the White House, which used the tool during the Open Government Initiative.

President Obama, however, may have "overpromised" on his ability to deliver social media-driven change in the way Washington does business, Stern mused:

> My general stance is that yes, it's baby steps at this point…There's a lot of legwork being undertaken…establishing the regulatory framework for all this kind of work and disseminating the tools and making sure everybody can use them in the government. There's a lot of moving pieces and I'm ultimately optimistic about where things are headed—it's just not as fast as I'd like. I totally empathize with those who run these projects. They're in a difficult situation and they've had to make things up as they go along. And the last thing is: it's possible that the President maybe overpromised early. Not deliberately but because perhaps he thought it would be easier to do more online than it is. I don't know—that's a judgment call.

FINANCIAL DIFFICULTY

Another reason for the limited success of the Obama Administration's social media efforts may have been that the amount of financial resources required, and the difficulty of implementing such a program, proved too demanding—despite initially appearing to be a solvable problem. Certainly, implementing costly social media to government would most likely lie outside realistic scenarios of a post-2010 Congress cooperating with the Administration. As demonstrated by the Grand Challenge science initiatives outreach described in chapter 6, attempts to accomplish effective crowdsourcing can be extremely challenging, and even with large grants from the MacArthur Foundation and elsewhere, a good solution may not be achievable. The inherent financial strains associated with such initiatives are no doubt exacerbated by the prolonged state of fiscal crisis that has afflicted innumerable public and private institutions across the United States. In particular, it is difficult to imagine the additional allocation of entrepreneurial resources in light of the automatic sequestration protocols that have begun more recently.

PERSONNEL LIMITS

Beyond the technical and financial dimensions is another possibility: that the team did not have the personnel to manage the task. Practically all humans seem to suffer from an optimism bias—in this case, that difficult problems can be solved because of exciting emerging technology and the existence of a core of committed believers. There is also the fact that problems may not scale well. What works in a small-scale test may not work when unfurled across a nation of more than 300 million people. Yet, at the end of the day, it may simply have been the case that the people who were in charge of the program were not able to carry out the dream as envisioned by President Obama and his social media advocates.

Another possible reason is that there were some talented people who could have implemented more collaborative use of social media, but they left the Administration before anything useful could be done. According to social media evangelist Laurel Ruma, the key is for each governmental department to employ "someone who is educated about social media tools," so they can "reach out to the public in these new and important channels." Ruma said, "You need to go where your audience is." With newspapers declining in popularity, "where are people getting their news and information?" Ruma asked. "Facebook. So you're going to have to understand how to use Facebook and how to get your news out there."[17] Some excellent people did leave the Administration earlier than perhaps planned, but it also is the case that enormously talented people are always ready to step in.

ALTERED PRIORITIES

Another possible reason for the failure of policy crowdsourcing to gain traction with the government could be that Administration social media-empowerment support-ers decided to pursue different courses of action. They could have decided that it was, after all, not wise to pursue a governmental policy by social media initiative. However, if this is the case, the rhetoric has not changed. Even in 2012, more than three years after Obama took office, the White House home page continued to urge visitors to become engaged with the Administration and share ideas and thoughts for the specific purpose of improving policy.

John Wonderlich commented that, in contrast with the Affordable Care Act negotiations, when President Obama and congressional leaders were trying to ham-mer out a multi-trillion dollar debt-reduction deal during the 2011 budget discus-sions, the White House tended to retain tight control over its communication with the public. "Where they are now, politically, they're not trying to reach out broadly and publicly unless it's a very carefully scripted message," Wonderlich said.

At the time, notwithstanding its claim of having the most transparent White House in history, the Administration refused to confirm when Obama was meet-ing with top officials in the House and Senate. "We're so serious about getting a deal done, as opposed to engaging in political theater...that we are going to have meetings that I'm not going to tell you about," White House spokesman Jay Carney told reporters at a press briefing.[18] He continued, "We do have meetings that we don't...I mean, we're trying to get a deal done here."

Under questioning by members of the press corps, President Obama's press sec-retary backed off a suggestion that secret, high-level debt negotiations were indeed taking place. "I am not saying there are some meetings scheduled with leaders that I'm not telling you about. That is not the case," Carney was quoted as saying. Yet President Obama did meet privately with House Speaker John Boehner in an unscheduled, unannounced meeting at the White House. Asked by media about the reported session, "Carney wouldn't even confirm it.... The press secretary declined to confirm or deny meetings that may or may not have happened," *Politico's* Josh Gerstein reported. Carney said that Obama aides believed "the greater interest of trying to reach a significant" budget deal justified the secrecy. The press secretary "went on to justify the secrecy by arguing that real-time information on who's meet-ing with the President and when aren't of much concern to the general public." Although the hour-by-hour narrative was of some interest to a small community, Carney claimed, that interest was "outweighed by the higher interest of accomplish-ing something."[19]

Such shifts prompted Wonderlich to note that "the presidency is a weird thing. It's such a public thing, everybody's entitled to their opinions about it; it couldn't be more politically intense. So, trying to do policy creation publicly in the White House is bound to be tricky."[20]

STRATEGIC MANIPULATION

An alternative possibility for the failed expectations of the Obama Administration's social media initiatives is that claiming that the Administration wanted citizen guid-ance for policy-making was a cynical exploitation of a popular trope. It is easy to believe that focus groups or other market testing showed that declarations of want-ing to hear the people's voice sold well among potential voters, and unprecedented amounts were spent on precisely this kind of research by the Obama campaign.

Wonderlich said the Administration's attempts at public interaction appeared to slide across a "spectrum of authenticity," ranging from "trying to reach out to just trying to look like [it was] reaching out." Politics, however, can ultimately limit the effectiveness of government policy crowdsourcing attempts, he said. "Is it a sign of weakness if you try to have a discussion about the right policy solutions?" he asked. "Does that symbolize you not knowing the correct answer? There are different con-straints there." Notwithstanding the existence of such restrictions, Wonderlich said there is no excuse for passing up opportunities to meaningfully involve the public in policy-making. "To say 'share your story' is often the easiest [thing to do] out there, but why can't they say 'share the solutions that you're aware of' or 'let's talk through the ways of solving this problem,' and in a structured way?"

In the long run, "imperfect processes" marred the White House's social media plan, because the Administration treated the results of its outreach "as though they were static," Wonderlich claimed. "If you have a Town Hall in a senior center, you are going to get a different set of results than if you go on Digg, the website; you are going to get a different set of issues."

For Wonderlich, the government's social media initiatives proved to be "just one-way communication." Ultimately, he said, the social media outreach amounted to "a narrow broadcast model communications effort." Expounding on this claim, he viewed the Administration's White Board series of videos (explaining government policy), and its Facebook Town Hall meetings, as "really just efforts to get the President's agenda articulated publicly and to reach the Internet better. It's not bad to try to reach people through the Internet, but it's really one-way communication," Wonderlich said. "They answer people's questions during the Facebook Town Hall, but that's hardly a dialogue. That's no more a dialogue than "Meet the Press" is a dialogue, or any of those kinds of shows."[21]

Another pertinent point needs to be raised in this context. If one considers the type of people who enter the White House through policy-related posts, it is to be expected that they already have been deeply involved in policy processes. When such people begin work in high positions, they have informed knowledge of what policy development directions are needed. They would naturally be reluctant to start with a blank slate and turn the matter over to the American public. However, they might readily turn to public opinion aggregation and discussion forums to consider ways to secure implementation or, even better, as a way to mobilize the public to implement the previously chosen solution. Indeed this may be one reason why so little traction has been gained for policy-making by the public, as President Obama has so often signaled he would like. In this regard, it is also the case that lots of insulting and off-topic material arrives on open forums, especially those with high visibility. As Alexander Howard says, "The federal government, Congress and the White House are pretty resilient to being insulted and denigrated at this point that it's just accepted and, to its credit, the White House posts things on Facebook and Google+ and get completely burned up every single time." He continued, "I mean, for the most innocuous things possible—pictures of the President hanging out with children or pictures of the dog, Bo, and those comments turn very political, very quickly. But they tolerate it; they're not actively moderating, for what I've ever been able to tell. Which is something that they really can't; that would fairly probably be called out as a violation of the First Amendment." Explaining the effect of this, he said, "That's one of the reasons that, I think, that the WhiteHouse.gov blog never allows comments, because it would be stuck with an impossible moderation challenge."

THE NONFEASIBILITY OF DIRECT MASS ENGAGEMENT

Political sociologist Irving Louis Horowitz once commented that "the vocabulary of human motive is infinite." People have myriad explanations for why they might do something, and justifications for action can be cut to fit nearly any purpose or conceptual framework; even a given individual might not know his or her reason for taking a certain action. In this case, it would be difficult to parse out the various motives driving the Obama Administration's decisions related to its social media initiatives, and, indeed, they may not even be clear to the actors themselves. Rather than focusing on the motives of those Obama team members who were involved in the initiatives, we can look at the idea itself.

Followed to its logical conclusion, failure to use social media for political guidance may in large part be due to serious reservations about the concept itself. Simply put, it turns out not to be a good idea. Such a statement flies in the face of enshrined American values—to say that the public should not be fully and effectively involved in policy is deemed offensive by many. Moreover, such a declaration goes against the decades-long evolution of policy, which has consistently encouraged greater public involvement in hearings, regulations, assessments, and processes. In fact, even suggesting such notions can at times be met with harsh denunciations for elitism, authoritarianism, and worse. (We hasten to add that simply because we believe that crowdsourcing of public policy directives is a bad idea does not mean that we are against representative democracy; quite the contrary, we are very much in favor of it.) Yet, we should not be dissuaded from inquiry simply because of the reflexive critiques of those who have not given thoughtful attention to the question at hand. In fact, allowing this to happen would likely yield the conclusion that democratic values are best served by insulating political leaders from the moment-to-moment passions of the crowd.

A "closed" government culture obstructs crowdsourcing, according to Ruma. "It's not just government-to-citizen, it's agency to agency, within each agency," she said in an interview.[22] "You have to create this open culture and I think that's why the Silicon Valley culture is pretty different. If you work for a start-up, it's expected that anyone in that start-up will be able to say to the CEO: 'hey, you know what? This is not working.'"

"So what we need to do," Ruma said, "is use these engagement strategies to create trust, to create understanding, and to empower those employees, so...they're not working in a constant state of hate and mistrust."

Another potential impediment to policy crowdsourcing is online security, according to Howard.[23] The reality is that "there definitely are cyber criminals, and actors and reactors who are also online and who have great interest in some of the policy being discussed," he said. "So there has to be some recognition that while involving the public is important, there also needs to be a preservation of some level of discussion of privacy, secrecy, etc."

The "danger" for "any entity that chooses to engage and use these platforms," Howard said, "is they are not wholly controllable. People can and will self-organize, aggregate. The risk is even greater if you say you are going to listen, and then don't, if you do say that you're going to collaborate and then don't take any time to actually engage." Explaining the complexities, he said, "I think that the challenge for this Administration—any Administration—is that the hyper-partisan atmosphere is just being fueled by the 24/7 media cycle, by the rapidity with which information flows online." He added, "That cycle now has become quite vicious in terms of how quickly information flows and divisions can be made based on lack of complete context. Unfortunately, that's not going to go away."

Howard said he sees an opportunity for any government to "offer more insight and ask for more feedback using the [social media] platforms, but also to recognize that if they do so, they're going to have to listen." Losing control of the conversation, however, simply is not palatable for many political organizations, he said. "How do you get effective negotiations, when often the kind of wheeling and dealing that historically has been important in closed rooms to get bills through is being increasingly shared?" The thing to recognize, he said, "is that the government doesn't own the tools, and that people can, and will, self-organize, using whatever platforms happen to be available. You don't control the conversation," Howard said. "If the politicians or any other entity tries to do that, it almost always comes back to bite them. It actually causes more attention to come back."[24]

Putting it more bluntly, Amelia Showalter, Director of Digital Analytics of Obama's 2012 campaign said, "You're trying to compare social to face-to-face contact. Look at the kind of shit that people say in comments on social media that they would never in a million years say to a person's face. It's just like a different kind of medium. It's not totally the real world. So I think that there is a place for all of this. But when people are actually making decisions and carrying out actions I think that social [media] doesn't always have the perfect application."[25]

In this regard, the volatile—and often vindictive—nature of citizen referendums comes into play in terms of nonfeasibility. In this sense, broad scale citizen engagement via social media for policy commitments becomes problematic in several ways. First, even the way questions are posed can frame the issue to lead to certain reactions or outcomes. Second, the speed of decision-making can lead to ill-considered decisions. Third, people's feelings about a topic are subject to great vicissitudes, and can shift to polar opposites within a matter of hours. None of these bode well for the prospect of directly harnessing public sentiment (as referendums), especially when the speed of decisions, as would be allowed by social media, can take place in a matter of moments. These problems were of profound concern, as we noted at the book's outset, to Plato and the ancient Greeks, no less than to the Founders of the United States. These concerns were articulated in *Federalist Papers* 9 and 10 (Alexander Hamilton again casting a long shadow). Despite their hoary pedigree, these problems remain highly pertinent today, when majorities are tempted to use democratic means to impose their preferences on groups who are in the minority. We return to this subject in the next chapter.

AN ABSENCE OF DESIGN

Yet another possible explanation for the failure of social media-assisted policy-making to take hold in the Obama Administration is that in the struggle for approval and votes, unserious and glib remarks were made about these topics. That is to say, the idea was just a transient one voiced by a top aide or speechwriter that then found its way into comments and declarations of the candidate and his supporters. Once the idea was introduced, it gained traction. After a short time, the campaigners found that they were digging themselves deeper and deeper into a hole. As the saying goes, sometimes the only way to get out of the hole seems to be to dig deeper. Although we do not find this to be a compelling explanation for what has happened with social media under the Obama Administration, it is a possibility that cannot be excluded.

ADDITIONAL CONSIDERATIONS

Putting it simply, we can say that feedback from social media-empowered citizens either shows support or opposition for a political leader's objectives. From the politician's viewpoint, then, social media input is to be much valued if it supports the goals of the political leader. Indeed, random social media expressions of support from the public are solicited by the White House, and such expressions even find their way to the White House home page. Citizens who choose to express support, may, in a few rare instances, find themselves invited to the White House for a photo opportunity with the President or have videos of them posted on the White House website. This was the case in late 2011 when President Obama was trying to rally support for his ultimately successful extension of the payroll tax relief.

Yet, if the social media commentaries run against a politician, then the commentaries are likely to be ignored, blunted, or countered. This is because, from a politician's viewpoint, having public involvement that opposes the politician's goals could impede the fulfillment of ideological objectives. Hence, the inputs from the public that are perceived to be problematic for the president would have to be defused. In fact, several chapters of this volume have been devoted to documenting how social media for policy-making may have been the banner headline for an activity, but did not fulfill the substance. Hence, we can conclude that unless the public input is uniformly in support of a political leader's position, any system that purports to draw on it will find ways to massage, filter, and neutralize nonsupportive viewpoints.

Turning to a management perspective, having public involvement can impede effective program administration. And even from the viewpoint of democratic politics, it could be that, if not fully and faithfully achieved, allowing public input could result in nondemocratic outcomes. That is to say, allowing a segment of the public to be involved in a policy decision, while other segments are not involved—either because of lack of interest or inability—cannot be seen as promoting democracy in the highest sense of the word. This last point goes to the heart of an important issue of public mobilization.

The United States has a representative form of government as enshrined in the Constitution. It is not designed to be run along the model of ancient Athenian democracy, in which citizens were supposed to have been frequently consulted by their elected leaders. Neither is it designed to be run according to a system in which the government is largely autonomous from popular will. Rather, it is designed to have a carefully crafted separation of contesting powers within the branches of government and periodic empowerment of the legislative and executive branches by the people. In point of fact, it is designed to have only intermittent consultation with the people. The primary form of consultation is achieved electorally every two years in the case of members of the House of Representatives, every four years in the case of the Presidency, and every six years in the case of members of the Senate. Another form of consultation lies in the First Amendment, which prohibits Congress from abridging the right of the people to "petition the government for redress of grievances." (More will be said later about White House petitions and social media.)

This form of government has brought to realization one of history's most brilliant, if underappreciated, dimensions of political imagination: freedom *from* politics. Specifically, it allows citizens in a democratic society to go about their daily lives without having to displace their energies in the pursuit of politics, while at the same time allowing them to exercise control at regular intervals. This is in stark contrast to many authoritarian and theocratic governmental systems that constantly mobilize their citizenry to support policy (or public sentiment, in the case of the death of North Korea's "dear leader" in 2011). No one has the right in these societies to be politically disengaged, neutral, or disinterested. There is no freedom to be uninvolved. What is the mark of governmental success and legitimacy in these societies? It is the very existence of forced mass demonstrations, either in the public square or in the ballot box. Such regimes see that 99 percent or so of the population support them at election time, and while few outsiders find this result credible, it does create the necessary, if ironic, gloss.

It is not only authoritarian governments that require the political engagement of their citizens. Australia, Argentina, Brazil, and seven other countries provide instances where voting in national elections is compulsory, and where people are subject to fine if they fail to cast a ballot. One consequence of such systems is that the victorious party is able to claim legitimacy for its policies. The right to be politically uninvolved, however, is trampled upon. Moreover, there is the argument that those who are less involved may be more ignorant of the issues, and therefore may make poor judgments compared with those who are steeped in political debates or who follow particular issues. (Although this rationale has in the past been used to bar participation in elections, the converse need not apply: people need not be forced to participate simply because they were prevented from doing so in the past.)

Ultimately, though, using social media for governmental guidance catches the advocates on the horns of a dilemma. In order for the system not to be gamed by special-interest groups, or driven by passionately committed advocates, widespread involvement and participation is required. Yet, except in times of crisis, most people do not wish to be encumbered by learning about vital, let alone arcane, issues or to be subjected to bombardments of propaganda from various sides (other limitations will be discussed later). So, at best, any social media input system can only be advisory. Nonetheless, even to the extent that it is advisory, such a system easily can be subject to capture or manipulation by special interests. As former Pentagon social media chief Sumit Agarwal told us,[26] it is unlikely that groups of outspoken individuals can be prevented from hijacking the debate. Agarwal, however, pointed out that the Defense Department was "not necessarily" putting up its policies or decisions for a referendum. "We're not saying, here's an issue, look at the serious number of votes, that group wins," he said. "So if someone is hijacking the conversation, what they really accomplish in the end is they simply devalue that communication channel, because we simply conclude that we're unable to derive reasonable signal, an unbiased signal from that particular interaction and so we don't necessarily accept as much outside input on that question." Thus, the use of social media for providing governmental inputs to policy direction remains quite limited, though not entirely useless.

Among the technologies' uses is taking the temperature, in a limited way, of the public, biased and incomplete as it would be. Another is to provoke public interest in an issue and then take charge of it. This is tantamount to the listening tour mentioned in the breakout box in chapter 8, in which a politician tours an area and allegedly listens to the public before responding with what is often an already established program or pronouncement. Social media for political participation can be used to legitimize decisions, or, as practiced by the Obama Administration, filtered to deal only with carefully chosen issues.

Top-Down Leadership and Pronouncements
about Social Media

How does the Obama Administration actually incorporate the platforms of social media into the dynamics of public participation? Given that any national government is composed of many people with a variety of viewpoints and takes many different actions in various domains, its effort must stand for many things. Adding complexity to the issue is the fact that those delegated with responsibilities may not always discharge them in the manner intended by those occupying higher rungs of leadership. Still, despite huge variability, there also tend to be points of concentration and consistency when presidents declare their intentions.

One declared intention of the Obama Administration was to pioneer how social media could be used to provide the federal government with guidance and advice. Yet, the initiatives it has undertaken in this direction have been dwarfed by its huge commitment to using social media as a way to propagate its views, recruit and organize supporters, and harness them as bulwarks against its political adversaries. From the vantage point of our tripartite description of modes of social media use for governmental purposes, the Obama Administration has prioritized the second—information dissemination and propaganda—relative to the third—adhering to citizen guidance concerning policy directions.

President Obama has certainly invited participation in a way that could be claimed to be using social media to gather viewpoints that might be of use to his Administration (the first of our three modes). Yet, a more detailed examination of these claims shows them primarily to be ways of harnessing the popular cachet of social media, embracing the widespread enthusiasm for these tools among the public and helping to attract attention to Administration views and accomplishments. Just as in the campaign, the use of social media becomes a news story in itself, so it is no surprise that the practice would continue. The Obama Administration has used social media events to attract public and press attention on the basis of the technology's novelty and seeming openness to the citizenry; but it actually serves as a forum from which Administration views can be expounded. It is news when the first "Facebook Town Hall" is held. It is news when the first "Electronic Town Hall" takes place. It is news when YouTube videos are used to disseminate Administration viewpoints. In all these cases, the "news" is a form of viewpoint transmission to audience segments as part of a larger pursuit of Obama Administration goals.

These events actually are not meaningful ways for the public to engage with the President. In fact, they are sometimes the opposite: they are used to defuse serious questioning of Administration policies. Rather than conducting a press conference with at least moderately inquisitive reporters, or holding an in-depth interview with specialists who wish to probe a topic, the President can maintain the option of responding to questions of his choosing. In this way, rather than having to defend more controversial lines of argument, he is able to use the interaction as an opportunity to rephrase and reiterate established Administration positions. In a tough press briefing, the President would have less ability to selectively control the flow of the discussion, were he to be confronted by competent, well-informed reporters or interviewers who could pursue his responses with detailed follow-up questions.

Instead, explanations of policies to the American public can frequently go unexamined. In the image-management business, calls for press conferences may be blunted by the response that the President has already addressed the concerns of the public.

Indeed, "Authoritarian Progressivism" and "New Authoritarianism" are among the negative characterizations that detractors use to attack the Obama Administration.[27] Ironically, such characterizations stand in stark contrast to the very image that President Obama sought to project during the Administration's early unrolling of engagement pronouncements. Moreover, rather than a distant authority figure, in public-presentation terms, President Obama seeks to project himself as a casual, regular fellow who loves sports and having a beer with the guys. The role social media can play often lies in making the President seem approachable and attractive—perhaps even a potential acquaintance.

SOCIAL MEDIA AND CITIZEN IMAGINATION: BRINGING THE PRESIDENT CLOSE

The idea that one can feel close to the President, especially one who is regarded as charismatic by his many admirers, can be powerfully appealing. We have seen how the thought of having personal (albeit mediated) communication with the President arouses the imagination of teens in the example of the "text the President about student debt" discussed in chapter 8. This closeness effect was captured by Kate Albright-Hanna, Director of Video for New Media for the Obama '08 campaign, who told us:

> One powerful thing that social media can do is make celebrities seem like normal people that we can relate to. It was what I think some of those photo shoots of Dubya Bush playing with his dogs and chopping wood on his ranch were trying to do. But the staged quality made it seem too fake and too far removed. When people are able to tell their own stories directly (even if in reality it is a third party doing the writing) it allows them to construct their own narratives of self and reframe their public presentation. Consumers of this social media feel like they are getting this information directly rather than through a publicist or the perspective of a journalist. It feels somehow personal—like you're both the journalist or celebrity friend with an inside scoop and that they are just a normal person who is talking to you about their day the way you might with a coworker. Periodically, people who are particularly adept at social media will tweet back or respond in other ways to average people who message them. Though it might only be one person out of the thousands that contacted them that week, it makes it seem as if that relationship exists in a more meaningful way than it really does.[28]

The imagination tends to be underestimated as a force in political science analysis, yet it has the power to stir nations to war. So too it can be a strong motivator for human behavior in politics. In this vein, social media can do much to bind media-savvy citizens to the leader. Obviously this is recognized by many heads of state, as pointed out earlier in the book concerning the rise of Twitter among them. Eve Wong, a technologically savvy anthropologist who participated in President Obama's Reddit session and (like most of the people she knows) watched his

Facebook Town Hall and other events online, told us, "We now can follow along and read 'private' conversations between politicians and their constituents via Twitter." She continued, "Being inculcated with this sense (justifiably or not) that we have direct contact, or at least a possibility for direct and instantaneous contact (like the Reddit thing, as good a chance as any other Average Joe), with our representatives and President seems to have caused a significant shift in our expectation, evaluation, and more importantly, *preference* for our relationships with them." Reflecting on changes over time, she added, "It seemed to me that it used to be once, that the desirable candidate for leadership was one who was decidedly NOT like us. It was someone better than our individual self-images, more educated, more...shiny and glittery somehow. But distant. Formal. No longer do we seek the authoritative leadership of a rigid and distant father-figure leader...instead we look for friends." Wong explained further, "We want our dream best friend. We want to LIKE them. Media and politics, like moieties, seem to be in constant didactics, changing and evolving with, against, and in spite of one another."[29]

SUSTAINING THE ENGAGEMENT

By contrasting the White House social media outreach described in this chapter with earlier case studies, we see that over time there has been an evolution in terms of initiatives that have been undertaken. There has been movement from the free-for-all of the Transition Team's Citizen's Briefing Book, to a greater exertion of control over the agenda. At one time, broad collections of citizen concerns were solicited in an attempt to inform policy-makers and to "crowdsource" potentially transformative ideas and engage the public in what at least had the appearance of steering policy via its collective voice. And President Obama continues to speak of the desirability of such activities. Yet, over time, social media efforts have shifted to targeted events to address specific issues or engage specific communities as well as to highlight the warmth and caring of the White House. In a sense, the procedure for the seemingly open forums is "ask me anything, but I will tell you what I want to say." By using social media, many in the audience are more likely to respond to the President by saying, in effect, "I had the opportunity to make my views known to the President of the United States. What a thrill" (a topic we pick up in the next chapter).

However, in these more contemporary social media events (which in effect seem to say, "ask me anything" or "tell me your concerns" about an issue) there is more the appearance rather than the reality of empowering citizens through social media. The divergence between perceptions and reality allows the Administration to head off citizen contestation of its priorities and instead provides it with an opportunity to explain and justify its positions to engaged audiences. It could be said that the Administration is using these moments to learn of public concerns, communicate with the citizenry, explain government perspectives, and respond to criticism. The cumulative effect is that the Administration can disseminate its message, a point that President Obama has repeatedly stressed as an area for improvement on his own part. Yet no matter the framework, in operational terms, contemporary social media forums limit citizen input in various ways. There are significant restrictions on the ways citizens can respond to or follow up on presidential statements during these forums. In this way, the presidential message, in a controlled manner, can be conveyed to the target audience, and tailored to the situation.

Yet given the small probability that one would have direct contact with the president, or even have one's questions selected from the multitude as meriting response, it is worth pausing to briefly explore the motives of people for getting engaged in social media politics (a topic worthy of its own book). As we conducted the research for this book, we were able to get a more in-depth perspective on this issue; we took steps to observe online discussions during and after such events, spoke to participants, and monitored communities such as Reddit to see how attitudes shifted over time. Selections from two of our interviews illustrate common viewpoints from people who are Redditors (individuals who identify as members of the Reddit online community) who engaged with President Obama's Ask Me Anything (AMA) session and found it meaningful at the time, even if later they were less enthusiastic about the interaction.

Michelle Welch, a Boston University graduate student, said participants were excited about being able to pose a question directly to a head of state, because,

> They can ask a question they believe is very insightful or that they believe is a harder question that hasn't been asked before or is not going to be asked by news media...as a Redditor you have more access and have the ability to ask that question you've been burning to ask him rather than just the stock news people or news site...I think with an AMA people feel like they have a direct link to the source. And they can actually sit there and ask a question that even if it is not answered by him they feel like they had this channel directly to him and they don't have to go through a third party...And it is not necessarily that he is going to answer you. You don't know if he is going to answer you. But just the fact that he took the time, some people felt OK, yeah, he took the time—he took the time to answer maybe ten or eleven questions. Yeah, that's not a lot but some people and I were kind of like, "Wow, he took thirty minutes out of his hectic schedule as President of the United States! Come on now."[30]

Denice Szafran, a visiting anthropology lecturer at the State University of New York at Geneseo, said Obama's participation in the AMA, "answering questions from John Doe," by itself gave the Redditors "the feeling that now they had a voice," that "somehow, some way, their concerns would be considered." Redditors were "excited" about the AMA, she said,

> because there was the President of the United States on Reddit and (that was) cool because Reddit is our community...He's talking to us and he's gearing the conversation to the specific group of people or some culture of people who expect this kind of communication. This is what we do...That synchronicity and the feeling that the President is addressing something that is of concern to you and probably several other people because they upvote this—that's exciting. Because you can't just fly to Washington and walk up to the front door of the White House and say, "Excuse me. Can I ask the President a question?"...I was really impressed that the President was talking to us.[31]

Later, after she read the transcript and evaluated President Obama's post-election actions, Szafran said she was disappointed because his AMA "was just talking points that we really could already find out in other places." And yet, she could not deny that the experience had been meaningful at the time and she still felt excited that she had participated.[32]

We sought to understand how, for participants, engaging directly with a political figure through social media is different from watching or listening to the same political figure speak in a press conference broadcast live on television or radio. From our interviews, we were able to tentatively identify six reasons why some individuals are drawn to social media political engagement.

The first is catharsis. Many denizens of the digital world are happy to use social media to express themselves since they, like most people, gain psychological relief by having the opportunity to at least articulate their views, even if no action is taken. The mere act of communicating their concerns, wishes and ideas provides pleasurable relief. Just having an opportunity to air a view is emotionally meaningful.

The second is a lottery effect. Even though it is unlikely that one's question will be chosen, it is always possible. The seemingly chance-based process through which questions are chosen adds to the attraction given the way random reinforcement impacts the human psyche (random reward is the most powerful form of operant conditioning, which helps explain the powerful appeal of gambling).

Third is the affiliative value of such participation. One joins with the group of other like-minded people to express a viewpoint. This can be done through voting, but also through collateral organizational efforts. This joins both the pursuit of a cause that an individual may care about with a sense of belonging to a group. (Group membership is also something that has been found to be psychologically gratifying and another powerful characteristic of humans).

Fourth, there is what might be called an "ego-grooming" effect. People feel that they are being somehow chosen or selected by the politician for special attention. Being attended to by a person of power is an ego-gratifying experience, as attested to by the many displays of commemorative photos taken with political leaders.

Fifth, there is a disintermediation effect: one has the sense that one can communicate directly with the top leader, without a lot of gatekeepers being in the way. As attractive as this is, it has the negative reciprocal in that if one does have an opportunity to connect with a person in power, but is subsequently ignored by that person, one feels hurt.

Finally, there is the moral dimension. This is much like voting where, in most cases, any one individual vote makes no difference. However, collectively the exercise of citizenship is important, and is deemed meaningful by the roughly half of the population that does take the trouble to vote. For those who feel responsible for the fate of the world, care about a particular policy, or who may consider themselves good citizens, the feeling that they are exercising their responsibilities diligently is fulfilling, even if they recognize that their particular contribution may not on its own have any import.

Many of these dimensions are related to the optimism bias that humans generally have, namely that they overestimate in a positive direction the likelihood of good things happening, and in this case, that would be through their own efforts. These factors can come into play to varying degrees for each engaged citizen. But their cumulative effect is to make social media efforts a worthwhile endeavor for both the political leadership and citizens who choose to participate in those efforts. Together, lots of positive (and at times negative) feelings can be generated, but it does take individual and group motivation to get citizens engaged with social media politics in the first place.

CONCLUSION: THE ROAD NOT TAKEN

To summarize this chapter, we have examined the motives for using social media for citizen engagement, and focused in particular on the theme of public involvement in national policy-making. We analyzed various explanations for the outcomes that have been observed. We have also contextualized the conflicting perceptions of President Obama as someone who exploits social media, even to the extent of being considered authoritarian, but who also uses the technologies in ways that many find thrilling, in enabling them to bring him vividly into their lives and to feel a personal connection with him.

Much of our analysis has focused on the growing gap between President Obama's declaration of intentions for the uses of social media and the ways they have actually been used by his Administration. While the reality of this gap seems difficult to refute, as we have alluded, there are many reasons to take comfort in the failure of the President to live up to his promises in this regard. As we will argue in the next chapter, even though departures from the commitment to social media-steering are disturbing to advocates of citizen engagement with policy, and even though the President has made gestures in that direction, it is better that that road not be taken.

CHAPTER 11

CONCLUSIONS AND IMPLICATIONS

BARACK OBAMA'S PRESIDENTIAL CAMPAIGN AND ELECTION IN 2008 APPEARED TO bring social media enthusiasts' dream of citizen participation in governmental policy-making closer to reality. But even with a second term of office in which to work, fulfillment of this vision remains a distant remnant of early term ambitions. A closer look yields a number of insights about the patterns underlying the complex phenomena associated with the balancing of Administration priorities with the pursuit of broader public engagement.

BROADER PATTERNS OF SOCIAL MEDIA REALITIES

An important overarching principle to bear in mind is that social media are just the latest in a long string of attempts at deploying technological solutions to political and social problems. The Obama Administration was not the first to have great expectations for communication technologies that would put governmental leaders in touch with their people. Most of them worked to a degree. While telephones, fax machines, and email all allowed greater user-centric contributions to both vertical and horizontal communities, they ultimately have not altered the hierarchical structures of executive decisions, high-level bargaining, influential lobbying, and bureaucratic agency that define the contours of major policy crafting. Despite the initial highly appealing technological ease and efficiency of these communication tools, none of them became the panacea anticipated by optimistic prognosticators. Moreover, policy elites quickly found ways to insulate themselves from these forms of pressure and persuasion.

Social media engagement will inevitably remain a permanent tool of presidential campaigns, transitions, and administration for the foreseeable future. The Obama operation has built a solid foundation for the Democratic Party's future interactivity with its voter base, and the Romney campaign's digital director, Zachary Moffatt, correctly points out that while Mitt Romney lost the 2012 election, his campaign's efforts have likewise established a large audience primed for social media outreach.[1]

Rebecca Heisler, Romney's Social Media Director, remarked that, "Who knows where we will be in a couple years in terms of digital and campaigns but I really see it being the core of everything...It is hard to imagine not having dedicated digital staffers within every [campaign] department in 2016."[2]

On a more basic level, the creation of a new standard landscape that necessarily involves social media should not cause us to lose sight of essential questions of information gathering, message broadcasting, and collaborative engagement.

Mistakenly, many succumb to the belief that governance fails to adopt the seemingly open, flexible, and engaging communication dynamics of the campaign trail. In fact, both Obama election campaigns and White House Administrations have sought to control not only the strategic objectives but also the communication modalities and content. This mistake has given rise to what we call the myth of the free-form social media campaign, a myth we described in chapter 3, which draws enthusiasm but entraps both the public and leadership in an illusory dance of citizen engagement. Further, investment in this myth leads to the conflation of a desire to make governance more responsive and transparent (worthy objectives, of course) with a belief that large heterogeneous groups with competing objectives will come together to happily embrace jointly agreed upon policies and nationwide objectives. Although constituting an attractive abstract intellectual concept, the combination of social media input and technological opinion reduction for policy decisions remains outside the bounds of the realizable, despite the oft-repeated shibboleth that politics is the art of the possible.

Real world evidence of this pattern can be observed in the progression and integration of technology acquisition by presidential candidates and administrations. Expectations were ambitious, but actual adoption of newer media technologies was incremental, disjointed, and, most critically, subsequently wrangled and restricted anytime it threatened to extend beyond the range of its operators' controls.

In addition to social media arising along a continuum of emergent technologies over time, these platforms—like their predecessors—illustrate the profound difficulties in discerning the motives of its users and designers at the individual, group, and mass public levels. The behavior of government officials, politicians, and citizens discussed throughout this book—behavior that swings between the two poles of high-minded motives and eliciting greater public involvement, on the one hand, and self-serving manipulation and selectivity of content and response, on the other—suggests that it is impossible to determine the true motives for the multiple social media undertakings we have described. In our estimation, however, some people probably have one set of motives, others the other, and some have a mixture of both. Moreover, it is likely that they start out with the high-minded motives, but once they discover how difficult it is to make them work, they gravitate to exploitative and manipulative uses of social media.

Not only are personal and organizational motives difficult to discern, the dynamics of causal mechanisms, variable relationships, and derivative results are likewise confounding to any potential investigation. When a change occurs that has coincided with use of social media, it is easy to assume that the social media were the cause, and even the enablers, of the change. Yet it is by no means clear that social media were either the cause or the enabler. In fact, it has been argued that the "Arab

Spring" in Cairo was actually inflamed by the Mubarak government's suspension of the Internet and the cellphone systems. By cutting people off, the argument went, people had to leave their apartments and go into the streets to find out what was going on. The presence of crowds in the streets fed the revolution.[3]

Likewise, we saw in the 2008 Obama campaign how the use of social media became a story in and of itself. News coverage of the candidate's social media use drove people to employ the various social media facilities themselves, resulting in phenomena such as "Obama Girl," in which Amber Lee Ettinger became a TV and Internet celebrity because of her Internet video "I Got a Crush on Obama," in which she expressed her admiration for the then-Illinois Senator.[4]

Despite the great difficulties in uncovering the specific inner workings of social media's operational contours, these technologies will continue to exercise a strong pull over the public imagination. Ever more exotic or popular uses of social media will continue to drive academic, journalistic, field-specific, and pop-cultural narratives. At a broader system level, data errors and inaccuracies will create problems in spheres as diverse as entertainment, employment, federal benefits, international events, and private relationships, but even correct data will expose people to risk due to its wide, and often careless, dissemination.

This trend, in turn, will further distort and highlight the seemingly critical role of social media in political activities. Another dimension is the privacy question. This issue poses a problem in five interlinked ways.

(1) The first is that becoming visible, or at least entering one's name on some list, makes an individual subject to bombardment with both general and targeted messages (and apparently one can get on these mailing lists even without ever having signed up for them). This in turn can result in intrusions on one's solitude or ordinary communication practices. Such intrusions can be as simple as receiving unwanted or a superabundance of messages from the Administration. It can also give one an eerie feeling that one's movements and communications are being surreptitiously observed.

(2) The second is the idea that data collected for one purpose is used for another. Data may be aggregated in ways unimaginable to the individual who provided it.[5] Thus one's information acquired in one domain can be placed in another without permission. Though such practices have a troubling element of powerlessness and taking of property (at least intellectual property) without permission, they also have a critical dimension of privacy violation. This includes not only one's own opinions, but group and interpersonal discussions, and the improper disclosure of the content of these communications to others.

(3) A third risk to privacy is vulnerability to manipulation due to asymmetrical knowledge; the targeter knows something about the target but the target does not know what this information is and to what purpose the targeter is putting it. Thus the target is open to manipulation, at least in principle, and has personal control over his/her knowledge usurped.

(4) In practical terms, there is a fourth risk that stretches beyond the question of attitudes and intrusion of messages to intrusions and threats at a physical

level. By contributing money or participating in social media, an individual's political views can become known, and that person may be targeted both positively and negatively by other groups. This can have the consequence, as well, of stifling public participation by those who are sensitive about their personal data, or public persona.

(5) Finally, there can be personal physical threats as well as psychological ones, due to one's participation in social media for political purposes. While such concerns smack of Orwell's *1984*-style dystopian world, it is not at all far-fetched. For example, the 2012 Obama campaign released the names of major donors to his opponent, Romney. President Obama's critics have suggested that this move was designed to encourage his supporters to take reprisals against the Romney donors. Whether this was the motive behind the action, the move, for some of those whose identities were revealed, did lead to threats, economic losses and a sense of physical danger. While the criticism in this case may be directed at the Obama campaign, it is an extensible problem when behavior and attitudes become both individually identifiable and readily collectible and transmittable. Looking toward the future, it is easy to anticipate that those with unpopular views could be threatened if they became easily locatable by hostile and aggressive individuals. Beyond the individual level, an entire organization could be exposed to economic risk as well, if its leaders were to take unpopular views.

Privacy is related to issues that operate at the system level, as well. These problems of complex technological systems that deal with human information have been studied by Edward Tenner, who concludes that it is impossible to predict the unintended and often negative consequences of advancing data systems.[6]

In terms of bureaucratic politics, we have observed some interesting phenomena in this book. In order to fulfill campaign promises, and carry out commitments made to attentive audiences of social media elites, political leaders find themselves having to establish offices to implement the social media revolution. However, as the political leaders come to realize that these newly established bureaucracies are a source of embarrassment, they push their own interests over and above those of their nominal masters. We can expect to see this cycle repeated in each new subsequent wave of promises, followed by disappointing realities of public input via technology. This happened to the science advisor under Presidents Johnson and Nixon[7] and, as discussed here, appears to have happened to the social media unit under President Obama.

Note that we are not talking about using social media to identify processual problems, corrupt officials, or other forms of waste and abuse; in fact, social media can be quite good at pinpointing these problems, just as the suggestion box was in an earlier era (and, according to Beth Noveck, continues to enjoy some utility in governmental offices) and the telephone 800 number that most organizations now have today to report problems. This area, however, is not what we are addressing. By contrast, we are talking about using the public as a source of policy preferences and decisions. For the purposes of political engagement and governance, the relevant questions revolve around analysis of the intentions and desires for transparency, the goals and pitfalls of civic engagement, the contours of inter-institutional and bureaucratic interaction, the quality of public information and the broader ability of digital media engagement to translate into offline political mobilization.

DIGITAL DIVIDE AND FUNDAMENTAL INEQUALITIES OF DIGITAL ENGAGEMENT

The digital divide/inequality of participation problem is a theme that underlies discussion at several junctures in this book, and here we examine it specifically. Although access to social media tools continues to grow, there are groups in society that would continue to be systematically excluded due to technological barriers, as well as barriers of many other kinds, including education, income levels, and physical condition. Even assuming equal interest, and officially available tools at public places such as community centers and libraries, a host of variables would put the most vulnerable and least articulate at a disadvantage were there to be strong influence exercised by social media over governmental affairs, at least for the foreseeable future. The problem was elegantly formulated by an anonymous federal official who was participating on an Office of Management and Budget blog designed to support President Obama's citizen engagement in policy initiative in 2009. The official said:

> I guess my one concern is about the (pretty big) slice of the population who are not technology literate...every day we receive dozens of letters that are hand or typewritten on old sheets of lined paper...But simply put, my grandmother after a few years can barely email and is never going to learn how to Twitter—and the same is true for millions of other Americans.
>
> Figuring out how to bridge the techno-literacy gap is going to continue to be a big issue. Google has the advantage that 100% of their customers know how to Google; Microsoft knows that 100% of their customers own a PC; and, Facebook knows that 100% of their customers have email. We [in the Government] unfortunately do not have those luxuries, and if we do not play a strong role bridging the gap (rather than widening it) it is going to have serious repercussions for whether a whole group of people feel like they have the opportunity to participate in government.[8]

The particular problem stated above has been echoed in a series of academic studies that have covered a vast variety of digital divides.[9] Even though structuring deliberation in various ways may reduce some forms of inequitable participation, such as giving women a greater voice in discussion,[10] it is difficult to foresee social media truly leveling the playing field in many other domains, such as technological ability, time commitment, and education.

There is another aspect to the digital divide, and that goes to the heart of just what people want from their citizen engagement. Not everybody, by any means, wishes to be involved in policy-making, via social media or otherwise, as mentioned above. Only a subset of even the engaged population active on the Internet will even be interested and aware of opportunities for direct government engagement occurring outside of their usual social media platforms. This means that there is a divide not only between digital and nondigital users but within the digital demographics;

there, great variations exist in how much people are interested in utilizing social media for political engagement. Many people just want to go on social media platforms to share photos, maintain relationships, and stay informed. Putting it rather directly, the White House's Macon Phillips said, "One of I think the biggest biases in a lot of government consultation is self-selection. Who on earth actually takes time to go and comment on a government site? And what kind of biases are you introducing just based on that behavior?"[11]

STRENGTHENING BUREAUCRACIES IN SURPRISING WAYS

One interesting question is whether bureaucracies resist social media input and steering. Folk beliefs—what one would expect to hear from the proverbial "person in the street"—would have it that they do. In fact, according to considerable evidence, the record is much more mixed; in some cases, bureaucracies have embraced social media as a tool to learn about the needs of their clients and to monitor them. To the extent they resist social media tools, this resistance may be no different in many respects than the resistance that organizations offer to any other innovation. Actually, it could be argued that their resistance to social media inputs from the public is far less than the resistance bureaucracies exhibit to attempts at structural modifications or other truly intrusive forms of change. This differential in resistance may be the result of an ironic consequence of social media-based citizen guidance. The argument here is that rather than weakening internal power structures of the bureaucracy, social media can strengthen them. Moreover, it can strengthen bureaucratic control over the citizenry, even if the original justification was the reverse.

The "irony of unintended consequences" argument plays out in the following manner: when people give feedback about issues and problems, the bureaucracy can respond. The mere act of response helps justify the bureaucracy's existence. If the bureaucracy responds positively, it can demonstrate that it has done something that the people wanted accomplished. Therefore, since the bureaucracy is doing something the people wanted done, its budgets are justified. The bureaucracy can even potentially make greater claims on the public purse on the basis of a "job well done" (as measured, of course, via social media). Hence, rather than seeing public input via social media as a threat (though sometimes it certainly can be), there are many reasons why it can also be in the bureaucracy's best interest to welcome public participation. In fact, the notion that people like being seen as part of a social network (thus the popularity, for instance, of photos, videos, and video conferencing on the web) ties in with the idea that it is beneficial for organizations to be seen as well as heard. This lesson has been well understood by politicians for over 2,000 years—witness the rulers' heads and names on the statuary and coinage of ancient Persia and Rome, and the prominence of governors' and presidents' names on official documents and signage; their names even appear on welcoming signs at airports and tollways, and their faces look out to the people from photos posted on myriad governmental bulletin boards. The same notion is behind many bureaucracies' attempts to engage people via

Facebook and Twitter, for instance, in order to be a meaningful part of citizens' lives, "to be part of the conversation."

Social media also help bureaucracies monitor their "clients." One such source of data for this purpose is the social media "chatter" that can be tapped into to learn what people are thinking about and what they are saying (a reason to encourage users to be engaged via Facebook and Twitter). Secondary data collection, such as location monitoring and network use by geography, can also be a useful information source for a bureaucracy. But more to the point is to directly request information from users via social media. Facebook pages by myriad organizations demonstrate this perceived value by bureaucracies.

More subtle forms of data are also available to bureaucracies about clients. Citizen reporting of problems, denunciations of wrongdoers, and identification of problems can assist a bureaucracy in seeing that subjects under its purview are being appropriately controlled. Social media magnify the surveillance ability of bureaucracies, in the name of serving clients. Further, collection of data via social media allows a bureaucracy to construct better narratives as to its effectiveness, ultimately aiding its quest for legitimacy.

Finally, social media input from citizens can help justify the service orientation of the organization in the eyes of the external political leadership (i.e., the president). By having summary data as well as poignant examples of service, the bureaucracy can at once demonstrate fealty to the goals of the political leadership and fend off pressure for political redirection.

Together, these trends result in the ironic consequences of further strengthening bureaucracies vis-à-vis the public rather than the other way around.

As we are enumerating longer term trends affecting social media and bureaucracies, we point out that despite the good intentions of those who design a system, those in power will seek to use it to advance their own influence and policies. This is an inherent characteristic of the way politics works. It is well established that those who work in the political staff system will manipulate available tools to the advantage of the political leader.[12] Despite attempts to use social media technology as a tool for the expansion of democratic processes and opportunities, the net effect of the technology is that it reproduces many of the same inequalities, privileging activist classes—particularly those in power and those in executive agencies—to an extent that prior media advances did not.

Terry Moe and William Howell argue that unilateral power is the single most defining feature of the modern presidency.[13] In their appraisal, presidents draw their power from the ambiguities associated with the American political contract. Most importantly, however, Moe and Howell posit that unilateral executive power is ever expansive, with the President continuing to push against the limits that would purportedly constrain executive action.

The evolution of information and communication technology interfaces demonstrates a clear progression toward the further consolidation of presidential power via the ability to selectively prompt, guide, and engage social media. Recent examples of the use of social media by the Obama Administration, as discussed, provide opportunities for presidents to use symbolic interactivity as substitutes for substantive engagement.

Blowback of Disappointed Supporters

We have already discussed the fact that in addition to outright opponents to the President's policies, the White House had to deal with criticism from former supporters who had felt the President had not carried through on his promises for social media engagement. These disappointed followers form a core of strident critics who in many ways are more difficult to bear for the President's staff than those who are ideologically opposed to his programs. This is all the more so since some of them initially worked hard on behalf of Obama. But a useful perspective on this dilemma was offered by Macon Phillips:

> When we came in I think there were a lot of people in the building who were like, "Well let's just set up a tool where the public can suggest all of these things that we should do! And vote on them! And we'll go do them." It turns out a lot of those ideas aren't actionable. And a lot of it is sort of—I think a lot of people want to elect people who will make those choices and not necessarily give that input. And that's understandable. But there are a lot of people out there who do have very valuable input to offer. And I think we still have a lot of work to do on sort of sorting between the two so we have more efficient online consultations. And yield products that are more easily sort of internalized here in the building.[14]

Misplaced Faith in the Wisdom of the People,
as Reflected in Plebiscites and Low-Interest Issues

Had there been policy-driving social media tools of the kind promised by President Obama, it is easy for many progressives to imagine that the causes they embrace would have quickly become Administration and thus national policies. These interests would presumably include marijuana legalization and sharp restrictions on the National Security Agency's ability to eavesdrop. Yet perhaps their expectations are misplaced. Conservatives would probably end up being the ones to cheer the use of such tools, at least on a tactical level, since plebiscites on these issues usually favor conservative causes. This is certainly what has happened in California, where the citizens have endorsed binding propositions banning gay marriages and racial considerations in college admissions. California's pattern is all the more striking in light of the state's voting heavily in favor of the Obama ticket in both elections. (Of course a conservative outcome of plebiscites is not a universal principle, as some liberal causes are vindicated through plebiscites.) Had promised social media tools for national policy setting been available, almost certainly key Obama Administration initiatives, first and foremost being the Affordable Care Act, would have been rejected. That said, conservatives would almost certainly not want to see the kind of social media steering dreamed of by many Obama activists since it goes against their fear of the passion of the mob and the moment.

Lack of public interest is also a problem. Important issues that do not immediately command widespread public interest can be misjudged as inconsequential due to the low rate of participation. Likewise, in such a setting a few voices can distort interpretations of the public's views. While earlier we showed how an organized group, such as the pro-marijuana legalization advocates, can quickly dominate social media-driven voting systems, other perturbations can occur when public concern is minimal to vanishing. For instance, in areas where there is modest public interest, even a tiny and disorganized group could dominate the policy outcome. And for topics where public interest may be quite small, the prospects are even bleaker that meaningful outcomes through participation could be forthcoming. That is, what if the government held a social media idea-fest for the public, but nobody came? The Office of Science and Technology Policy (OSTP), the Executive Office of the President agency charged with science policy, found an approximate answer in the winter of 2010. For six weeks, from February 5 to March 19, it sought to fulfill the public engagement levy of the Open Government Initiative (discussed above). Along with other federal agencies, it used an online brainstorming platform to gather public input for how to create a "collaborative, and participatory government" at OSTP. Remarking on the results, the OSTP observed that it "had 23 commenters, who posted 29 ideas, 144 votes, and 26 comments."[15] From the vantage point of deliberative democracy, it is important to inquire what it would mean to have government action on a policy issue informed by the views of a handful of anonymous citizens who happened by a website.

SOCIAL MEDIA MODELS OF BEHAVIOR: "ECONOMIC ACTOR" VIS-À-VIS "TECHNOCRATIC CITIZEN"

The "economic actor" model is based on the idea that people act in their own best interest to maximize gain and minimize loss. The idea of the pure *homo economicus* extrapolates to the "invisible hand of the market," which creates wealth and allows the best possible technology, goods, and services to be produced, in turn maximizing happiness. Transplanting this template from the world of economics to the world of politics, one can readily imagine the value of social media for policy-making: people put forward ideas, the best one wins, and over the long term, benefits and happiness are maximized for the society. The transplant, however, ignores several factors. Social media engagement for decision-making, at least as currently conceived, is driven by the will of the majority, which has several shortcomings. Among them are that minorities and people who do not wish to participate will find themselves at a disadvantage. The economic model, moreover, is predicated on the idea that competition will make some more efficient players win out over those who are less efficient. This may make sense in economic competition among corporations, but few would want to have that as a model for determining governmental policy. It also ignores the social scientific understanding of biases in decision-making. Dimensions such as risk aversion, distortions in relative judgment, and social pressure have only recently come to the surface in terms of social-psychological influences on decision-making. How can social media rate one person's severe risk-aversion as less important than another's mild risk-aversion? Perhaps interest in social media for governmental decision-making is itself an instance of an added factor, namely optimism bias, the premise that people assume things will work out better than they are actually likely to (which, it is worth noting, appears to affect not only social media participants but social media system designers as well).

Social media model advocates harken back to the hoary notion that "if only you have the right technology or technique, you can solve the problems of civilized life" (echoing thinkers such as Jacques Ellul[16]). But this tantalizing technocratic vision implies that value conflicts are due simply to either a lack of clear communication among individuals or severe moral failings on the part of the people with whose values one does not agree. (The explanation of resistance usually starts with the former but then migrates to the latter.) The technocratic dream is that there is a state of unity between information and values that can be realized through the application of the right technique. This dream often appears realizable: people can agree on a desirable future state in the abstract, but disagree on its details. Further, people can agree on a problem's definition but not on its solution. For example, practically everyone agrees that people should have shelter. But deciding as a matter of policy what kind of shelter, where it should be, and who should pay for it sparks wide disagreement.

Another conflict point in the technocratic approach arises from insensitivity to interest-group politics, or at least the calculus of the human heart. When constructing the White House opinion aggregation systems, designers apparently failed to attend to the problems of sampling bias (which plague all public opinion surveyors). Repeatedly, they were quickly hijacked when a specialized group, in particular the advocates of marijuana legalization, used their superior organization to dominate the social media input process.

Yet, in some quarters, faith in technocratic visions of direct democratic participation in national decision-making remains undiminished. In an August 2012 speech, Eric Schmidt, a top Google executive and longstanding supporter of Obama, described the world as becoming "fully automated" as a consequence of governments' struggles to manage successfully an ever-widening scope of society-wide problems. Part of this full automation, he believes, will be the development of a comprehensive model of how citizens directly engage with governments for services and beyond. "All of the known technical and societal issues" would be revealed in the process of designing this comprehensive model, including, Schmidt said, resistance to innovation (which by implication would include overcoming any resistance to the comprehensive model's implementation).[17] This brave new world of technological modeling for democratic governance is quite stark but also quite illuminating, reflecting as it does a profound faith in a tool-based solution to questions that often are driven by considerations of human passion and power. If all factors are known, the pertinent question is what need have we of leaders? Or, for that matter, what need would there be for citizen engagement?

Another shortcoming with many social media information gathering practices, such as voting on policy preferences, is that they assume that attitudes are basically stable and only need to be tapped. But people frequently revise their opinions, especially through their interaction with others, and what they think about topics can vary dramatically and quickly. Moreover, the communication process itself affects attitudes: even if people begin a deliberation, there is a strong tendency for arguments to become polarized. This is a well-known process in argumentation in which, rather than coming to a meeting of the minds, contending parties tend to alienate and irritate each other, escalating their rhetoric, making reconciliation more difficult. Second, people judge matters in relative terms. Hence positions become heavily dependent, not on the decisions themselves but on the outcomes as seen relative to those of others. To take a simple instance, Jo may be glad to receive a gift of $10 from Mo, and Jo is happy until discovering that Mo gave Jo's best friend a gift of $100.

Therefore, in a sense, there is another profoundly flawed aspect of an ideal of using social media to drive policy: it will always be subject to the same passions and limitations residing at the base of every important and significant policy issue that is related even slightly to values as opposed strictly to data. Data can be very helpful in understanding problems, and other things being equal we are in favor of having the best data. But data alone generally cannot resolve divergent interests and conflicting values. Neither are we against social media for various governmentally related uses, including problem reporting. (In fact, we are enthusiastically for it, especially in areas such as process improvement and constituent communication.) We also recognize that participation in social media forums for policy has many positive corollaries, as demonstrated in the work of Daniel Halpern,[18] including enhancing one's sense of empowerment and community belongingness among those who use such services. But can social media, at least as it has been embodied under the Obama Administration, be a substitute for the tough and often idiosyncratic business of politics?

It has been said that war is a continuation of politics by other means, but it could equally be said that politics are a form of warfare carried on by other means. The idea that the world's problems could be solved by Twitter and Facebook is remote, in fact equally as remote as was the prospect in the mid-1970s of solving problems by relying on the Warner Cable Qube system. (This cable system allowed connected citizens to vote on local issues and communicate directly with mayors and other officials.[19])

Yet the enthusiasm for social media in a governmental policy setting is guided at least partly by magical thinking about the way the world works now and how it will work in the future. The mirage of an ideal world created by social media is enticing. Somehow, the imaginative metaphor goes, the honest sweat on the brow of the working person will be distilled into wisdom through computer data processing. Today's variation is to rely on this being done in a "cloud." Every earlier communication technology was greeted by seers who perceived the mirage of human perfection hovering near the horizon; the printing press, telegraph, telephone, radio, television, and standalone computer, each had such a reception. When each new generation of skeptics pointed out that comparable promises of human perfection had been uttered before, the seers would say, "This time it is different."

We hasten to add that we do believe in technological progress, and see manifold evidence of it everywhere. We also believe that there have been many social media-related changes for the better in human rights and other policy domains. In fact, as we have said before, social media bestows many advantages in the governmental sphere. These include enhanced information availability, as well as the ability to improve governmental processes and communicate with government officials. We have also noted that interaction among social media users on governmental forums can be gratifying for participants, if not necessarily in terms of policy outcomes.

CIVIC CULTURE AND EMPOWERMENT

Though we are not sanguine about the prospects of social media for direct involvement in setting national policy, we do find the impulse for setting up such a system laudable. While we have pointed out some of the negative consequences of (frustrated) participation, it is also important to highlight some of what appear to us to be positive aspects. Macon Phillips declared, "If [WeThePeople] petitions are fostering a debate that might not otherwise take place about the issues Americans care about, that's a positive thing."[20] Though he did not elaborate as to why it would be a "positive thing," Daniel Halpern, as noted, has shown[21] that when Americans participate in online political discussions and related activities that have an interaction effect with others, they feel more empowered and interested in the policy process. Another benefit has been proposed by Stephen Coleman and Peter Shane,[22] who hold that such participation trains citizens in activism so that they can become more articulate in terms of interests and influence-exertion, and socializes them to expect greater participation through better social media instantiations when they become available.

We should also spotlight a fascinating change in American culture: the increasing amount of work that is done collaboratively. This means that both the federal government's internal processes and its opening the gates to external input from citizenry is likely to become more interactive and dynamic. Consequently, some of the approaches that have not worked well may, as a result of generational change and improving social-technical systems, come to play a large role in the policy process. Phillips reflected this view, saying:

> People who have been in college in the last five years or in grad school tend to have worked together on papers using tools like GoogleDocs. And it is obvious to them, "Well of course! I'm doing a group project or I'm putting together a party for tomorrow night or I need a list of something. Let's all just jump on together and kind of work and our cursors are different colors and move around the pages." And that sort of thing. That's a cool technology but the underlying collaborative ethic is much more interesting. And we have a generation of smart people who are moving through these experiences that are inherently collaborative. And it wasn't like that when I was in college. It certainly wasn't like that for people who are older than I am. So as you're looking at sort of the nature and impact of digital technology on government I think you should really examine fundamental questions of government. About collaboration, and consultation, and coordination. And then sort of look at what is happening with the next generation of leaders and what they are taking for granted in terms of how to be collaborative.
>
> I think some of that will change as we see a generational shift. And I think some of that is changing with these very policy makers who are saying, "Wow there are all these new communities and tools!" But you have to make them easy. You have to make them easy for them to adopt. Because as much as I think my work is interesting and busy, these folks are dealing with just such incredibly complex and serious issues. And you have to be able to present the value of why collaborating and getting new input is the right thing to do.[23]

While we believe his assessment is on target, the enduring tension over political control means that these forms of engagement, for the general citizen, will continue to restrict their access to the levels of power and detailed agenda-setting.

COVERT ACTIVITIES AND HIDDEN CONSEQUENCES

Just as it is important to recognize the collateral benefits of social media engagement, attention must also be directed to questions of the ultimate use and level of privacy of social media-generated data, including byproducts and transactional sources of data arising from network usage. What may be colloquially called paranoia about Big Brother affects both the level of participation and quality of participation in social media. As perception governs behavior, the imagined risks and felt concern play an important role in how social media are (and are not) used by the citizenry. Thus we touch here on revelations concerning covert data collection and possible misuses of data repositories.[24] As described by Phil Howard[25] and earlier by senior author Katz,[26] the increased use of telecommunication technology, including social media, means that ever greater amounts of private information are being collected and stored. These "data shadows" can be used for policy development, website analytics, and polling. But they could also be used for tracking and monitoring citizens in ways that make many people uncomfortable or even agitated. Perceptions of monitoring can chill expression, including protests and whistleblowing.

Yet beyond hidden uses of the data is the mere fact that the social media expression enterprise is increasingly conducted in proprietary spaces, such as Facebook, Google, LinkedIn, and Zillow. This trend is dismaying given that companies who promoted themselves and their products through the posturing of the democratic utopian rhetoric and who, in the case of Facebook and Google,[27] have been involved in fostering Obama Administration activities for public engagement. Micah Sifry adds a valuable perspective to this when he argues:

> Citizens should not have to sign up for a private corporation and share personal information with them in order to participate in civic engagement...So what we need is an initiative to create online public space that's genuinely public. Holding a Town Hall meeting on Facebook is not an acceptable alternative. First of all, you have to be a member of Facebook to join that, and not everybody wants to or should be forced to join a private company's platform to engage in a public conversation.[28]

IS THERE A FUTURE FOR PRESIDENTIAL SOCIAL MEDIA?

A few words are in order about the future of social media and its role under new presidential leadership. As to social media's role in future administrations, we heard conflicting views. Some, such as online public advocate Alan Rosenblatt, foresee that social media for citizen engagement will naturally grow in importance, led by the petitions process and its progeny. Others, such as Obama Transition Team staff member Dan McSwain, hold that social media for meaningful citizen engagement can only happen with top-level political support and backed by technical resources and leadership. Asked if social media for engagement would be an inevitable part of any future administration, he responded firmly:

> I don't think it is inevitable and I don't think it will be inevitable going forward. I think it is a dangerously wrong mindset to assume that the federal government would or will continue to be taking steps in the right tech direction without a lot of

people pushing for it...I don't think this is something that would have happened on its own just because Obama was the first digital president...One thing that really became clear to us was that a government website at rest tended to stay at rest. This concept of inertia in government tech absolutely holds.[29]

Our view is that social media technology cannot and will not be ignored; it is simply too useful to presidents in terms of gathering information and especially for message propagation. It is also an extremely convenient way to micro-target certain constituencies. Yet the efforts to keep it operating in high gear are costly, and future presidents may not want to keep up President Obama's intensity in doing so. Interest in other national conversations or town halls, in which citizens can directly express their policy preferences, has proven to be a costly lesson in terms of citizen engagement and not one to be soon repeated. We can also expect continuing "open government," transparency and free-form citizen input efforts from executive branch agencies. Yet, as McSwain argues, without strong pressure from the top, these efforts are likely to bear little fruit.

CLOSING REMARKS

SUMMING UP THE BIG PICTURE

2008 marked a watershed point when the potential of social media as a consequential public engagement tool moved from a discussion topic to being used in an attempt to guide national policy. Driving this shift was Barack Obama's apparent personal commitment and his coterie of advisors and supporters. Radio, television, and the World Wide Web can each lay claim to serving as the pivotal political communication platforms of prior elections, and each has been used as outreach to the electorate. Likewise, the postal service, telegraph, and telephone have all served as ways for the public to have input to the White House. But never has such a broad-based attempt to gather public opinion occurred as it has under President Obama and his drive to use social media. Credit must be given for the attempt. Yet the modality of use quickly converged to using social media tools to broadcast governmental objectives and reach out to citizens through conduits of nonbinding input. Events became more carefully controlled in terms of the citizen input coming to him. This provides the White House with a decided structural advantage in using these forums for message propagation. (But these events also showcase Obama as being a "savvy operator" in the digital domain, as described in chapter 3 by his 2008 campaign's New Media director, Teddy Goff. It is remarkable that he allowed himself to be so publicly experimental in engaging with the social media, and sets a high standard by which his successors will be measured.)

After more than five years in office, and with reelection secured, the promised realization of mass public input through technological platforms remains unfulfilled. As critics—and many supporters—have learned, the Obama Administration has readily embraced social media tools to advance preexisting objectives, but it has not used the technology for any true exercises or experiments in large-scale pure democracy. This point is illustrated in the case studies and interviews discussed above. Whether these patterns have arisen intentionally or unintentionally is for other studies to determine. But our analysis of the events is clear with respect to the limits of fostering public engagement: a federal government will not use social media tools for mass exercises in direct, participatory democracy. In addition to being hampered by logistical difficulties, such exercises present tangible risks to the integrity of democratic processes. Thus we draw the distinction between falling short of the soaring rhetoric of engaging the public in mass decision-making, which is notable, and the advisability of implementing such a system. From what we are able to discern, it is better that the full-blown promise was not able to be realized, for reasons delineated below.

IMPLICATIONS FOR FUTURE DIRECTIONS

Conventional logic may intuitively suggest that social media platforms are beginning to wear thin in the public imagination as users face a relentless barrage of information from political, commercial, and personal sources. Could social media thus wither as a format of political discourse and participation? Despite sustained cultural criticism, confessions of personal failure, and acknowledged problems from addiction to suicides, the technology is integral to the fabric of modern life. After all, similar criticisms of radio and television have been insufficient to halt their popular embrace. Social media usage will be no different, and seems destined to become an entrenched fixture of political life. Individual platforms such as Facebook, Twitter, Foursquare, Reddit, or Vine may evolve, shift, or vanish, but similar interfaces will continue to play an expansive role in campaigns, transitions, governance, and in the broader spheres of public attention, opinion, and mobilization.

One reason for this persistence is that popular expectations for political figures to deploy social media technology will remain robust. Candidates who eschew social media engagement will run the risk of being castigated as out-of-touch, aloof, elitist, or archaic. Certainly, embracing social media is no guarantee against such characterizations, as evidenced by the candidacies of John Kerry and Mitt Romney, but neglecting to adopt the technology is a virtual guarantee for marginalization at best, and invisibility at worst. Along with amplifying and prolonging gaffes of perceived public disconnect (we may mention, drawing from recent presidential contests, tea-pot tempests over endive planting, Windsurfing, Swiftboating, The 47 Percent of Americans who Pay No Income Tax, Binders Full of Women, or friendships with NASCAR team owners) the very inability to converse in the *lingua franca* of social media interactivity will be a liability in its own right. Moving forward, presidential candidates—and presidents in office—must rise to the expectations of basic fluency in the technology of social media interfaces. These expectations will percolate vertically, and candidates for national, state, and local offices will increasingly find themselves devoting substantial efforts toward social media engagement. Furthermore, the vertical flow of expectations will be multidirectional, as innovations at state and local levels will influence larger-scale campaign and governance initiatives.

A second reason for the persistence of social media in the political sphere is that they do, in fact, as evidenced by the examples in this book, serve as highly effective conduits for information collection, agenda broadcasting, and mobilization. Despite the prolific popular conversation about the superfluous spread of information, political actors can demonstrate that their social media strategies do, in fact, generate voter turnout, raise money, enhance prominence, and mobilize active supporters.

The caveat to the benefits for elite actors in this overall dynamic is that individual and group empowerment conceptualizations will not dissipate—people and organizations will continue to seek openings for active challenges to elite power structures. A social media arms race of sorts is a likely outcome, as elite and popular actors attempt to steer conversations and wrest control of individual social media platforms. Innovative groups will enjoy the best chances of attaining and consolidating positions of authority and prominence in the political mediascape, but such prominence will always be at risk of cooption and erosion by elite actors and power structures.

PERILS OF SOCIAL MEDIA STEERING

There are serious drawbacks to social media for guiding governmental action. The fundamental question of whether crowdsourcing and true democracy is actually a good way to run the government calls into question the entire enterprise of using social media tools to inform governmental opinion. Plato's misgivings about popular steering stemmed from profound concerns, not simply about operational inefficiencies, but about actual harm to the society at large. Ironically, in his wary perspective, on matters of statecraft and social organization it is broad, unfettered attempts at inclusivity across a society that undermine the ongoing viability of that very society. The fact is, we have a constitutional form of government, and much can be said for it; as noted elsewhere, there is no technological reason that some earlier forms of communication technology could not have been used to guide policy, minute by minute—for instance, through the telephone, a communication device that was developed in the late 1800s.[30]

The Obama Administration's efforts with the Online Town Hall highlights the problem of trying to guide political systems through a tightly linked social media voting/policy assessment; in such exercises, the silent majority's interests tend to be ignored, while the passions of special interests dominate. Thus, representative government with periodic electoral checks by the populace is a fairer way to secure the interests of the general public. History suggests it is not possible to design game-proof systems. In other words, as we saw with the marijuana-legalization question raised in the Online Town Hall and the Citizen's Briefing Book experiments, people can manipulate systems to serve themselves and their interest group. This is by no means unique to social media: it happens throughout political systems, despite carefully controlled conditions and laws enforced by regulatory commissions and judicial bodies. Just as the gambling industry finds that people continually come up with new ways to get around rules, "netizens," citizens of the Internet, will also continue to figure out ways to manipulate social media-based political systems to their advantage.

This assertion is not solely applicable to the present Administration—the risks of careless mass engagement persist across time and technology. Past presidential Administrations have all displayed astute wariness of the reach, scale, and depth of public engagement through media platforms. The same seems true of the present incumbent, and there's no reason to expect that to change in the future.

A Prospect that Remains on the Horizon

Social media applications remain an unutilized tool of citizen self-governance, the lofty words of President Obama and other technology enthusiasts notwithstanding. The hope that they would make a meaningful change in the way the federal government draws upon the public for involvement in fundamental public policy decisions remains just that: a hope, but not a change.

Another point, mentioned earlier, is the obvious limits to time, resources, and intellectual focus. When confronted by rational calculation, competing priorities, and empirical realities, many idealistic proposals, despite being predicated on eminently praiseworthy sentiments, founder. Thus, for a leading scholar of the field, Stephen Coleman, the technology of social media for participation is part of a teleological vision for "e-citizenship," namely, "a democratic space where anyone can stake a claim to be heard and respected and all proposals have a chance of being acted on."[31] As we have sought to point out, and as the White House learned when it undertook to conduct its program to petition the government, even for information concerning official positions, any attempt along these lines will become quickly swamped with people demanding input. This experience is borne out in other domains, such as when well-intentioned people attempt to counteract the ever-renewing claims of Holocaust deniers, 9/11 "Truther" conspiracy theorists, or intelligent design advocates. Those who seek to advance rational arguments that rely on the full spectrum of empirical evidence, and abide by the rules of the logic of scientific inquiry, find that the fight is exhausting as their opponents constantly shift the grounds of the argument and the rules of engagement. Every claim that so easily falls from the lips of a claimant, rationalists find, requires a response, and sometimes a detailed one. This has been the experience when empirically based arguments have been brought to bear on entrenched groups who themselves have numerous supporters. Under the Coleman scenario, it is likewise the case that every proposal requires a response, which takes resources. One can readily imagine how much more difficult the situation would be if "all proposals" would have to be considered for action. It becomes a legitimate question as to whether this kind of world is actually good, what the costs are to the group or society, and what other desirable social objectives are being forfeited by the displacement of resources. But this is a conundrum encountered by every large-scale system that aims for democratic participation and fair treatment of all. Although the desire for equal representation and an equal voice is on some levels quite laudable, it would be a mistake to overlook the operational costs and realities, as well as the distortion that these values entail, when making sophisticated decisions about complex issues.

A further consideration is that social media cannot be viewed as comprising a panacea to intra-group disagreement. Despite the feelings of individual empowerment and well-being that citizen participation in governmental administration can potentially engender, leaders are put in place to lead, and, ultimately, to persuade. Standing aside neutrally while advising the public, "here is the issue, now you decide," is not part of a leader's job description. Given few people's willingness to weigh in meaningfully on a policy issue (as opposed to "slacktivism," that is, simply registering an opinion in response to the urging of a third party, such as via an online petition, which even then is done in small proportions), it is important that leaders take positions to protect the interests of those who are less decisive or less able. Jefferson and Hamilton may have been opposed on the issue of citizen participation in democracy, but they saw eye-to-eye on this point, despite their otherwise venomous differences.

Although we have presented some successes of President Obama in the social media arena, we have found that progress toward the ambitious goals for citizen participation remains modest. Others who have looked at this topic from a multinational viewpoint have found similar results: for instance, a detailed 2012 analysis of online political consultations concluded that "their democratic potential is nowhere near to being realized."[32] We agree with this sentiment. But is the vision of governmental policy setting espoused by former presidential candidate Obama just around the corner? In our opinion, and for the reasons we have given, we see that the day when social media applications will be a significant tool of citizen influence over US governmental policy remains far distant, if not entirely out of the question. This remains the case despite the undoubted continuing attempts to find ever-better ways to engage the public via social media at all levels, not the least of which will be at the level of presidential politics and policies.

Two additional points need to be reinforced in terms of social media use for steering national policy. First, despite the fact that progress has been modest, and often yielding puzzling results, it does not mean that those who have been working on the inside have not been making considerable exertions to achieve success. The Obama White House social media experts are dedicated and smart. The results to date speak to the intractability of the problem rather than individual shortcomings on the part of staff.

Second, there are structural questions on the sociological, political, and legal levels. As noted, though partly explained by technical and economic conditions, it appears inevitable that only a small minority of citizens would be willing to engage in policy-steering by social media. This situation of course raises important questions about the fairness and democratic nature of the grand experiment of using social media for major policy. But it is merely the matter of the upwelling of opinions from the citizens. Neither is it, or at least it should not be, a question of political will. There must also be administrative structures and budgetary allocations. Whether genuinely intended or not, expressed desires for greater transparency and public involvement are circumscribed by the realities of elite entrenchment, bureaucratic gridlock, and the risks to executive message control of free-form public participation. And of course another important element is the master control on all the dreams of drawing the American people into frequent disquisitions on national policy, and that is the United States' constitutional-representative form of government.

Thus, as we conclude our investigation, we continue to see social media as a mirage insofar as they can be used to have the wishes and ideas of the general public play into the macro-level decisions and choices of policy-makers. The mirage has an appealing, refreshing, even energizing image; hovering as it does on the horizon, it seems real and reachable. But even as we press our way toward it, even after our struggle over obstacles and expenditure of time and fortune, it eludes us, and remains as far away as when we started.

Appendix: Scholarship of Digital Media and the American Political Landscape

THIS APPENDIX BRIEFLY DISCUSSES SELECTED THEORETICAL STUDIES THAT SPEAK TO our analyses of presidential politics and citizen engagement. They address the twin demands of power and legitimacy that drive political communication in general, and apply specifically to our three modalities of social media communication (which, as formulated in chapter 2, are information gathering, broadcasting and propagandizing, and deliberative engagement). The theories we examine here shed light on how participation and persuasion can enhance the legitimacy and exercise of presidential power. (Power and legitimacy, while often contrasted, far more often work hand-in-glove across our three areas of concern.) We look first at theories of how information and communication technology (ICT) might affect democracy.

The Democratizing Potential of Information and Communication Technologies

Many theorists believe that advances in communication technologies offer a great opportunity for broad swaths of the citizenry to at last gain meaningful access to the important decision-making processes that have traditionally been dominated by elites. (Elites can of course encompass everyone from heads of large Silicon Valley tech firms to bosses of major labor unions.) Especially when it comes to digital technology, some claim that the unique user and community-centered aspects of digital media technology, and thus its decentralized structures, offer hope for meaningful deliberative activities.[1] Daniel Kreiss offers support for this viewpoint when he shows how digital media expertise altered Democratic Party processes, from the expansion and streamlining of fundraising to the harnessing of more efficient platforms to mobilize for rallies, turnout initiatives, and other offline events.[2] This, in turn, enabled increased oversight of policy development and implementation practices. Daniel Halpern's experiments suggest that even if participants on White House and US government Facebook and YouTube pages do not receive responses from authorities, they find that deliberations with other commentators raise their sense of self-efficacy.[3] David Karpf illustrates how backchannel networking can create informal institutions that mimic—or compete with—formal channels of political communication.[4] Karpf's most recent volume explains the emergence of greater deliberative and participatory opportunities resulting from the coalescence of "organizational substrates" (individual loci for multi-issue mobilization) and the processes of "sedimentation" (the cumulative building of human infrastructure, tactics, and reputation). He also underscores backchanneling's importance, arguing that while modern political networks may appear more opaque, they are also more porous and amenable to deliberative opportunities within their organizational frameworks.[5] Erik Bucy and Kimberly Gregson study the relationship between forms of participation and their resultant empowerment, concluding that media participation entails "active" and "passive" modes of *participation*, and "symbolic" and "material" modes of *empowerment*. Although digital media engagement is generally associated with passive participation and symbolic rewards, it may actually serve a valuable function as a provider of frequent, ongoing access points.[6] Opportunities to take advantage of such access points enable the continued mass perception of a responsive government. Their line of inquiry certainly resonates with our findings concerning the importance of vicarious and symbolic participation for social media users in presidential forums.

At both the individual level and on a society-wide basis, Manuel Castells has spread a broad theoretical cloak, capturing and uniting many disparate aspects.[7] His sophisticated analysis incorporates levels ranging from neurological to international data, and formulates the notion of mass self-communication. This, he says, "enhances the opportunities for social change, without however defining the content and purpose of such social change. People, meaning ourselves, are angels and demons at the same time, and so our increased capacity to act on society will simply project into the open who we really are in each time/space context."[8] He sapiently observes that power can only be exercised through communication. Although we find this notion vital to understanding uses of social media, we do not embrace essentialist arguments about human nature, personality, or our "true selves." Rather we see attitudes and behaviors, especially communication patterns, emerging from situational variables and interaction across networks. This approach aligns much more with views of Kenneth Gergen[9] and other social constructionists who see meaning arising out of interpersonal communication. The constructivist perspective aids in understanding social media's communitarian aspects and utility for political activism. It also recognizes the often contentious nature of communication. The fact that values, goals, and satisfaction are derivative of interaction explains why increased communication, rather than allowing problems to be productively resolved, often uncovers new problems and sources of friction. This perspective suggests that while social media platforms may succeed as tools for information gathering or agenda broadcasting, the ensuing discord undermines their ability to engender more meaningful collaborative participation. While we cannot delve into the many significant angles of topics such as personal efficacy here, we can posit them as backdrops against which many of the uses of social media for governance discussed in this volume play out.

PRACTICAL LIMITATIONS TO DELIBERATIVE DEMOCRACY

Manifold rationales and examples envision a strong future for advancing ICTs as democratizing tools. Yet there is ample reason for pause and concern about such prognostications. One shortcoming of more optimistic deliberative scholarship is that its postulates rest on the constructive support of formal institutions. Such works are, from many angles, derivatives of Habermasian discourse ethics[10] framed in the context of emerging media technologies. A subset of scholars offer a more nuanced perspective, arguing that digital media activity constitutes a new sphere of contested deliberative terrain, subject to the actions and influences of competing actors in an increasingly complex operational landscape.[11] In terms of actual applications, Beth Noveck, the US Deputy Chief Technology Officer for Open Government,[12] presents a fascinating case study about using self-selected individuals to increase the quality level of patents by involving them in the evaluation of proposed patents. Her system, which was implemented by the federal government, depends on the virtues enunciated by Jurgen Habermas in terms of clear, rational, and open debate and a commitment on the part of all community members to produce quality discourse. Again, the presence of such prerequisites assumes a political terrain that is considerably less complex than the convoluted reality.

POLITICAL COMMUNICATION SCHOLARSHIP

Some scholars have taken note of these complexities, developing theories that argue that the Internet and other novel variants of communication technology are overrated commodities, vulnerable to discrimination in access, inequalities of skill, reflexive communication (i.e., seeking information and reacting to information based on preexisting preferences), corporate domination, or increasingly sophisticated state surveillance.[13] After more than a decade of rather narrow focus on the application of digital media technology to deliberative discourse ethics, more recent scholarship has embraced a diversity of theoretical pathways. Matthew Hindman's[14] penetrating work reveals how discourse remains concentrated among a few major (often corporate) actors, and the idea of a citizen voice being heard remains as remote as ever. He explains that control of political matters is not diminishing, but rather undergoing a formatting change: "the Internet is not eliminating exclusivity in political life; instead it is shifting the bar of exclusivity from the *production* to the *filtering* of political information."[15] In addition to altering the positioning of gatekeepers, Hindman argues that participatory imbalances of voice and reach are further magnified online when one considers actual readership, as opposed to the simple creation, of political information.[16] In a May 2013 interview, Hindman told us that even in the few years since his book was written, the situation has deteriorated further. Blogging has been normalized and professionalized, with virtually no chance of an ordinary person gaining a significant audience: "there is now a total lockout of non-professionals at the top of blogosphere."

Other scholarship supports the emergence of more skeptical appraisals. Bucy and Gregson, while noting the relevance of certain types of passive participation, nevertheless raise critical questions about actualized versus perceived efficacy, questions that strike at the heart of social media's impact as a tool of deliberative democracy. Kay Schlozman, Sidney Verba and Henry Brady find that online forms of engagement reproduce the socioeconomic stratification of offline forms.[17] This stratification is less pronounced among younger (and newer) users, but technology merely reduces the gap—it does not erase it. Peter Dahlgren and Margaret Kohn both argue that deliberative models of digital engagement favor existing channels of elite communication.[18] Hubertus Buchstein argues that the Internet is more useful for understanding opinion-formation than it is for understanding actual decision-making, with less impact as a creator of new spheres than as a support to existing institutions of information flow.[19] Lincoln Dahlberg finds that offline limits to inclusivity will circumscribe online deliberative space.[20] Continuing with the concept of the ongoing role of offline factors, Karpf holds that organizational strength depends not only on leadership strength but also on membership network strength, which varies considerably based on whether its members are "issue grazers" or "niche specialists," as well as the match between membership type and the operational outlook of the organization.[21] Øystein Sæbø, Jeremy Rose, and Leif Skiftenes Flak examine the importance of information control, asserting that authorities can selectively choose formats and topics that promote agendas or target involvement in manageable ways.[22] Stephen Coleman and Peter Shane illustrate the presence of institutional barriers to deliberative potential due to the rise of new intermediaries.[23] James Bohman goes a step beyond Dahlgren and Kohn, arguing that a vibrant deliberative sphere of digital media engagement is only possible with the support of formal institutions, maintaining that institutions are necessary because they can establish norms of equal access and community conduct.[24]

While Karpf and Kreiss provide compelling insights into the detailed mechanics of expanded opportunities for deliberation and participation, it should be emphasized that they approach these questions from the perspectives of actors and organizations who are proactively mobilizing around citizen-centered objectives. Our analysis addresses such questions with an eye toward formally empowered actors engaged in the practice of governance rather than citizens engaged in the practice of advocacy. Getting their candidate elected helps alignment campaigns,[25] but once the candidate is elected solidarity quickly frays in terms of what specific objectives and tactics should be pursued. As our case studies and interviews illustrated, the opportunities for fissure are markedly more prominent during the years between elections, and the alignment that engenders normally fluid participatory dynamics is much more vulnerable to friction, backlash, and counter-reactive controls. Absent the existential common grounds of an election, and the limited collective that consists exclusively of campaign or Administration proponents, the resolution of such alignment breakdowns over public input becomes massively more complex.

Lastly, many deliberative scenarios rest on the specific preconditions of open access and responsive legal structures. While such baselines can be established under experimental conditions, they do not exist "in the wild" of ordinary human existence. Thus experts are likely to encounter substantial difficulties in transposing findings from controlled settings to the rough-and-tumble world of politics, and social media are not exempt from this cautionary note.

PRESIDENTIAL SCHOLARSHIP

Subfields of American political studies also offer insights for our work. While these theories were developed without reference to social media phenomena, they nevertheless point to underlying forces and broader dynamics of power and legitimacy.

The pioneering work of Richard Neustadt on the "persuasive presidency" held that while presidents could issue direct appeals, using force weakens the president. Samuel Kernell challenges Neustadt, arguing that the president's ability to "go public" can supplant the pluralist imperative of bargaining to accomplish key objectives.[26] Though Kernell agrees that going public is a last resort, he articulates the realities of the individualized presidency, the rising number of active players in complicating bargaining processes, and the advent of technology in facilitating direct public appeals. Examining these factors through the lens of social media suggests that digital media formats constitute a further extension of the original concept of "going public." This vision suggests that the increasingly overt, individualized presidency would be accordingly effective at embracing social media tools for information gathering and policy broadcasting in particular.

William Howell argues that collaborative bargaining models err by placing the president on the periphery of policy-making.[27] Most importantly, Howell sees that presidents can exercise a wealth of unilateral powers, circumventing Congress, for example, via executive orders or recess appointments. These kinds of unilateral moves can be aided by social media platforms simply as a tool of public appeal; yet they can also tap the act of engagement as part of a larger strategy by consolidating executive power by using social media to secure a strong base of public support for the person of the president. Whereas Kernell focuses more on the application of presidential power in accordance with strategically selected issues, and "climate," Howell considers distal patterns as largely dependent on the president's own initiative. Applying this model, presidents can deploy social media interfaces to expand the parameters of information acquisition and policy broadcasting, with no significant growth in meaningful collaborative communication.

In applying different theoretical models to the potential outcomes of the White House's digital media outreach projects, it is worthwhile to move beyond the individual dynamics of unilateralism, bargaining, or public appeals and examine the broader complexities of the universe in which every president must operate. Analyzing the personal qualities and political environs that influence the presidency, Fred Greenstein offers four analytical dimensions, which, though predating the emergence of digital media forms, are nonetheless helpful to understanding the questions and problems at hand. These are: (1) though having greater formal and informal powers at their disposal, modern presidents risk greater backlash if they miscalculate the application of these powers; (2) despite being the primary agenda-setters of national policy, modern presidents inevitably set unreachable expectations; (3) while having the resources of larger administrative staffs, modern presidents are also more vulnerable to the dissent or indiscretions of their staffs (and here we would add the nature of digital media and contemporary journalism as further exacerbating factors); and (4) although they enjoy far greater visibility than any individual legislator, modern presidents are far more exposed to scapegoating.[28]

Greenstein's encapsulations are not only prescient—they coordinate well with the potential outcomes offered by other theorists. The reception of an online petition, interactive news feed, blog, or tweet could easily prompt backlash based on misapplied content, timing, wording, placement, or other factors. The ease of using social media technology could easily invite overestimation of feasible policy goals or hasty commitment to ill-conceived policy positions. The issue of larger staff is likewise related to the ease of use with respect to social media technology—larger staff create more points of access, which, in turn, engender a far wider array of opportunities for individual misjudgments to affect the presidency at large. And, certainly, the broad, horizontal nature of social media platforms and their very public integration with news outlets, aggregator sites, and other sharing interfaces allows for prolific criticism of the president from virtually infinite points of origination. The president certainly benefits from the expanded resources of the modern White House, but is also more prone to errors and risks that can undermine his legitimacy and power.

Offering one of the more comprehensive forays into combined analysis, Stephen Skowronek's concept of "political time" is useful for considering the dynamics of a presidency and the challenges before it. This concept considers a president's ability to lead as a function of not just initiative or circumstances, but political reality in the context of major events, public mood, and electoral cleavages.[29] Broader economic, social, and geopolitical externalities collide with the prior legacies of the White House, Congress, and the electorate to create eras of "political time" in which specific "political orders" are ascendant, descendant, or stable.[30] Skowronek describes these eras as: (1) disjunction (when a deteriorating political order is no longer capable of addressing national issues); (2) reconstruction (when a new political order has been installed); (3) articulation (when an existing political order has been affirmed); and (4) preemption (when a dominant political order is in conflict with the White House and, at times, the public). In a disjunctive model, the pursuit of any social media initiatives by the president would constitute little more than an afterthought to a failed administration. In a reconstructive model, the president would be able to successfully implement ambitious social media-based outreach programs, and would be freer to expand the reach of these programs into new terrain with more consequential policy relevance. In the category of articulation, the president's pursuit of new digital engagement strategies could trigger opposition, either from his base, or from the opposing party. A preemptive president could expect the pursuit of social media engagement projects to be similarly caught in a web of criticism between his own base and his opposition. Obviously, it is yet unclear whether Barack Obama is presiding during a period of articulation or preemption, but what is clear is that his digital engagement strategies—along with many other policies—are subject to reactive critique from both his base and his opposition, limiting his maneuverability, but never severely impeding his power as chief executive.

MEDIA AND PUBLIC OPINION SCHOLARSHIP

How presidents use the media to influence public opinion and voter behavior has been deeply explored. Benjamin Page and Robert Shapiro contend that media's ability to shape public opinion is negligible compared to larger, less controllable events such as the economy or wars.[31] With reference to our "homo economicus" model discussed in chapter 11, Anthony Downs, as well as Donald Kinder and D. Roderick Kiewiet, hold that public opinion and electoral decisions are shaped by rational, utility-maximizing actors.[32] In contrast, Angus Campbell, Philip Converse, Warren Miller, and Donald Stokes see public opinion and voter behavior as irrational phenomena, shaped largely by socialization and, often, by misperceptions of one's factual environs.[33] John Zaller, building on the work of Converse et al., sees the media as an intermediary between voters and elites.[34] Further, by determining the exposure and salience of issues, media play a major role in shaping public opinion, and the public responds to these formulations (the "Receive-Accept-Sample," or RAS model). Shanto Iyengar and Donald Kinder have explicated the priming, framing, and agenda-setting processes of the media in affecting public opinion.[35] Samuel Popkin sees the media actors playing an intermediary role by pushing the public to form opinions based on "information shortcuts."[36] An argument made by strong social media optimists[37] is that advancing communication technologies will be able to finally break elite and special interest controls, and allow the foundational beliefs of the public to directly affect major policy decisions. However, there is little reason to believe that the phenomena of priming, framing, agenda-setting, RAS-based information processing, and information shortcuts are invalidated in digital media formats simply because of the relative nascence of the interface. The link between media and public opinion research as they collectively relate to contemporary social media engagement questions is perhaps better illustrated in the context of even earlier mass media scholarship. Harold Lasswell's seminal 1948 work on mass media provides some of the most persistently relevant guidance on the relationships between mass media platforms, government power and popular behavior. He ascribes three roles to mass media institutions: *surveillance* of people, organizations and events, *interpretation* about meanings, context and consequences, and *socialization* of the populace through the conveyance of basic shared values and ideological orientations. In Lasswell's appraisal, these three functions of mass media ultimately serve a purpose that symbiotically integrates the objectives of elite actors and institutions, namely, the continued popular support of existing power structures. The dynamics of information flow and elite actors combine with the dynamics of gratification, perceptions of security and vicarious participation, thus confirming, en masse, ongoing commitment to the status quo of the political system. Lasswell's profound insights should be considered when analyzing the dynamics of information flow and mass participation in the context of social media. Furthermore, his theories of mass media functions suggest that the actual extent of social media's divergence from traditional mass media should be scrutinized more closely. Lasswell's three functions of mass media resurface not only in the television and public opinion research of Iyengar, Kinder, Zaller, and others, but also in our case studies and other examples, where modalities of information gathering, propaganda and collaboration can ultimately be harnessed for purposes very much in line with his modeling. Therefore, they will likely remain powerful components in any efforts to alter or expand the landscape of information gathering, policy broadcasting, or collaboration with the public.

CIVIC ENGAGEMENT SCHOLARSHIP

We can also draw on the corpus of American political theory to place civic engagement theories in the context of social media technology. Robert Putnam argues that civic engagement has eroded due to declining social capital, citing the decreased robustness of associational bonds, but he does not explicitly distinguish between formal and informal modes of associational life.[38] Yet this distinction is essential for comparing engagement via older and newer media forms. It is conceivable that despite the erosion of traditional patterns of associational life, less formal emergent patterns could be indicative of a greater ability to meaningfully engage with the public on important policy issues given the innovative information flows of new communication platforms. Like Putnam, Verba, Schlozman, and Brady also decry the decline in American civic life, but offer an additional consideration—associational networks are likely to be sought out by the more educated, affluent segments of the citizenry who are also more likely to be enmeshed in networks already versed in civic skills.[39] It should be asked whether social media formats offer any such opportunities to either develop these necessary networks or help imbue citizens with new civic skills. While social media are often viewed as independent, autonomous, free-form modes of communication, Theda Skocpol, Marshall Ganz, and Ziad Munson provide a helpful counter-narrative to this view.[40] They contest Toqueville's notions that the country has been built (and from the perspective of his followers today, rests) on a bedrock of voluntary, spontaneous, localized participatory networks. By extension, contrary to this thesis of organic aggregation and action, one could question social media's role as an associational "glue" that allows people to join together for community activities. Indeed, given their belief in federal leadership of communities, might not social media become an avenue through which viable civic networks may materialize? This is a point of profound concern, and a topic that we considered in the final chapter.

The consensus on the value of civic engagement is not universal. Morris Fiorina argues that the growth in access to civic participation forums has witnessed a parallel growth in dissatisfaction with government.[41] The net result is that more extreme elements of the population participate in public conversation at disproportionately high levels. Fiorina's warnings highlight the difficulty that any administration might encounter with a truly open online engagement platform. Such a platform could be counterproductive by offering a forum to fringe elements, exacerbating friction without fostering either mutual understanding or policy progress, undermining the hope that these new tools would promote meaningful engagement on important national issues.

DIGITAL MEDIA AND TRANSPARENCY

In recent years, general theorizing about deliberative democracy has yielded research on the specific possibility that social media platforms can engender more responsible, competent, and accountable institutions of state power. John Carlo Bertot, Paul T. Jaeger, and Justin M. Grimes argue that despite their risks of being disruptive or unwieldy, ICTs have the potential to foster government transparency through "a combination of political will and technology."[42] Jaeger and Bertot, in a companion study, explain that Barack Obama "campaigned with a heavy focus on information policy," and included promises of greatly increased government transparency and "new means of access to government information."[43] Their study echoes calls for parallel exertions of political will and innovation, focusing largely on structural and regulatory logistics. Regulatory modernization was emphasized in a later paper by Bertot, Jaeger, and Derek Hansen, who express concern that an obstacle to transparency is the inability of regulatory practices to keep pace with ICT advancement.[44] Just as scholars of deliberative democracy too often neglect the critical normative questions of mass participation, much of the recent scholarship on ICT-enabled transparency suffers from a similar lapse, dwelling on the mechanical questions of technology and organization rather than the more difficult question of whether mass participation is desirable in the first place.

TAPPING THE ORGANIZING POWER OF SOCIAL MEDIA

The growing use of the Internet and the World Wide Web by governments for delivering information and services to citizens has led scholars such as Jaeger to claim that e-government has at least theoretically made it possible for "a great number of people over a wide distance to participate in the democratic process."[45] Castells analyzes the transformative qualities of evolving power and network relationships.[46] Katz's analysis, a decade earlier,[47] considers the process of extending oneself through communication media and amplifying oneself and laying an interpersonal basis for the large-scale transformations through digital devices (especially mobile ones) and network infrastructures. Social media gave engaged citizens the power to meet virtually, a crucial step in facilitating political discussion and raising awareness of collective problems.[48] However, Zaller, Iyengar, Kinder, and others soberly remind us that information flows overwhelmingly from elite actors and institutions who can wield the influence associated with their prominence and resources.[49]

What we can conclude from this literature review is that the uses of social media for citizen engagement are integral to a longer-standing set of democratic trends that are fostered by advances in communication technology. These trends, which sometimes operate in conflict with one another, include free-expression, inclusion, deliberation, behavioral monitoring, and social control. Thus the analysis we present in this volume both fits with and expands upon a body of scholarship addressing political power, information, participation, and citizenship.

NOTES

1 INTRODUCTION AND OVERVIEW

1. Remarks by the President Presenting New Management Agenda, July 8, 2013, http://www.whitehouse.gov/the-press-office/2013/07/08/remarks-president-presenting-new-management-agenda (July 17, 2013); emphasis added.
2. This wide-ranging collection of significant personalities includes Google's Eric Schmidt, Facebook's Chris Hughes, Harvard's Robert Putnam and Lawrence Lessig, and the former head of the Federal Communications Commission (FCC) Julius Genachowski.
3. John Perry Barlow, "Is there a there in Cyberspace?" *Utne Reader* 68 (1995): 53–56; Y. Benkler, *The Wealth of Networks: How Social Production Transforms Markets and Freedom* (New Haven: Yale University Press, 2006); Stephen Clift, "E-democracy, E-governance and Public Net-Work," Publicus.net (2003) http://www.publicus.net/articles/edempublicnetwork.html; Stephen Coleman and John Gøtze, *Bowling Together: Online Public Engagement in Policy Deliberation* (London: Hansard Society, 2001), 39–50; A. Michael Froomkin, "Habermas@discourse.net: Toward a Critical Theory of Cyberspace," *Harvard Law Review* 116, no. 3 (2003): 749–873; Daniel Lathrop and Laurel Ruma, *Open Government: Collaboration, Transparency, and Participation in Practice* (Sebastopol, CA: O'Reilly Media, 2010); Gwanhoo Lee and Young Hoon Kwak, "An Open Government Maturity Model for Social Media-Based Public Engagement," *Government Information Quarterly* 29, no. 4 (2012): 492–503; Tim O'Reilly, "Government As a Platform," *Innovations* 6, no. 1 (2011): 13–40; Mark Poster, "The Internet As a Public Sphere?" *Wired* January (1995): 19–27; Douglas Rushkoff, *Open Source Democracy: How Online Communication Is Changing Offline Politics* (London: Demos, 2003); Don Tapscott, Anthony Williams, and Dan Herman, *Government 2.0: Transforming Government and Governance for the Twenty-First Century* (Austin: nGenera Insight, 2008), http://wiki.dbast.com/images/a/aa/Transforming_govt.pdf (August 15, 2013).
4. Gerald Stourzh, *Alexander Hamilton and the Idea of Republican Government* (Palo Alton: Stanford University Press, 1970); Lance Banning, "Jeffersonian Ideology Revisited: Liberal and Classical Ideas in the New American Republic," *The William and Mary Quarterly* Third Series, 43, no. 1 (January 1986): 3–19.
5. Ronald Chernow, *Alexander Hamilton* (New York: Penguin, 2004).
6. Philip N. Howard, *New Media Campaigns and the Managed Citizen* (New York: Cambridge University Press, 2006), 184–189; Examples of the fragments that create data shadows could range from overt expressions of support for a candidate on social media profiles or comments on a major political news story, to more subtle indicators

of preference, such as Amazon purchasing history, reviews on Yelp, or details on home or car ownership.

7. Howard, *New Media Campaigns and the Managed Citizen*, 187.

8. "The people, especially when moderately instructed, are the only safe [sic], because the only honest, depositaries of the public rights, and should therefore be introduced into the administration of them in every function to which they are sufficient;" Thomas Jefferson to Adamantios Coray, October 31, 1823.

9. Hamilton's coauthor of the *Federalist Papers*, James Madison, wrote, "Had every Athenian citizen been a Socrates, every Athenian assembly would still have been a mob. *Federalist No. 55*. Jacob E. Cooke, *The Federalist* (Middletown, CT: Wesleyan University Press, 1961), 374.

10. For an erudite treatment of this topic, see Fred Turner, *From Counterculture to Cyberculture: Stewart Brand, the Whole Earth Network, and the Rise of Digital Utopianism* (Chicago: University of Chicago Press, 2008).

11. Thus it is the political reception and use of this idea that is our focus, rather than the testing and evaluation of formal social scientific hypotheses. Though we offer snapshots of clashing theoretical perspectives, our emphasis is decidedly on the exploration of a topical area rich with consequences for political activity and the nature of citizenship.

2 SITUATING SOCIAL MEDIA AND CITIZEN PARTICIPATION IN THE OBAMA ERA

1. Morton Frisch (ed.), *Selected Writings and Speeches of Alexander Hamilton* (Washington, DC: American Enterprise Institute, 1985).

2. Thomas Jefferson to George Washington, 1786. Quoted in Henry J. Perkinson, *Two Hundred Years of American Educational Thought* (New York: David McKay, 1976), 44.

3. We also use it to include digital communication that is used for social (i.e., human centric) communication among people. Hence modalities such as email would be encompassed by our term. Nowadays email is not necessarily a horizontally integrated tool; it is integrated into people's communication devices and profiles and other sites that are socially mediated, and thus can be included in our broader connotation of the phrase "social media" that a strict constructionist might disagree with. But we find this broader connotation useful, and that an attempt to restrict the term's usage would also reduce its heuristic power in this context.

4. Michael Powell, "Obama, the Populist," *New York Times*, April 1, 2008, http://the caucus.blogs.nytimes.com/2008/04/01/obama-the-populist/ (August 13, 2011).

5. "A Call to Serve": Remarks in Mt. Vernon, IA. December 5, 2007, http://www .presidency.ucsb.edu/ws/?pid=77024 (August 12, 2013).

6. Barack Obama in Indianapolis, IN. April 30, 2008, http://www.youtube.com/watch? v=WyNzC9W2C8Q (July 21, 2013).

7. Caroline McCarthy, "Gore: Electrifying Redemption, Thanks to the Web," *CNET*, November 7, 2008, http://news.cnet.com/8301-13577_3-10087795-36.html (December 28, 2011).

8. Arianna Huffington, of the left-leaning Huffington Post website, claimed: "If not for the Internet, Barack Obama would not be President or even the Democratic Nominee," *New York Times*, November 7, 2008, http://bits.blogs.nytimes.com/2008 /11/07/how-obamas-internet-campaign-changed-politics/ (December 30, 2011).

9. Antonio Jose Vargas, "Obama Raised Half a Billion Online," *Washington Post*, November 20, 2008, http://voices.washingtonpost.com/44/2008/11/20/obama _raised_half_a_billion_on.html (September 5, 2011).

10. Kate Albright-Hanna, interview, May 31, 2013.

11. Barack Obama, Remarks by the President in Welcoming Senior Staff and Cabinet Secretaries to the White House, January 21, 2009, http://www.whitehouse.gov/the -press-office/remarks-president-welcoming-senior-staff-and-cabinet-secretaries -white-house (August 12, 2013).

12. Within political science, several books have highlighted the impact of the Internet on elections. Phil Howard's *New Media Campaigns and the Managed Citizen* (New York: Cambridge University Press, 2006) provides an important analysis of the shadows of data created by campaigning; Costas Panagopoulos (ed.), *Politicking Online: The Transformation of Election Campaign Communications* (New Brunswick, NJ: Rutgers University Press, 2009) includes detailed empirical analysis of the Internet in the 2008 election. Bruce A. Bimber and Richard Davis's *Campaigning Online: The Internet in U.S. Elections* (New York: Oxford University Press, 2003) follows the same tradition, as does Kirsten Foot and Steven M. Schneider's *Web Campaigning (Acting with Technology)* (Cambridge: MIT Press, 2006). Our focus is much less on election cycles and much more on the governance process, except where the former intersects with social media for citizen engagement.

13. See endnotes 2 and 3 in chapter 1.

14. Gianpietro Mazzolini (ed.), Julianne Steward, and Bruce Horsfield, "The Media and the Growth of Neo-Populism in Contemporary Democracies," *The Media and Neo-Populism: A Contemporary Comparative Analysis*, ed. Gianpietro Mazzoleni, Julianne Steward, and Bruce Horsfield (Westport, CT: Greenwood, 2003), 1–20.

15. David Sarno, "Obama, the First Social Media President," *Los Angeles Times*, November 18, 2008, http://latimesblogs.latimes.com/technology/2008/11/obama-the-first.html (April 25, 2012).

16. David Carr, "How Obama Tapped into Social 'Networks' Power," *New York Times*, November 10, 2008, http://www.nytimes.com/2008/11/10/business/media/10carr .html?_r=2&oref=slogin&ref=business&pagewanted=print (August 4, 2011).

17. Vargas, "Obama Raised Half A Billion Online."

18. Needless to say, there are many other conceptualizations of the relationship between the government and social media information flows. For instance, Nam proposes a tripartite division: purpose (image-making or ideation), collective intelligence type (professional knowledge or innovative ideas), and strategy (contest, wiki, social networking, or social voting). Taewoo Nam, "Suggesting Frameworks of Citizen-Sourcing via Government 2.0," *Government Information Quarterly* 29, no. 1 (2012): 12–20.

19. Macon Phillips, interview, July 16, 2013.

20. Howard, *New Media Campaigns and the Managed Citizen*, 187–189.

21. For a broader review of these topics, see Stephen Coleman and Peter M. Shane (eds.), *Connecting Democracy: Online Consultation and the Flow of Political Communication* (Cambridge, MA: MIT Press, 2012).

3   DIGITAL MEDIA AND ELECTORAL POLITICS: AN ABBREVIATED HISTORY

1. Sidney Blumenthal, *The Permanent Campaign* (New York: Simon and Schuster, 1982); Norman Ornstein and Thomas Mann, *The Permanent Campaign and its Future* (Washington, DC: American Enterprise Institute Press, 2000).

2. Daniel Kreiss, *Taking Our Country Back: The Crafting of Networked Politics from Howard Dean to Barack Obama* (London: Oxford University Press, 2012.).

3. Stephen Ponder, *Managing the Press: Origins of the Media Presidency, 1897–1933* (New York: Macmillan, 1999).

4. Diana Owen and Richard Davis, "Presidential Communication in the Internet Era." *Presidential Studies Quarterly* 38, no. 4 (2008): 658–673.

5. James E. Katz and Ronald E. Rice, *Social Consequences of Internet Use: Access, Involvement, and Interaction* (Cambridge: MIT Press, 2002).

6. Richard Wiggins, "The Unnoticed Presidential Transition," *First Monday* 6 (2001): 1–8.

7. See: Robert E. Denton, *The 1996 Presidential Campaign: A Communication Perspective* (Westport: Praeger, 1998); and Diana Owen, Richard Davis, and Vincent James Strickler, "Congress and the Internet." *The Harvard International Journal of Press/Politics* 4, no. 2 (1999): 10–29.

8. The 1996 Election cycle coincided with Executive Order 13011, issued in July 1996. This order directed the various component agencies of the executive branch to establish communication systems for interagency support, sharing information and best practices, and reducing redundancies (cited in Owen and Davis, 2008, 661).

9. Rita Kirk Whillock, "Digital Democracy: The'96 Presidential Campaign," in *The 1996 Presidential Campaign: A Communication Perspective*, ed. R. E. Denton (Westport: Praeger, 1998), 179.

10. Bruce A. Williams and Michael X. Delli Carpini, "Monica and Bill All the Time and Everywhere: The Collapse of Gatekeeping and Agenda Setting in the New Media Environment," *American Behavioral Scientist* 47, no. 9 (2004): 1208–1230.

11. White House Memorandum on Electronic Government. December 17, 1999, www.gsa.gov/…/ogp/egov_memo_12_R2E-cL-l_0Z5RDZ-i34K-pR.doc (August 5, 2013).

12. David Almacy, interview, July 22, 2013.

13. Almacy, interview.

14. Declan McCullagh, "Expert Analyzes White House Site," *Wired*, January 23, 2001, http://www.wired.com/print/politics/law/news/2001/01/41325.

15. Jimmy Orr, interview, August 5, 2013

16. Orr, interview.

17. Almacy, interview.

18. Orr, interview.

19. Almacy, interview.

20. Almacy, interview.

21. Wendy Macias, Karen Hilyard, and Vicki Freimuth, "Blog Functions as Risk and Crisis Communication during Hurricane Katrina," *Journal of Computer-Mediated Communication* 15, no. 1 (2009): 1–31.

22. Douglas Kellner, "The Katrina Hurricane Spectacle and Crisis of the Bush Presidency," *Cultural Studies↔ Critical Methodologies* 7, no. 2 (2007): 222–234.

23. Teddy Goff, interview, July 18, 2013.

24. Brian Stelter, "The Facebooker who Befriended Obama," *New York Times*, July 7, 2008, http://www.nytimes.com/2008/07/07/technology/07hughes.html?pagewanted=all (April 15, 2011).

25. Ellen McGirt, "How Chris Hughes Helped Launch Facebook and the Barack Obama Campaign," *Fast Company*, April 1, 2009, http://www.fastcompany.com/magazine/134/boy-wonder.html (March 6, 2011).

26. McGirt, "How Chris Hughes Helped."

27. James E. Katz, "I Media, la Democrazia, e l'Amministrazione Obama: La Speranza, Senza Cambiamento?" *Comunicazione Politica* (Bologna) 10, no. 3 (2009): 421–431.

28. Katz, "I media."
29. Kreiss, *Taking our Country Back.*
30. Jose Antonio Vargas, "Obama Raised Half a Billion Online," *44: Politics and Policy in Obama's Washington: The Washington Post,* November 20, 2008, http://voices.washingtonpost.com/44/2008/11/obama-raised-half-a-billion-on.html.
31. Katz, I media.
32. Katz, I media.
33. Katz, I media.
34. Katz, I media.
35. The Elegantologist, "Fashion Police," Easy and Elegant Life, January 19, 2009, http://easyandelegantlife.com/2009/01/fashion-police/ (December 30, 2011).
36. Chris Hughes, "Moving Forward on My.BarackObama," November 7, 2008, http://groups.dowire.org/groups/us/messages/topic/2PDYZilSlHatn7BRvu0Mzc (July 21, 2013).
37. Kreiss, *Taking our Country Back.*
38. The practice of tracking voters on strike lists and following up on their progress dates back well over a century. In the yesteryear of more dubious election practices, precinct and ward bosses retained the services of various strains of "volunteers" and "contractors" to provide the necessary "encouragement" that ensured proper turnout.
39. See: Lois Beckett, "Everything We Know (So Far) about Obama's Big Data Tactics," *ProPublica* (November 29, 2012), http://http://www.propublica.org/article/everything-we-know-so-far-about-obamas-big-data-operation; Ruby Cramer, "Messina: Obama Won on the Small Stuff," *BuzzFeed* (November 9, 2012), http://http://www.buzzfeed.com/rubycramer/messina-obama-won-on-the-small-stuff-4xvn; Jon Ekdahl, "The Unmitigated Disaster Known as Project ORCA," Ace of Spades HQ (November 8, 2012), http://ace.mu.nu/archives/334783.php; Sasha Issenberg, "How President Obama's Campaign Used Big Data to Rally Individual Voters," *MIT Technology Review* (December 19, 2012), http://www.technologyreview.com/featuredstory/509026/how-obamas-team-used-big-data-to-rally-voters.
40. Eric Fehrnstrom, interview, July 16, 2013.
41. Fehrnstrom, interview.
42. Rosenblatt, interview, July 30, 2013.
43. Rosenblatt, interview.
44. Jeff Howe, interview, August 6, 2013.

4 FRAMING THE "PEOPLE'S WHITE HOUSE": CROWDSOURCING AND THE CITIZEN'S BRIEFING BOOK

1. David Carr, "How Obama Tapped into Social Networks' Power," *New York Times,* November 9, 2008, http://www.nytimes.com/2008/11/10/business/media/10carr.html (May 2, 2012).
2. There are some fascinating parallels between this case and President Obama's bid to address the nation's schoolchildren in the fall of 2009. Though the Administration argued that the President merely wanted to encourage and inspire young people, he was roundly criticized by those who disagreed with his ideology for attempting to propagandize a new generation of potential Democratic voters. Though not identical, both instances suggest a disconnect over an insensitivity to power relationships when the White House is attempting to "get its message out."

3. Jeff Howe, "The Rise of Crowdsourcing," *Wired*, June 2006, http://www.wired.com/wired/archive/14.06/crowds.html (June 3, 2011).

4. Daren Brabham, "Crowdsourcing as a Model for Problem Solving: An Introduction and Cases," *Convergence: International Journal of Research into New Media Technologies* 14, no. 1 (2008): 75–90.

5. Alek Felstiner, "Working the Crowd: Employment and Labor Law in the Crowdsourcing Industry," *Berkeley Journal of Employment and Labor Law* 32, no. 1 (July 5, 2011), http://works.bepress.com/alek_felstiner/1 (December 29, 2011).

6. Jeff Howe, interview, August 6, 2013.

7. "About the Project," in *Peer to Peer* website, no date, http://peertopatent.tumblr.com/abouttheproject (December 31, 2011).

8. Beth Simone Noveck, *Wiki Government: How Technology Can Make Government Better, Democracy Stronger, and Citizens More Powerful* (Washington, DC: Brookings Institution Press, 2009), 13

9. Geoff Brumfiel, "US Patent Office Ponders Peer Scrutiny," *Nature*, May 15, 2006, http://www.nature.com/news/2006/060515/full/news060515–4.html (August 13, 2013).

10. Noveck, *Wiki Government*, 18.

11. Noveck, *Wiki Government*, 20.

12. Office of the President-Elect, "Your Seat at the Table," December 5, 2008, http://change.gov/newsroom/entry/seat_at_the_table/ (July 13, 2011).

13. Office of the President-Elect, "Your Seat at the Table."

14. Kate Albright-Hannah, "Inside the Transition: Technology, Information and Government Reform," January 19, 2009, http://change.gov/newsroom/entry/inside_the_transition_technology_innovation_and_government_reform/.

15. CIOL Bureau, "Obama Team Goes Online with Salesforce: Change.gov Website Provides Open Forum for American People to Present their Ideas to the President-elect and Cabinet," January 19, 2008, http://www.ciol.com/Enterprise/News-Reports/Obama-team-goes-online-with-Salesforce/19109114941/0/ (December 30, 2011).

16. Valerie Jarrett, "Introduction to the Citizen's Briefing Book," *YouTube video file*, January 14, 2009, http://www.youtube.com/watch?v=KEVZCNp-66c (July 12, 2011).

17. Dan McSwain, "Wrapping up the Citizen's Briefing Book," *Change.gov*, January 16, 2009 http://change.gov/newsroom/entry/wrapping_up_the_citizens_briefing_book/ (May 2, 2012).

18. Michael Strautmanis, "Thank You for Contributing to the Citizen's Briefing Book," *YouTube video file*, January 16, 2009, http://www.youtube.com/watch?v=jCK9X7rYExc (June 5, 2011).

19. Dan McSwain, interview, August 12, 2013.

20. McSwain, interview.

21. Nancy Scola, "White House Opens 'Office of Public Engagement,' Releases Citizen's Briefing Book," *techPresident*, May 11, 2009, http://techpresident.com/taxonomy/term/5772 (September 14, 2011).

22. The Office of Public Liaison, "Citizen's Briefing Book: To President Barack Obama from the American People," 2009, http://www.whitehouse.gov/sites/default/files/microsites/Citizens_Briefing_Book_Final2.pdf (May 31, 2011).

23. McSwain, interview.

24. The White House, "The President Introduces the Office of Public Engagement," YouTube video file, May 8, 2009, http://www.youtube.com/watch?v=dx7ZIdvr5fM (June 27, 2011).

25. Nancy Sutley, "Nancy Sutley Reacts to the Citizen's Briefing Book," *YouTube video file*, February 22, 2009, http://www.youtube.com/watch?v=J5dKG-3kVhE (May 25, 2011).

26. Sam Stein, "Obama's Citizen's Briefing Book changes the flow of information," *The Huffington Post*, January 15, 2009, http://www.huffingtonpost.com/2009/01/15/obamas-citizens-briefing_n_158035.html (August 13, 2011).

27. Nancy Scola, "White House Opens Office of Public Engagement, Releases Citizen's Briefing Book," *techPresident*, May 11, 2009, http://techpresident.com/taxonomy/term/5772 (September 14, 2011).

28. Macon Phillips, interview, July 16, 2013.

29. David Almacy, interview, July 22, 2013.

30. McSwain, interview.

5   WHITE HOUSE ONLINE TOWN HALL

1. Cheryl Stolberg, "Obama's Interactive Town Hall Meeting," The Caucus: The Politics and Government blog of *The New York Times*; "Obama's Interactive Town Hall Meeting," *New York Times*, November 10, 2008, http://thecaucus.blogs.nytimes.com/2009/03/26/obamas-interactive-town-hall-meeting/ (June 15, 2011).

2. Mark Lacey, "History is Made by an Old-Fashioned Chief.gov," *New York Times*, November 9, 1999, http://www.nytimes.com/1999/11/09/us/history-is-made-by-an-old-fashioned-chiefgov.html?pagewanted=all&src=pm (December 18, 2011).

3. The White House, "Transparency and Open Government: Memorandum for the Heads of Executive Departments and Agencies," January 21, 2009, http://www.whitehouse.gov (February 3, 2011).

4. "Engage and Connect," http://www.whitehouse.gov/openforquestions/ (December 28, 2011).

5. "Engage and Connect," http://www.whitehouse.gov/openforquestions/ (December 28, 2011).

6. The White House, "Online Town Hall," *YouTube video file*, March 26, 2009, http://www.youtube.com/watch?v=YPPT9pWhivM (July 21, 2011).

7. David Sarno, "Obama Addresses Marijuana Questions in Online Town Hall," March 26, 2009, http://latimesblogs.latimes.com/technology/2009/03/obama-addresses.html (December 29, 2011).

8. Sarno, "Obama addresses."

9. Mitch Wagner, "Obama's Online Town Hall was a Failure of Crowdsourcing," Information Week Government Blogs, April 9, 2009, http://www.informationweek.com/blog/main/archives/2009/04/obamas_online_t.html (February 10, 2011).

10. Jose Antonio Vargas, "The Clickocracy: Normalizing the Internet," *The Washington Post*, March 26, 2009, http://voices.washingtonpost.com/44/2009/03/26/normalizing_the_internet.html (May 7, 2011).

11. The White House, "Online Town Hall."

12. Wagner, "Obama's Online Town Hall was a Failure of Crowdsourcing,"

13. Jeff Howe, "Obama and Crowdsourcing: A Failed Relationship?" *Wired*, April 1, 2009, http://www.wired.com/epicenter/2009/04/obama-and-crowd/ (September 13, 2011).

14. Howe, "Obama and Crowdsourcing: A Failed Relationship?"

15. Jeff Howe, interview, August 6, 2013.

16. Micah Sifry, interview, July 24, 2013.

17. John Wonderlich, interview, June 24, 2011.

18. David Stern, interview, June 27, 2011.

19. Stern, interview.

20. Laurel Ruma, interview, August 4, 2010.

21. "Engage and Connect," http://www.whitehouse.gov/openforquestions/ (December 28, 2011).

22. Stephanie Condon, "Marijuana Dominates Questions for Obama's YouTube Q&A," CBS News. January 27, 2011, http://www.cbsnews.com/8301-503544_162-20029808 -503544.html (December 28, 2011).

23. Sumit Agarwal, interview, August 9, 2010.

24. Ruma, interview.

25. Nate Silver, "Gallup Poll is First to Find Plurality Support for Marijuana Legalization," Five Thirty Eight Blog, NYTimes.com, October 18, 2011, http://fivethirtyeight .blogs.nytimes.com/2011/10/18/gallup-poll-is-first-to-find-plurality-support-for -marijuana-legalization/ (January 15, 2012).

26. Agarwal, interview.

27. Ruma, interview.

28. Sifry, interview.

29. See: Peter Dahlgren, "The Internet, Public Spheres, and Political Communication: Dispersion and Deliberation," *Political Communication* 22, no. 2 (2005): 147–162; Margaret Kohn, "Language, Power, and Persuasion: Toward a Critique of Deliberative Democracy," *Constellations* 7, no. 3 (2002): 408–429; Lincoln Dahlberg, "The Internet and Democratic Discourse: Exploring the Prospects of Online Deliberative Forums Extending the Public Sphere," *Information, Communication & Society* 4, no. 4 (2001).

30. Jennifer Earl and Katrina Kimpor, *Digitally Enabled Social Change: Activism in the Internet Age* (Cambridge: MIT Press, 2011).

31. Sifry, interview.

32. Wonderlich, interview.

6   GRAND CHALLENGES: CROWDSOURCING A VISION FOR SCIENCE AND TECHNOLOGY

1. American Association for the Advancement of Science, "Join the Conversation on the Future of Science," April 20, 2010, http://promo.aaas.org/expertlabs/grandchal lenges.html (August 3, 2011).

2. The White House, "Open Government Directive," December 8, 2009, http://www .whitehouse.gov/open/documents/open-government-directive.html (June 2, 2011); The White House, "Open Government Initiative," December 8, 2009, http://www .whitehouse.gov/open/ (June 2, 2011).

3. Vivek Kundra, "Remarks at Federal Chief Information Officer Council," September 20, 2010, http://www.scribd.com/doc/37802876/201009-Kundra-IT-Management -Federal-CIO-Council (December 30, 2011).

4. American Association for the Advancement of Science, "White House, Via AAAS's Expert Labs, Asks Scientists and Engineers for Their Collective Wisdom," April 13, 2010, http://www.aaas.org/news/releases/2010/0413expertlabs.shtml (December 31, 2011).

5. Anil Dash, "The Most Interesting New Tech Startup of 2009," A Blog About Making Culture weblog, August 14, 2009, http://dashes.com/anil/2009/08/the-most -interesting-new-tech-startup-of-2009.html (March 13, 2011).

6. Gillian Reagan, "Dash to D.C.! Tech Guru Will Head Gov't Incubator, Digitize Democracy," *New York Observer*, November 18, 2009, http://www.observer.com/2009/media/dash-dc-tech-guru-will-head-govt-incubator-digitize-democracy (July 25, 2011).

7. American Association for the Advancement of Science, "Independent Effort to Help Policy-Makers Tap 'Cloud Expertise,' Social-Media Pioneer Anil Dash Says," November 18, 2009, http://www.aaas.org/news/releases/2009/1118expert_labs.shtml (March 13, 2011).

8. Dash, "The Most Interesting New Tech Startup of 2009."

9. Reagan, "Dash to D.C.!"

10. Nancy Scola, "An Interview with Anil Dash, Director of Expert Labs," *techPresident*, April 2, 2010, http://techpresident.com/blog-entry/interview-anil-dash-director-expert-labs (September 13, 2011).

11. Anil Dash, interview, June 27, 2011.

12. Expert Labs, "Grand Challenges Responses," 2010, spreadsheet, https://spreadsheets.google.com/ccc?key=0Akb-7yx3DGIbdFFwX2hvTWN2U2dEN2tXcmExNUVRekE&hl=en#gid=0 (June 2011).

13. Anil Dash, "Grand Challenges: the First Results," weblog post, April 14, 2010, http://expertlabs.org/2010/05/grand-challenges-the-first-results.html (July 7, 2011).

14. Dash, interview.

15. Expert Labs, "Year One Final Report," May 31, 2011 unpublished manuscript.

16. ThinkUp, "New Ideas from Your Online Conversation," http://thinkupapp.com/ (no date), http://thinkupapp.com/ (November 11, 2011)).

17. Nancy Scola, "ThinkUp in the Wild," *techPresident*, October 5, 2010, http://techpresident.com/category/categories/expert-labs (October 29, 2011).

18. Alexander Howard, interview, August 4, 2011.

19. Open Government Initiative, "ExpertNet: Background and Principles," no date, http://expertnet.wikispaces.com/Background+and+Principles (August 14, 2011).

20. Howard, interview.

21. Micah Sifry, "The Obama Disconnect: What Happens When Myth Meets Reality," *techPresident*, December 31, 2009, http://techpresident.com/blog-entry/the-obama-disconnect (July 26, 2013).

22. David Plouffe, *The Audacity to Win: The Inside Story and Lessons of Barack Obama's Historic Victory* (New York: Viking Press, 2009).

23. Anil Dash, Expert Labs Evolution. March 9, 2012, http://expertlabs.org/2012/03/evolution.html (September 21, 2013).

24. Anon. Internet strikes back: Anonymous' Operation Megaupload explained, RT.com, http://rt.com/usa/anonymous-barrettbrown-sopa-megaupload-241/ (September 21, 2013).

25. Alexis Ohanian, "Jan. 18, 2012—The Net Decides We Won't Live With Infamy," *Wired*, January 25, 2012, http://www.wired.com/business/2012/01/guest-ohanian-sopapipa/ (September 21, 2013).

26. David Plouffe cited in Sifry, "The Obama Disconnect."

27. Kathleen Hall Jamieson, Ed., *Electing the President, 2008: The Insiders' View* (Philadelphia: University of Pennsylvania Press, 2009).

28. Ari Melber, "The Nation's Full Interview with David Plouffe," YouTube video file, December 17, 2009, http://www.youtube.com/watch?v=OCwgeRumlXk&feature=player_embedded (December 31, 2011).

29. Nick Judd, "White Boards and Goolsbee vs. Obama and Babies," *techPresident*, June 29, 2011, http://techpresident.com/short-post/white-boards-and-goolsbee-vs-obama-and-babies (November 11, 2011).

30. John Markoff, Obama Seeking to Boost Study of Human Brain. *New York Times,* February 17, 2013, http://www.nytimes.com/2013/02/18/science/project-seeks-to-build-map-of-human-brain.html?pagewanted=all&_r=1& (September 21, 2013).

7   THE SUPREME COURT VACANCIES AND THE HEALTHCARE DEBATE

1. Ariane DeVogue, "White House Prepares for Possibility of 2 Supreme Court Vacancies," *ABC News,* February 4, 2010, http://abcnews.go.com/Politics/Supreme_Court/white-house-prepares-possibility-supreme-court-vacancies/story?id=9740077 (August 31, 2011).
2. Peter Baker and Jo Becker, "Speeches Show Judge's Steady Focus on Diversity and Struggle," *New York Times,* June 4, 2009, http://www.nytimes.com/2009/06/05/us/politics/05court.html (December 27, 2011).
3. Mitch Stewart, "Stand with Sotomayor," *techPresident,* May 31, 2009, http://techpresident.com/feed-item/stand-sotomayor (December 30, 2011).
4. Peter Baker and Jeff Zeleny, "Obama Picks Kagan, a Scholar but not a Judge," *New York Times,* May 5, 2010. www.nytimes.com/2010/05/11/us/politics/11court.html?pagewanted=all (August 12, 2013).
5. Nancy Scola, "Organizing for Elena: Dems Launch Kagan Confirmation HQ," *techPresident,* May 20, 2010, http://techpresident.com/blog-entry/organizing-elena-dems-launch-kagan-confirmation-hq (December 12, 2011).
6. Organizing for America, "Introducing Elena Kagan," *Video file,* no date, http://my.barackobama.com/page/content/kaganforjustice-video (December 30, 2011).
7. William S. Strong, interview, September 11, 2013.
8. Kate Albright-Hanna, interview, May 31, 2013.
9. Macon Phillips, "Facts Are Stubborn Things," White House Blog, August 4, 2009, http://www.whitehouse.gov/blog/Facts-Are-Stubborn-Things (December 30, 2011).
10. FoxNews.com, "White House Move to Collect 'Fishy' Info May Be Illegal, Critics Say," August 7, 2009, http://www.foxnews.com/politics/2009/08/07/white-house-collect-fishy-info-illegal-critics-say/ (December 30, 2011).
11. FoxNews.com, "White House Move."
12. Katharine Seelye, "Talk of 'Enemies List' in Health Care Debate," *New York Times,* August 5, 2009, http://thecaucus.blogs.nytimes.com/2009/08/05/talk-of-enemies-list-in-health-care-debate/?scp=3&sq=macon%20phillips%20and%20%22fishy%22&st=cse (July 12, 2011).
13. FoxNews.com, "White House Makes Security Changes to Web Site Following Complaints Over E-Mails," August 17, 2009, http://www.foxnews.com/politics/2009/08/17/white-house-makes-security-changes-web-site-following-complaints-e-mails/ (September 28, 2011).
14. Jeff Zeleny, "Thousands Rally in Capital to Protest Big Government," *New York Times,* September 12, 2009, http://www.nytimes.com/2009/09/13/us/politics/13protestweb.html (August 22, 2011).
15. Susan Davis, "White House Steps Up Messaging Effort on Health Care," *Wall Street Journal,* August 10, 2009, http://blogs.wsj.com/washwire/2009/08/10/white-house-steps-up-messaging-effort-on-health-care/ (September 13, 2011).
16. The White House, "Get the Facts about the Stability and Security You Get from Health Insurance Reform," Health Insurance Reform Reality Check, http://www.whitehouse.gov/realitycheck/ (December 30, 2011).

17. The White House, "Nancy-Ann DeParle Takes Your Questions on Health Care," *YouTube video file*, September 10, 2009, http://www.youtube.com/watch?v=cUepZ qc8S10&feature=relmfu (December 30, 2011).

18. Alex Howard, interview, August 4, 2011.

19. Chip Reid, "Obama Reneges on Health Care Transparency," *CBS News*, June 1, 2010, http://www.cbsnews.com/stories/2010/01/06/eveningnews/main6064298 .shtml (September 21, 2011).

20. Ben Smith, "The Summer of Astroturf," *Politico*, August 9, 2010, http://www.politico .com/news/stories/0809/26312.html (September 22, 2011).

21. Josh Gerstein, "White House Transparency a Casualty of Budget Talks," *Politico*, July 6, 2011, http://www.politico.com/blogs/joshgerstein/0711/White_House_transparency _a_casualty_of_budget_talks.html (November 12, 2011).

22. *ABC News*, "Transcript: Diane Sawyer Interviews Obama," ABC World News With Diane Sawyer, January 25, 2010, http://abcnews.go.com/WN/Obama/abc -world-news-diane-sawyer-diane-sawyer-interviews/story?id=9659064# .Tv-fdlZxSSo (December 31, 2011).

23. Jeff Howe, "Crowdsourcing and the President: A Failed Marriage?" http://www .crowdsourcing.com/cs/2009/04/crowdsourcing-and-the-president-a-failed-mar riage.html. (August 13, 2013); Kobza, Kim. "FCW Insider: How to Improve the Virtual Town Hall," *Federal Computer Weekly*, March 30, 2009, http://fcw.com /blogs/insider/2009/03/assessing-virtual-town-hall.aspx (August 13, 2013).

24. Lawrence Lessig, "Open Transition Principles," December 2, 2008, http://www .lessig.org/2008/12/open-transition-principles/ (August 13, 2013); Tim O'Reilly, "Put change.gov Under Revision Control!" O'Reilly Radar, November 28, 2008, http://radar.oreilly.com/2008/11/change-gov-revision-control.html (August 13, 2013).

25. Kate Albright-Hanna, interview, May 31, 2013.

8 SOCIAL MEDIA MODALITIES: EXAMPLES AND PATTERNS FROM THE OBAMA WHITE HOUSE

1. Beth Noveck, "Open Government," Lecture at Princeton University's Center for Information Technology and Policy, October 20, 2009.

2. Specifically, the idea is: "If 2,000,000 of the total number of Federal Employees each spend two hours on the Save Award, then the total cost of the Save Award can be estimated based on an hourly rate. Estimating at a rate of $30 per hour, the total cost is $120,000,000. The Save Award must then save more than $120,000,000 in order to break even. By this estimate, savings greater than $120,000,000 must be generated in order for the Save Award to pay for itself." Source: http://saveaward2011.ideascale .com/a/dtd/Make-Save-Award-Pay-for-Itself/265698–10760 (January 8, 2012).

3. http://www.whitehouse.gov/ (January 9, 2012).

4. http://www.whitehouse.gov/ (January 6, 2012).

5. Josh Clark, "How Hillary Clinton works," no date, http://history.howstuffworks .com/american-history/hillary-clinton2.htm (January 7, 2012).

6. Signature Quotes: Politics: Hillary Clinton, http://www.urbin.net/EWW/sigs/HRCsigs .html (January 7, 2012).

7. http://www.whitehouse.gov/engage (January 6, 2012).

8. http://www.whitehouse.gov/blog/2011/10/03/good-problem-have-raising-signature -threshold-white-house-petitions (April 23, 2012).

9. https://petitions.whitehouse.gov/how-why/terms-participation (July 13, 2013).

10. Macon Phillips, "A Good Problem to have: Raising the Signature Threshold for White House Petitions," http://www.whitehouse.gov/blog/2011/10/03/good-problem-have-raising-signature-threshold-white-house-petitions (August 3, 2012).

11. Kenneth Laudon, *Dossier Society: Value Choices in the Design of National Information Systems* (New York: Columbia University Press, 1986).

12. Unidentified Flying Objects——Project Blue Book, US National Archives, http://www.archives.gov/foia/ufos.html (August 16, 2013).

13. https://wwws.whitehouse.gov/petitions#!/response/searching-et-no-evidence-yet (January 7, 2012).

14. http://www.whitehouse.gov/ (January 16, 2012).

15. http://www.dailydot.com/politics/white-house-we-people-petition-response/ (September 13, 2013.)

16. https://petitions.whitehouse.gov/petition/shutdown-petitionswhitehousegov/r5Wbx5hx (July 13, 2013)

17. https://petitions.whitehouse.gov/response/its-time-legalize-cell-phone-unlocking (posted March 23, 2013.)

18. http://www.ntia.doc.gov/files/ntia/publications/ntia_2012_dmca_letter_final.pdf (posted March 23, 2013)

19. Alex Howard, interview, July 18, 2013.

20. Macon Phillips, interview, July 16, 2013.

21. Kori Schulman, "White House Office Hours," July 26, 2011, http://www.whitehouse.gov/blog/2011/07/26/white-house-office-hours (August 3, 2013).

22. Matt Compton, "President Obama Hangs Out with America," January 30, 2012, http://www.whitehouse.gov/blog/2012/01/30/president-obama-hangs-out-america (July 12, 2013).

23. Obama's reaction invoked shades of the clamorous job-seekers who had filled Lincoln's White House waiting room and whom he tried to assuage. "A delegation once called on Mr. Lincoln to ask the appointment of a gentleman as commissioner to the Sandwich Islands......they urged that he was in bad health and a residence in that balmy climate would be of great benefit to him." Lincoln responded, 'Gentlemen, I am sorry to say that there are eight other applicants for that place, and they are all sicker than your man.'" Francis F. Browne, *The Every-Day Life of Abraham Lincoln* (New York: N.D. Thompson Publishing Co., 1886), http://lincoln.lib.niu.edu/cgi-bin/philologic/getobject.pl?p.5424:408.lincoln (August 16, 2013).

24. Compton, "President Obama."

25. D. J. Saul, "A Look Inside Obama's (Social) White House," *The Next Web*, February 16, 2013, http://thenextweb.com/socialmedia/2013/02/16/a-look-inside-obamas-social-white-house/ (August 3, 2013).

26. Saul, "A look inside."

27. Teddy Goff, interview, July 18, 2013.

28. Steven Muller, interview, July 17, 2013.

29. Kate Albright-Hanna, interview, May 31, 2013.

30. Esther Zuckerman, "Reddit Founders Wants Site to Become an 'Expected Campaign Stop'" (sic.), August 31, 2012, http://www.theatlanticwire.com/technology/2012/08/reddit-founders-wants-site-become-expected-campaign-stop/56389/ (August 4, 2013).

31. http://www.theatlantic.com/technology/archive/2012/08/on-obamas-reddit-appearance/261758/ (August 4, 2013).

32. Peter DiSilvio, interview, July 25, 2013.

33. Alan Rosenblatt, interview, July 30, 2013.

34. http://mashable.com/category/dosomething.org/ (July 28, 2013).
35. Muneer Panjwani, interview, August 5, 2013.
36. Panjwani, interview.
37. Marah Lidey, interview, July 30, 2013.
38. Lidey, interview.
39. http://www.dosomething.org/president/ (July 28, 2013).
40. http://www.dosomething.org/president/ (July 28, 2013).
41. Lidey, interview.
42. Panjwani, interview.
43. DoSomething.org, "This Teen's Convo with President Obama," (n.d.) http://www .dosomething.org/blog/teen-text-president-obama (August 4, 2013).
44. Executive Order 11494 (November 13, 1969).
45. http://www.whitehouse.gov/social (July 23, 2013).
46. CNN.com, "Clinton Ok'd Using Lincoln Bedroom For Contributors," February 25, 1997, http://www.cnn.com/ALLPOLITICS/1997/02/25/clinton.money/ (August 11, 2013).
47. The White House Social, http://www.whitehouse.gov/social (July 27, 2013).
48. Kyle Midura, "Vt teacher invited to State of the Union Tweetup," January 25, 2012, http://www.wcax.com/story/16598039/vt-teacher-invited-to-state-of-the-union -tweetup (July 28, 2013).
49. Kori Schulman, "Announcing the State of the Union Tweetup at the White House," January 17, 2012 http://www.whitehouse.gov/blog/2012/01/17/announcing-state -union-tweetup-white-house.
50. Wes Barnett, "White House Creates Social Media Trend to Pressure House Republicans on Payroll Tax Extension," December 21, 2011, http://politics.blogs .foxnews.com/2011/12/21/white-house-creates-social-media-trend-pressure-house -republicans-payroll-tax-extension (May 19, 2012).
51. For example, M. MacGrath, "Beyond Behaviour Management: Manage or Motivate?" *Education Review* 19, no. 1 (2005): 57–64; Kathleen A. FitzPatrick, "An Investigative Laboratory Course in Human Physiology using Computer Technology and Collaborative Writing," *Advances in Physiological Education* 28 (2004): 112–119.
52. The 2013 State of the Union, http://www.whitehouse.gov/state-of-the-union-2013 (August 13, 2013).
53. "Get Updates and Share your Story," WhiteHouse.gov http://www.whitehouse.gov /webform/get-updates-and-share-your-story (August 16, 2013).
54. *We Know Health Care is Personal. It's Your Care*, http://www.whitehouse.gov/mycare (August 16, 2013).
55. http://www.whitehouse.gov/healthreform/stories.
56. http://www.whitehouse.gov/mothersday/affordable-care-card (May 19, 2012).
57. This point was elegantly made in the classic study *Union Democracy*. Seymour Martin Lipset, Martin Trow, and James S. Coleman, *Union Democracy: The Internal Politics of the International Typographical Union* (New York: Free Press, 1956). The endpoint of this fear was classically characterized by Talmon as human life becoming "based upon the assumption of a sole and exclusive truth in politics. It may be called political Messianism in the sense that it postulates a preordained, harmonious and perfect scheme of things, to which men are irresistibly driven, and at which they are bound to arrive. It recognizes ultimately only one plane of existence, the political. It widens the scope of politics to embrace the whole of human existence." Jacob Leib Talmon, *The Origins of Totalitarian Democracy* (Boston: Beacon, 1952), 1–2.

9 Propagation of Social Media Modalities in the Federal Government

1. Daily Caller.com, "The Government Has No Idea How Many Agencies It has," May 3, 2013, http://dailycaller.com/2013/05/03/the-government-has-no-idea-how-many-agencies-it-has/ (August 10, 2013).

2. Obama'08, campaign handout, "Barack Obama on Technology and Innovation," http://www.whitehouse.gov/files/documents/ostp/opengov/Conversation+on+Participation.html (July 27, 2013).

3. Obama'08, campaign handout.

4. Federal Web Managers Council, "Putting Citizens First: Transforming Online Government: A White Paper Written for the 2008–2009 Presidential Transition Team," September 2008, http://www.webmasters.ne.gov/Federal_Web_Managers_Council_White_Paper.pdf (December 31, 2011).

5. Federal Web Managers Council, "Putting Citizens First."

6. Federal Web Managers Council, "Putting Citizens First."

7. Beth Noveck, interview, September 14, 2011.

8. The White House, "Transparency and Open Government. Memorandum for the Heads of Executive Departments and Agencies," January 21, 2009, http://www.whitehouse.gov (June 2, 2011).

9. The White House, "Open Government Directive," December 8, 2009, http://www.whitehouse.gov/open/documents/open-government-directive.html (June 2, 2011).

10. The White House, "Open Government Directive."

11. We noticed that in 2011, it was asserted in online discussion boards that the NASA Buzzroom was taken down due to its having frightened people about an impending "near-miss" of the Earth by a passing asteroid. Whether the rationale for the site going offline was correctly reported, even the allegation highlights the difficulties of mixing citizen engagement with official governmental outlets.

12. Dave McClure, "Associate Administrator for Citizen Services and Innovative Technologies, Testifies on Federal Agency Use of Web 2.0 Technologies," July 10, 2010, US House of Representatives Committee on Oversight and Government Reform, http://www.gsa.gov/portal/content/158009http://www.gsa.gov/portal/content/158009 (October 13, 2012).

13. Conor Friedersdorf, "The Obama Administration's Abject Failure on Transparency," *The Atlantic*, February 2 2012, http://www.theatlantic.com/politics/archive/2012/02/the-obama-administrations-abject-failure-on-transparency/252387; C. J. Ciaramella, "Least Transparent Administration in History," *Free Beacon*, January 18, 2013, http://freebeacon.com/least-transparent-administration-in-history/ (August 18, 2013).

14. Governmental official, interview, August 8, 2010. The official initially agreed to speak on the record and for quotation in this book. After 30 minutes of interviewing, the official asked for anonymity and that comments not be used although the discussion continued off the record. Comments are used here only up to the point when the official asked for anonymity.

15. Energy.gov, "Tomorrow: Department of Energy to Announce Philips Lighting North America Wins L Prize Competition," August 2, 2011, http://energy.gov/articles/tomorrow-department-energy-announce-philips-lighting-north-america-wins-l-prize-competition" (December 30, 2011).

16. "Apps for Healthy Kids," http://www.appsforhealthykids.com/ (December 31, 2011).

17. Flu.gov, "Public Service Announcements (PSA) Campaigns," http://www.flu.gov /psa/(December 31, 2011).

18. USA.gov, "And the USA.gov Video Contest Winner is…", http://www.usa.gov /contest/rules.shtml (December 31, 2011).

19. Vivek Kundra, "Vivek Kundra Testimony on Data Driven Performance," December 10, 2009, http://www.cio.gov/pages.cfm/page/Vivek-Kundra-Testimony-on-Data-Driven -Performance (December 31, 2011).

20. Daniel Terdiman, "Obama's open-government director opens up," *CNET*, December 8, 2009, http://news.cnet.com/8301–13772_3–10411479–52.html (December 31, 2011).

21. Noveck, interview.

22. Alice Lipowicz, "Budget Cuts Hit E-Gov Efforts Hard," *Federal Computer Week*, May 25, 2011, http://fcw.com/articles/2011/05/25/egov-budget-cuts-fedspace-data .gov.aspx (December 30, 2011).

23. Vivek Kundra, "Letter to Senator Tom Carper," May 24, 2011, http://www.federal newsradio.com/pdfs/0524_egov_carper.pdf (January 1, 2012).

24. Ed O'Keefe, "Open Government Sites Scrapped Due to Budget Cuts," *The Washington Post*, May 24, 2011, http://www.washingtonpost.com/blogs/federal-eye /post/two-open-government-sites-scrapped-due-to-budget-cuts/2011/05/24 /AG0UBABH_blog.html (December 27, 2011).

25. Nick Judd, "Departures Continue Among White House Tech Staff," *techPresident*, July 8, 2011, http://techpresident.com/taxonomy/term/6082 (December 28, 2011).

26. Alex Howard, interview, July 12, 2013.

27. Alan Rosenblatt, interview, June 24, 2011.

28. John Wonderlich, interview June 24, 2011.

29. Wonderlich, interview.

30. David Stern, interview, June 27, 2011.

31. Rosenblatt, interview.

32. Micah Sifry, interview, July 24, 2013.

33. Macon Phillips, interview, July 16, 2013.

34. Howard, interview.

35. Howard, interview.

36. Meenal Vamburkar, "Obama Faces Toughest Grilling About Drones, Not From The Media, But In A Google+ Hangout," February 15, 2013, *mediaite.com*, http://www .mediaite.com/online/obama-faces-toughest-grilling-about-drones-not-from-the -media-but-in-a-google-hangout/ (August 18, 2013).

37. "President Barack Obama pointed his finger at patent trolls, people and businesses who file patents and use them to aggressively sue others who produce potentially competing products, during a Google Hangout Thursday afternoon. 'They don't actually produce anything themselves,' said Obama of patent trolls. 'They're just trying to essentially leverage and hijack somebody else's idea and see if they can extort some money out of them.'" Alex Fitzpatrick, "Obama: Patent Trolls Hijack Others' Ideas to 'Extort Some Money' Mashable," February 14, 2013, http://mash able.com/2013/02/14/obama-patent-trolls/ (August 18, 2013).

38. White House Office of the Press Secretary, "FACT SHEET: White House Task Force on High-Tech Patent Issues," http://www.whitehouse.gov/the-press-office /2013/06/04/fact-sheet-white-house-task-force-high-tech-patent-issues (August 18, 2013).

39. Howard, interview.

40. Neha Prakash, "Icelanders Approve Crowdsourced Constitution," October 23, 2012, http://mashable.com/2012/10/23/iceland-approve-constitution/ (July 27, 2013).

41. Euractiv.com, "Icelanders Back First 'Crowdsourced Constitution,'" October 22, 2012, http://www.euractiv.com/enlargement/icelanders-opens-way-crowdsource-news -515543 (July 27, 2013).

42. Tom Ginsburg, "Iceland: End of the Constitutional Saga?" April 5, 2013, *HuffingtonPost.com*, http://www.huffingtonpost.com/tom-ginsburg/iceland-end-of -the-consti_b_3018127.html (August 19, 2013).

10 ANALYTICAL PERSPECTIVES

1. Andrew Chadwick, "Explaining the Failure of an Online Citizen Engagement Initiative: The Role of Internal Institutional Variables," *Journal of Information Technology & Politics* 8 (2011): 21–40.

2. Micah Sifry, interview, June 14, 2010.

3. Sifry, interview.

4. Tony Romm, "OMB: Social network polls, rankings should not be used as the basis for policy," *The Hill,* April 7, 2010, http://thehill.com/blogs/hillicon-valley /technology/91003-omb-social-network-polls-rankings-should-not-be-used-as-the -basis-for-policy (September 20, 2013).

5. Vivek Kundra and Michael Fitzpatrick, "Enhancing Online Citizen Participation Through Policy," Open Government Initiative, the White House, June 16, 2009, http://www.whitehouse.gov/blog/Enhancing-Online-Citizen-Participation -Through-Policy (September 14, 2013).

6. John Wonderlich, interview, June 24, 2011.

7. Sifry, interview.

8. Nancy Scola, "Obama's New HealthCare.gov: A Look at What's Inside," *techPresident*, July 1, 2010, http://techpresident.com/blog-entry/obamas-new-healthcaregov-look -whats-inside (September 17, 2013).

9. Social media official, US Department of Defense, interview, February 19, 2010. The official agreed to be interviewed only on condition of anonymity, saying "I am not obviously allowed to speak for the department."

10. Neil Sroka, Social Media Director, US Department of Commerce, April 10, 2010.

11. Social media official, US Securities and Exchange Commission, interview, April 10, 2010. The official agreed to be interviewed only on condition that his name not be used.

12. Alex Howard, interview, August 4, 2011.

13. The Associated Press/Huffington Post, "Obama Twitter Town Hall: President Answers Your Questions," *Huffington Post*, July 6, 2011, http://www.huffingtonpost .com/2011/07/06/obama-twitter-town-hall-_n_890985.html#s304091&title=The _White_House (December 30, 2011).

14. MSNBC, "Obama: Congress Shouldn't Toy with Debt Limit," July 6, 2011, http:// www.msnbc.msn.com/id/43658349/ns/politics-white_house/t/obama-congress -shouldnt-toy-debt-limit/#.TvinMFZxSSo (April 25, 2012).

15. Alan Rosenblatt, interview, June 24, 2011.

16. David Stern interview, June 27, 2011.

17. Laurel Ruma, interview, August 4, 2010.

18. Josh Gerstein, "President Obama's muddy transparency record," *Politico*, March 5, 2012.

19. Gerstein, "President Obama's muddy transparency record."

20. Wonderlich, interview.
21. Wonderlich, interview.
22. Ruma, interview.
23. Howard, interview.
24. Howard, interview.
25. Amanda Showalter, interview, July 6, 2013.
26. Sumit Agarwal, interview, August 9, 2010.
27. Fred Siegel and Joe Kotkin, "The New Authoritarianism," *City Journal*, January 6, 2012, http://www.city-journal.org/2012/eon0106fsjk.html (January 9, 2012).
28. Kate Albright-Hanna, interview, May 31, 2013.
29. Eve Wong, email to James E. Katz, June 7, 2013.
30. Michelle Welch, interview, September 13, 2013.
31. Denice Szafran, interview, August 27, 2013.
32. Szafran, interview.

11 CONCLUSIONS AND IMPLICATIONS

1. Zachary Moffatt, interview, July 18, 2013.
2. Rebecca Heisler, interview, August 8, 2013.
3. Spencer Ackerman, "Egypt's Internet Shutdown Can't Stop Mass Protests," *Wired*, January 28, 2011, http://www.wired.com/dangerroom/2011/01/egypts-internet-shutdown-cant-stop-mass-protests/.
4. "I Got A Crush on Obama——Obama Girl," *YouTube Video file*, November 29, 2008, http://www.youtube.com/watch?v=lqdgPojYOFc (January 17, 2012).
5. Kenneth Laudon, *Dossier Society: Value Choices in the Design of National Information Systems* (New York: Columbia University Press, 1986).
6. Edward Tenner, *Why Things Bite Back: Technology and the Revenge of Unintended Consequences* (New York: Random House, 1997).
7. James E. Katz, *Presidential Politics and Science Policy* (New York: Praeger, 1976).
8. http://www.whitehouse.gov/files/documents/ostp/opengov/Conversation+on +Participation.html (July 27, 2013).
9. Ronald E. Rice has published sapiently on this topic. For instance, see: Katie E. Pearce and Ronald E. Rice, "Digital Divides from Access to Activities: Comparing Mobile and PC Internet Users," *Journal of Communication* 63, no. 4 (2013): 741–755. For helpful and comprehensive summaries of first-order and second-order digital divide studies, see: Karine Barzilai-Nahon, "Gaps and Bits: Conceptualizing Measurements for Digital Divides," *The Information Society* 22, no. 5 (2006): 269–278; and Sanjeev Dewan and Fred J. Riggins, "The Digital Divide: Current and Future Research Directions," *Journal of the Association for Information Systems*, 6, no. 12 (2005): 298–337.
10. Christopher Karpowitz, Tali Mendleberg, and Lee Shaker, "Gender Inequality in Deliberative Participation." *American Political Science Review* 106, no. 3 (2012): 533–547.
11. Macon Phillips, interview, July 16, 2013.
12. George Reedy, *The Twilight of the Presidency: An Examination of Power and Isolation in the White House* (New York: World Publishing, 1987).
13. Terry M. Moe and William G. Howell, "The Presidential Power of Unilateral Action," *Journal of Law, Economics, and Organization* 15, no. 1 (1999): 132–179.
14. Macon Phillips, interview, July 16, 2013.
15. Office of Science & Technology Policy-Open Government Plan. http://www.white house.gov/open/around/eop/ostp/plan (August 8, 2013).

16. Jacques Ellul, *The Technological Society*, trans. John Wilkinson (New York: Knopf, 1964).

17. Eric Schmidt address to FOCAS meeting, August 5, 2012, FOCAS2012, Towards Open and Innovative Governance, Email from Charlie Firestone, Aspen Institute, August 6, 2012.

18. Daniel Halpern, "Towards a Networked Public Sphere: How Social Media Triggers Civic Engagement Through News Consumption and Political Discussion" (PhD dissertation, Rutgers University, May 2013).

19. John Carey and Martin Elton, *When Media Are New: Understanding the Dynamics of New Media Adoption and Use* (Michigan: University of Michigan Press, 2010).

20. Phillips, interview.

21. Halpern, "Towards a Networked Public Sphere."

22. Stephen Coleman and Peter M. Shane (eds.), *Connecting Democracy: Online Consultation and the Flow of Political Communication* (Cambridge: MIT Press, 2012), Chapter 17.

23. Macon Phillips, interview, July 16, 2013.

24. US House of Representatives, "Oversight Hearing on the Federal Bureau of Investigation," June 13, 2013, Washington: US GPO; Lindy Royce-Bartlett, "Leak Probe has Chilled Sources, AP Exec Says," *CNN*, June 19, 2013, http://www.cnn .com/2013/06/19/politics/ap-leak-probe (July 24, 2013).

25. Philip Howard, *New Media Campaigns and the Managed Citizen* (New York: Cambridge University Press, 2006).

26. James E. Katz, "Telecommunications Privacy Policy in the U.S.A.: Socio-Political Responses to Technological Advances," *Telecommunications Policy* 12, no. 4 (1988): 353–368.

27. http://bits.blogs.nytimes.com/2013/06/20/daily-report-the-deepening-ties -between-the-n-s-a-and-silicon-valley/?_r=0; http://www.nytimes.com/2013/06/08 /technology/tech-companies-bristling-concede-to-government-surveillance-efforts .html?pagewanted=1&_r=1&ref=global-home

28. Micah Sifry, interview, July 24, 2013.

29. Dan McSwain, interview, August 12, 2013.

30. Ithiel de Sola Pool, *Forecasting the Telephone: A Retrospective Technology Assessment* (Norwood: Ablex, 1983).

31. Page 391 in Stephen Coleman and Peter M. Shane (eds.), "Making the E-Citizen: A Sociotechnical Approach to Democracy," in *Connecting Democracy: Online Consultation and the Flow of Political Communication*, ed. Stephen Coleman and Peter M. Shane (Cambridge: MIT Press, 2012), 379–393, 391.

32. Coleman and Shane, "*Connecting Democracy*," 3.

APPENDIX: SCHOLARSHIP OF DIGITAL MEDIA AND THE AMERICAN POLITICAL LANDSCAPE

1. See: Barbara Becker and Josef Wehner "Electronic Networks and Civil Society: Reflections on Structural Changes in the Public Sphere," in *Culture, Communication, Technology: Towards an Intercultural Global Village*, ed. Charles Ess (New York: State University Of New York Press, 2001), 65–87; Thomas F. Gordon and Gernot Richter, "Discourse Support Systems for Deliberative Democracy," *Electronic Government* (2002): 325–334; James E. Katz and Ronald E. Rice, *Social Consequences of Internet Use: Access, Involvement, and Interaction* (Cambridge: MIT Press, 2002); Zizi

Papacharissi, "The Virtual Sphere the Internet as a Public Sphere," *New Media & Society* 4, no. 1 (2002): 9–27.

2. Daniel Kreiss, *Taking Our Country Back: The Crafting of Networked Politics from Howard Dean to Barack Obama* (London: Oxford University Press, 2012).

3. Daniel Halpern, "Towards a Networked Public Sphere: How Social Media Triggers Civic Engagement Through News Consumption and Political Discussion" (PhD dissertation, Rutgers University, May 2013).

4. David Karpf, *Beyond Citizen Journalism: Weigelgate, JournoList, and the Shifting Media Ecology of America* (Paper presented at the APSA Annual Meeting Paper, 2010), Washington, DC.

5. David Karpf, *The MoveOn Effect: The Unexpected Transformation of American Political Advocacy* (London: Oxford University Press, 2012), 19–21.

6. Eric Bucy and Kim Gregson, "Media Participation A Legitimizing Mechanism of Mass Democracy," *New Media & Society* 3, no. 3 (2001): 357–380.

7. Manuel Castells, *The Rise of the Network Society: The Information Age: Economy, Society and Culture* (New York: Wiley, 2000).

8. Manuel Castells, *Communication Power* (New York: Oxford University Press, 2012), 1481.

9. Kenneth Gergen, "Mobile Communication and the Transformation of the Democratic Process," in *Handbook of Mobile Communication Studies*, ed. James E. Katz (Cambridge: MIT Press, 2008), 297–310.

10. See: Jürgen Habermas, *The Theory of Communicative Action: Volume 2: Lifeword and System: A Critique of Functionalist Reason*, vol. 2 (Boston: Beacon Press, 1985); *The Structural Transformation of the Public Sphere: An Inquiry into a Category of Bourgeois Society* (Cambridge: MIT Press, 1989).

11. See: Lincoln Dahlberg, "Rethinking the Fragmentation of the Cyberpublic: From Consensus to Contestation," *New Media & Society* 9, no. 5 (2007): 827–847; James S. Fishkin, "Virtual Public Consultation: Prospects for Internet Deliberative Democracy," *Online Deliberation: Design, Research, and Practice*, ed. Todd Davies and Seeta Peña Gangadharan (Palo Alto, CA: Center for the Study of Language and Information, Stanford University, November 2009), 23–35; http://odbook .stanford.edu/viewing/filedocument/40; T. Witschge, "Examining Online Public Discourse in Context: A Mixed Method Approach," *Javnost-Ljubljana* 15, no. 2 (2008): 75.

12. Beth Noveck, *Wiki Government: How Technology Can Make Government Better, Democracy Stronger, and Citizens More Powerful* (Washington: Brookings, 2009).

13. See: Lincoln Dahlberg, "The Corporate Colonization of Online Attention and the Marginalization of Critical Communication?" *Journal of Communication Inquiry* 29, no. 2 (2005): 160–180; Lincoln Dahlberg, "The Internet and Democratic Discourse: Exploring the Prospects of Online Deliberative Forums Extending the Public Sphere," *Information, Communication & Society* 4, no. 4 (2001): 615–633; Shanthi. Kalathil and Taylor Boas, *Open Networks, Closed Regimes: The Impact of the Internet on Authoritarian Rule* (Washington: Carnegie Endowment, 2010).

14. Mathew Hindman, *The Myth of Digital Democracy* (Princeton: Princeton University Press, 2009).

15. Hindman, *The Myth of Digital Democracy*, 13.

16. Hindman, *The Myth of Digital Democracy*, 17–18.

17. Kay Lehman Schlozman, Sidney Verba, and Henry Brady, "Weapon of the Strong? Participatory Inequality and the Internet," *Perspectives on Politics* 8, no. 2 (2005): 487–509.

18. Peter Dahlgren, "The Internet, Public Spheres, and Political Communication: Dispersion and Deliberation," *Political Communication* 22, no. 2 (2005): 147–162; Margaret Kohn, "Language, Power, and Persuasion: Toward a Critique of Deliberative Democracy," *Constellations* 7, no. 3 (2002): 408–429.

19. Hubertus Buchstein, "Bytes that Bite: The Internet and Deliberative Democracy," *Constellations* 4, no. 2 (2002): 248–263.

20. Dahlberg, "The Internet and Democratic Discourse."

21. David Karpf, *Advocacy Group Activity in the New Media Environment* (Paper presented at the Political Networks Conference, Duke University, 2010).

22. Øystein Sæbø, Jeremy Rose, and L. Skiftenes Flak, "The Shape of eParticipation: Characterizing an Emerging Research Area," *Government Information Quarterly* 25, no. 3 (2008): 400–428

23. Stephen Coleman and Peter Shane, *Connecting Democracy: Online Consultation and the Flow of Political Communication* (Cambridge: MIT Press, 2011).

24. Bohman, James. "Expanding dialogue: The Internet, the Public Sphere and Prospects for Transnational Democracy." *The Sociological Review* 52, no. s1 (2004): 131–155.

25. Kreiss, *Taking Our Country Back*, 196.

26. Richard Neustadt, *Presidential Power* (New York: Wiley 1960); Samuel Kernell, *Going Public: New Strategies of Presidential Leadership* (Washington: CQ Press, 1997).

27. William G. Howell, *Power Without Persuasion: The Politics of Direct Presidential Action* (Princeton: Princeton University Press, 2003).

28. Fred I. Greenstein, "Introduction: Toward a Modern Presidency," in *Leadership in the Modern Presidency*, ed. Fred I. Greenstein (Cambridge: Harvard University Press, 1988), 1–6. For additional delineation of formal and informal presidential powers, see: Jeffrey Tulis, "The Two Constitutional Presidencies," in *The Presidency and the Political System*, ed. Michael Nelson (Thousand Oaks: Sage, 2009), 1–32.

29. Stephen Skowronek, *Presidential Leadership in Political Time: Reprise and Reappraisal* (Lawrence: University Press of Kansas, 2008).

30. It is critical to emphasize that an individual political order can include multiple presidents from either party—the conceptualization of a political order rests more on cohesive national outlook than on individual party-based presidential terms.

31. Benjamin I. Page and Robert Shapiro, *The Rational Public: Fifty years of Trends in Americans' Policy Preferences* (Chicago: University of Chicago Press, 1992).

32. Anthony Downs, *An Economic Theory of Democracy* (New York: Harper & Row; 1957); Donald R. Kinder and D. Roderick Kiewiet, "Sociotropic Politics: The American Case," *British Journal of Political Science* 11, no. 2 (1981): 129–161.

33. Angus Campbell, Philip Converse, Warren Miller, and Donald Stokes, *The American Voter* (New York: Wiley, 1960).

34. John R. Zaller, *The Nature and Origins of Mass Opinion* (New York: Cambridge University Press, 1992).

35. Shanto Iyengar and Donald R. Kinder, *News that Matters*, rev. ed. (Chicago: University of Chicago Press, 2010); Zaller, *The Nature and Origins of Mass Opinion*.

36. Samuel L. Popkin, *The Reasoning Voter: Communication and Persuasion in Presidential Campaigns* (Chicago: University of Chicago Press, 1994).

37. Howard Rheingold, *The Virtual Community* (Cambridge: Addison-Wesley, 1993); Zizi Papacharissi, "The Virtual Sphere 2.0: The Internet, the Public Sphere and Beyond," in *Routledge Handbook of Internet Politics*, eds. Andrew Chadwick and Philip Howard (New York: Taylor & Francis, 2009), 230–245.

38. Robert Putnam, *Bowling Alone: The Collapse and Revival of American Democracy* (New York: Simon & Schuster, 2000).

39. Sidney Verba, Kay Lehman Schlozman, and Henry Brady, *Voice and Equality: Civic Voluntarism in American Politics* (Cambridge: Harvard University Press, 1995).

40. Theda Skocpol, Marshall Ganz, and Ziad Munson, "A Nation of Organizers: The Institutional Origins of Civic Voluntarism in the United States," *American Political Science Review* 94, no. 3 (2000): 527–546.

41. Morris P. Fiorina, "Extreme Voices: A Dark Side of Civic Engagement," *Civic Engagement in American Democracy* 395 (1999): 405–413 in Theda. Skocpol and Morris P. Fiorina, *Civic Engagement in American Democracy* (Washington: Brookings Institute Press, 1999).

42. John Carlo Bertot, Paul T. Jaeger, and Justin M. Grimes, "Using ICTs to Create a Culture of Transparency: E-government and Social Media as Openness and Anti-Corruption Tools for Societies," *Government Information Quarterly* 27 (2010): 264–271.

43. Paul T. Jaeger and John Carlo Bertot, "Transparency and Technological Change: Ensuring Equal and Public Access to Government Information," *Government Information Quarterly* 27 (2010). 371–376.

44. John Carlo Bertot, Paul T. Jaeger, and Derek Hansen "The Impact of Policies on Government Social Media Usage: Issues, Challenges and Recommendations," *Government Information Quarterly* 29 (2012): 30–40.

45. Paul T. Jaeger, "Deliberative Democracy and the Conceptual Foundations of Electronic Government," *Government Information Quarterly* 22, no. 4 (2005): 702.

46. Castells, *Communication Power*.

47. James E. Katz and Mark Aakhus (eds.), *Perpetual Contact: Mobile Communication, Private Talk, Public Performance* (Cambridge: Cambridge University Press, 2002).

48. Lawrence K. Grossman, *The Electronic Commonwealth* (New York: Penguin, 1995).

49. Iyengar and Kinder, *News that Matters*.

INDEX

Printed in the United States of America